Sexual Customs in Rural Norway

A Nineteenth-Century Study

Sexual Customs in Rural Norway

A Nineteenth-Century Study

by

EILERT SUNDT

Translated and Edited by

ODIN W. ANDERSON

Iowa State University Press / Ames

Odin W. Anderson is professor of sociology at the University of Wisconsin-Madison and emeritus professor, Graduate School of Business and Department of Sociology, University of Chicago.

Originally published as *Om sædeligheds-tilstanden i Norge* (1857)

♾ Printed in the United States of America on acid-free paper

First edition, 1993

Library of Congress Cataloging-in-Publication Data

Sundt, Eilert Lund, 1817–1875.
[Om sædeligheds-tilstanden i Norge. English]
Sexual customs in rural Norway : a nineteenth-century study / Eilert Sundt ; translated by Odin W. Anderson.—1st ed.
p. cm.
Translation of: Om sædeligheds-tilstanden i Norge.
ISBN 0-8138-0588-0 (alk. paper)
1. Norway—Moral conditions. 2. Sex customs—Norway. 3. Norway—Rural conditions. 4. Illegitimate children—Norway. I. Title.
HN520.Z9M6713 1993
306.7′09481′09034—dc20 90-28458

To Professor Einar Haugen

CONTENTS

FOREWORD

How would Eilert Sundt have fitted into the social scientific world of today? Remarkably well one would imagine. After all, for almost the whole of his working life he was supported by government research grants, and there is nothing odd about that in today's social scientific world. Admittedly, in Sundt's case the grants were fought over in an unusually public place—the Norwegian Parliament. With these grants Sundt researched a wide range of topics that are still of interest, including poverty; the position of women; the role of the family; sexual behavior; the treatment of minorities; demographic, economic, and social change; alcohol abuse; crime and delinquency; education; the history of art (especially domestic architecture); and the minutiae of everyday culture.[1] His methods too would not have been out of place in the 1990s, for he took great pains with his methodology, being something of an innovator in this area. He conducted several large-scale surveys and much of his work was of a statistical nature. Aware that this would reduce his readership, he made a tremendous effort to make his tables as palatable as possible, describing in detail how they were constructed and why they were necessary. Sundt, too, was a great believer in fieldwork and did a lot of interviewing. For instance, from December 1850 to the summer of 1857 Sundt reckoned that he was working in the field on some 754 days. Widely read in French, German, English, and, of course, in the Scandinavian languages, Sundt adopted a multidisciplinary approach with much drawn from the fields of history, geography, sociology, linguistics, economics, demography, etc.

It is, however, not so much what Eilert Sundt did in the way of social science, nor how he did it, that makes him such a remarkable figure. Why he stands out is because he carried out his research well *over a century ago,* it being published in the years 1850–1873. Where today there are well-worn paths was then uncharted territory. Had his work not

1. A comprehensive selection of Sundt's work was brought out by the Oslo publisher Gyldendal in eleven volumes from 1974 to 1978. The last volume contains a comprehensive index to the entire collection (pp. 183–342). It consists of several sections. Going through these is the best way to grasp the vast range of Sundt's interests. It is a pity it is in Norwegian only.

been confined to a language understood in his lifetime by but a few million people and relatively speaking by even fewer today, he would have been widely recognized as a founding father of social science. Empirically his work can be set firmly alongside that of Henry Mayhew, Le Play, and Charles Booth. His findings on suicide foreshadowed those of Durkheim[2] and he was one of the first to apply the findings of Charles Darwin to social phenomena. Given all this, it is hardly surprising that one feels it so necessary to get the works of Sundt into the hands of scholars worldwide. Essentially, however, we must evaluate Sundt's writings in two ways: first for the concrete information they give to us of a world long lost and second for the insights they provide on those topics that are as of much interest today as they were in his lifetime.

For social historians there is little doubt that Sundt is a major source. More today, one might argue, than at an time in the past. For remarkably he dealt with topics that are of very considerable interest to historians today and he dealt with them in a way that gives one great confidence in his findings. Take for instance the topic covered in this volume. It was one to which Sundt returned again and again. Superficially it would seem to be as rooted in the 1850s as crinolines and stovepipe hats. As Sundt inveighs against the iniquities of the lower classes, with their self-inflicted wounds of sexual promiscuity and general fecklessness, one wonders if his work more properly belongs in one of those volumes of sermons that were produced in such large numbers a century or so ago. For he does seem bound by his class and his times. But get behind the language; pay close attention to *what* he is saying and not so much *how,* in some instances, he is saying it and the radical nature of his thinking is very apparent. Sundt was a controversial figure in his lifetime, often a sign that something important is being said. Indeed the debates in the Norwegian Parliament over the renewal of his grant were bitter towards the close of his career. And it was that same Parliament that had nurtured him for so long that, to all intents and purposes, brought his career to a close in 1869 when the vote went against him: 51–47.

It would, of course, be wrong to present Sundt as above criticism. He usually worked on several projects at the same time. He was quick to publish. Perhaps too quick so that, as has been pointed out, "much of his work appears in the form of interim reports."[3] And though many of his works are linked one with another, his findings rarely support a

2. Jon Elster, *Dagbladet,* 30 October 1978; Nils Christie, *Eilert Sundt som fanteforsker og sosialstatistiker* (Oslo: University of Oslo, Institutt for Sosiologi, 1958), 15.

3. Stein Ugelvik Larsen in his introduction to Eilert Sundt, *Harham: et eksempel fra fiskeridistrikterne* (Oslo: Universitets-forlaget, 1971), 11.

coherent body of theory. Here one should, perhaps, make an exception of some of his demographic work, notably that which appeared in his book *On Marriage in Norway.*[4] In the present volume Sundt characteristically darts from one topic to another, a product it might be said of his "enormous and infectious intellectual curiosity."[5] Chapter 2, for instance, comes rather out of the blue and it is not until one has come almost to the end of it that one begins to see how it fits into the book as a whole.

This book was published at a time when the number of births outside marriage was still rising, by whatever measure one chooses to adopt. It was to peak in the 1870s at about the time of Sundt's death after a rise that had begun a century before. By the 1960s the rate was below even mid-eighteenth century levels, but it then rose with enormous rapidity to the unprecedented levels of today. For the number of illegitimate births are now approaching the number of marriages (to use Sundt's preferred measure) with 30 percent of all births occurring outside marriage (Fig. F.1). No doubt this would have fascinated Sundt as much as the topic did

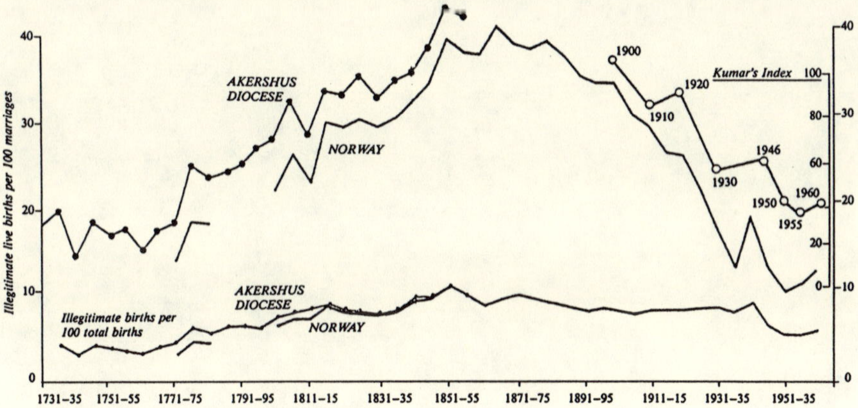

Fig. F.1. Illegitimate live births per 100 marriages and per 100 total births in Norway, 1801–1965 and in Akershus diocese, 1731–1860, together with an index of the "Illegitimacy Level" in Norway, 1900–1960 (from Michael Drake, "Norway" in *European Demography and Economic Growth,* ed. W. R. Lee [London: Croom Helm, 1979], 303).

4. For the only English translation, see that of Michael Drake: Eilert Sundt, *On Marriage in Norway* (Cambridge University Press, 1980).

5. Elster, *Dagbladet.*

in his own day. No doubt too he would have been interested to see that the regional variations—especially the markedly lower levels of births outside marriage in the southwest of the country, to which he drew attention—are still in evidence today. One can be sure that Sundt would see the problem in the round, as a social phenomenon to be analysed rigorously within a multidisciplinary framework. But above all one knows he would have taken just as great pains to make sure that any study he undertook would reach the widest possible audience as, indeed, he did with this one.

University of Tromsø MICHAEL DRAKE

PREFACE

The study by Eilert Sundt of sexual customs in rural Norway was published in three parts in 1857, 1864, and 1866. In 1976 Gyldendal Norsk Forlag published all three in one volume as *Fakkel-bok, Verker i Utvalg 4:* Eilert Sundt, *Om Sædeligheds-tilstanden i Norge,* the volume I used. Considering both relevance and expense, I have translated only the book published in 1857, which contains the major contribution of Sundt to the subject. The books published in 1864 and 1866 are essentially expansions of the 1857 book with more detail on data and methods. The 1864 publication is called *Continued Contributions Regarding the Moral Conditions in Norway.* The 1866 publication is called *On Moral Conditions in Norway, Third Report.*

In my translation of the text, I have tried to be true to the author's style, preserving most of the sentence complexities and mannerisms that characterize the original. Modern readers may need to exercise patience not only with the sentence length but also with the moralistic tone that intrudes. With readability in mind, I have enclosed Sundt's original footnotes—some of them quite lengthy—in parentheses and incorporated them into the text; my own notes—including page references to the sources cited—are enclosed in brackets throughout. A concern for readability was also the basis for the editorial decision not to number the text section by section, as Sundt did in the original; occasional subheadings will serve as guideposts to readers.

I have presented Sundt's own terms, sometimes abbreviated, for currency and measures, and offer the following explanation:

Term	*Abbreviation*	*Meaning*
spesiadaler	spd.	coin used until 1873, worth about one dollar U.S.
ort		old Norwegian coin
mark, *pl* merker		early Norwegian coin, worth about 20 cents U.S.; also used for weight, about one-half pound

Term	*Abbreviation*	*Meaning*
daler		Norwegian bank note and coin used until 1875, worth about one dollar U.S.
skilling	sk.	Norwegian coin; there were 120 sk. in one spd.
shilling		colloquial term used for a small unit, such as 10 cents U.S.
bismerspund	bpd.	unit of weight, about 12 pounds
voger		unit of weight, about 36 pounds
alen		unit of length, about two feet

Readers may notice variations in orthography for certain place-names, as the Norwegian language had not yet stabilized by the middle of the nineteenth century; ø and ö, for example, were used interchangeably for some time. While in the main I have adopted modern Norwegian spelling, I have let some variations stand.

ACKNOWLEDGMENTS

Einar Haugen, Emeritus Professor, Harvard University, was professor of Norwegian at the University of Wisconsin-Madison when I was a student there from 1932 to 1938. In my sophomore year at the university I started to take courses in Norwegian language and literature from Haugen. Aspiring to emulate him, I became interested in philology. Although my interest in his chosen field pleased him, he gently cautioned me that academic opportunities were so few that he doubted I could make a living. Being a practical person with no private income, I turned to an only slightly more practical field—sociology.

Since those early days, Einar and I have been colleagues and friends and kept in touch. He directed me to Eilert Sundt's work after I became interested in sociology and kept encouraging me to translate *Om Sædelighets-tilstanden i Norge.* Even though it took fifty years to get to the endeavor, I warmly dedicate this translation to Einar Haugen.

I wish to acknowledge the helpful financial support from Norges Almenvitenskapelige Forskningsråd (NAVF, the Norwegian Research Council for Science and the Humanities) for clerical assistance and a publication subsidy. I am particularly grateful because NAVF does not normally make grants to applicants who are not Norwegian citizens.

Professor Arvid Brodersen also has my thanks for encouraging me since 1935 to undertake a translation of Sundt. He graciously consented to write an afterword.

I thank the Department of Sociology, University of Wisconsin-Madison, and the university for providing my salary while engaged in this translation, no small subsidy to an endeavor that was a labor of love for both Norway and the history of sociology. I also wish to acknowledge the interest and support of Professor Aage Sørensen (now at Harvard University), who was chair of the department.

Sundt wrote his book in Dano-Norwegian of that time and used an occasional local-dialect expression now uncommon. This caused me some difficulties that I cleared up in consultation with Harald S. Naess, Professor of Scandinavian Studies, University of Wisconsin-Madison.

Finally, I wish to thank Nancy Klatt for her careful and painstaking typing of my handwritten translation for publication.

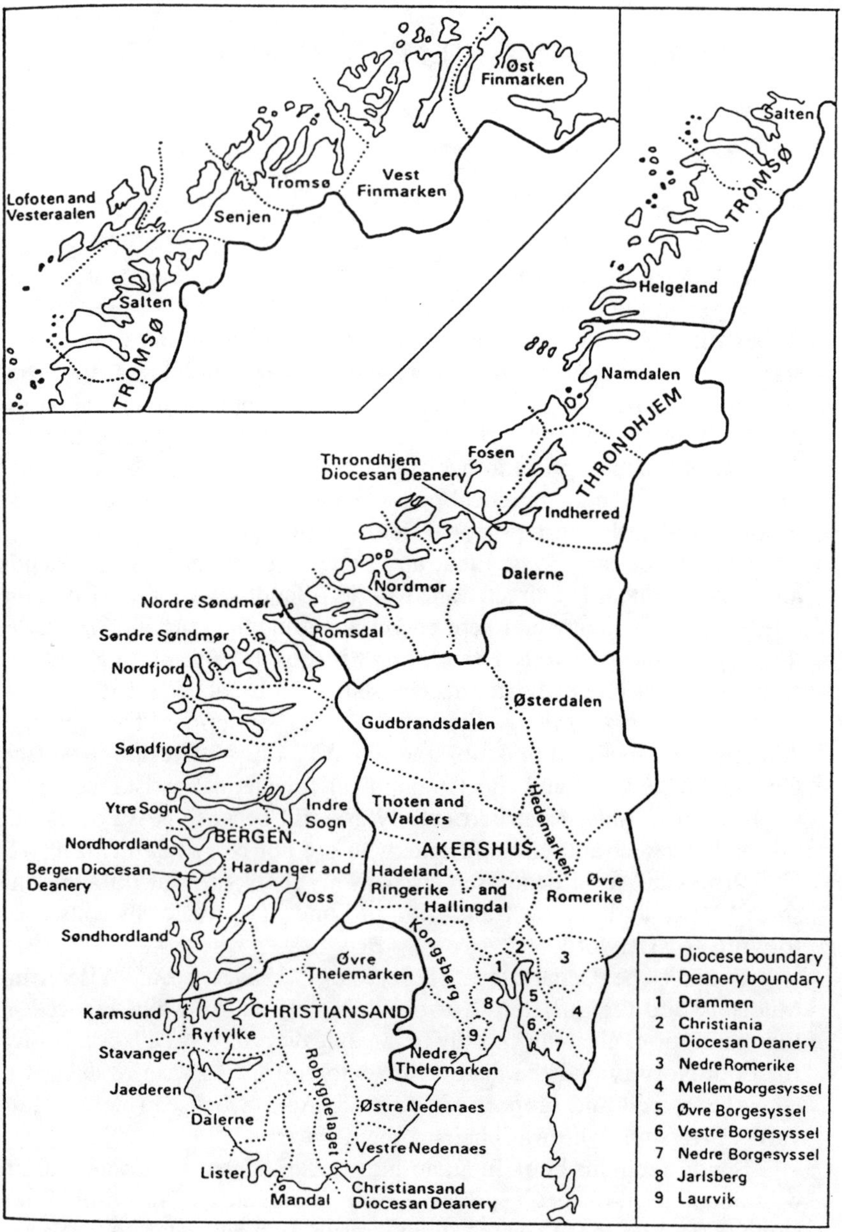

The dioceses and deaneries of Norway c. 1850 (Reprinted, by permission, from Eilert Sundt, *On Marriage in Norway,* translated and introduced by Michael Drake. © 1980 by Cambridge University Press).

Sexual Customs in Rural Norway

A Nineteenth-Century Study

1

Differences among Districts

IN 1851 the number of live births in Norway was 44,899; in 1852 the number was 44,219; in 1853, 46,039; in 1854, 48,896; and in 1855, 49,541. Of these children, many were born out of wedlock: in 1851, 4,090; in 1852, 4,220; in 1853, 4,144; in 1854, 4,533; and in 1855, 4,603. Accordingly, from one year to another, between four and five thousand births were illegitimate, or about one-eleventh of all births that occurred in the country. These are the numbers. But what is the reality behind these figures? For a long time, indeed too long a time, I wondered if it would be possible to describe these conditions in reports which could be made public. But now I am disclosing them, and I will depend on the discerning reader to find in my writing valid grounds for my doing so.

As an illustration, here are parts of my 1851 travel reports to the Department of Education.

EXAMPLES OF A HIGH DEGREE OF IMMORALITY

I stayed for two days in ______ (one of the unqualifiedly dissolute rural settlements at that time in the parish of Fron in Gudbrandsdal). The first day I spent mostly with cotters [farm laborers who in return for a cottage, sometimes with and sometimes without a patch of land, provided labor services]. In the first cotter's cottage I visited, the man and wife were preparing to cross the Laugen and cut brush in the very high but almost treeless mountainside which I had observed, and which reminded me of a similar mountainside down in the valley, where a few days before I had walked up and down in order to convince myself that the Gudbrandsdal forests are in the process of being completely destroyed. I saw a large area there where the ax had felled a mighty forest and where the knife was now cutting away each sapling that had grown up. The condition of the forest became a subject for conversation between the cotter and myself. He complained that so many people now occupied the land, that there was no longer enough wood and lumber for anybody. Later we came to speak of the relationship between the landlords and the cotters, and he now complained about the callousness of the farmers who refused to let people clear the land, and who kept poor people out of the tracts of forest which they had shared among themselves. But when I pointed out to him the contradiction inherent in his complaints (about the limited supply of woodlands on the one hand and about the farmers' measures to preserve what was left of the resources), he remarked that he "did not understand that, he had no mind for such matters." But he did have a "mind for such matters," since in his childhood a forest still stood on the stretch of land along the river where now he and many other cotters laboriously dug up roots for firewood, a forest which the growing number of cotters had helped to destroy through the land unfortunately being held in common. He had a good mind for such matters, but in this community had become accustomed to blame others for evils and could see malice in every effort that did not serve selfish and short-sighted ends.

In the next cotter's cottage I came to, there was poverty, but much was still "salvageable." The wife at home did not complain about her lot. "Mostly there is only starvation for poor folks, because the landlords are so hard that they will not let people live."—"How can you talk like that, my dear woman?"—"All right, now you just listen, there is a girl who lives with us with two children. She has nothing, and when she takes her children out with her early in the morning, she may go around at least half the community, and when she comes home in the evening, she may have hardly three merker [see Preface] of flour, so hard-hearted are they. And now she cannot go more than every third day, otherwise they will say she goes too regularly. But that means there is no more than one mark of flour for three people, and that is not enough to live on."—"But, how is it that the girl has two children?"—"Well, she has had five, but one is dead and one is a servant, and one is herding this summer, and it's a carpenter who is the father of all of them."—"But does he not take care of the mother and the children?"—"He? No, he drinks up almost every shilling he makes, and he makes plenty, for he is the best carpenter in the community, and it is quite something when she is able to get 12 shillings or so."—"Are these people still together?"—"Yes, that they are, because now in the summertime she has a place in the hayloft. I understand he is there sometimes, and he will surely continue to be around when he has finished a little cottage hereabouts, which he is building for her."

The next person I met was a woman who was weeding a potato patch. She told me her story. Eight years ago she had had to leave her servant position when she was pregnant. For three years she wandered around the community with her child, until she finally got its father to marry her, but they still had no place to go; he was only a farm laborer and owned nothing. They had rented a potato patch from a cotter, but weren't able to fertilize it and therefore it did not do well.

In the next cotter's cottage, I found a couple of impoverished elderly people who were in addition burdened by a sickly grown-up son. I admit I grabbed the opportunity to escape this sad scene when, quite fortuitously, a brisk, young, and pleasant-looking boy appeared. I engaged him in conversation and heard that in the previous year he had gotten a croft. He was not married yet but "nevertheless had a woman now"; that is, a girl he had worked with some years earlier and had a child by. He now intended to marry her in the near future.

The next person I met was a woman who carried a child on her back and led with one hand a somewhat older child and with the other a goat, which she wanted to tether on a little patch of grass beside the public road. She was married; she had had the first child before she was married, the other soon after. Now she and the husband were lodged with other people and sought to sustain themselves by day labor; but the wife's worn appearance brought me to believe, as had been reported, that a number of such families had actually suffered starvation that spring.

Hardly 50 paces farther on I met another woman who also carried a child on her back and led one by the hand and whose story was exactly the same: the older child before, the younger immediately after marriage, and in vain still seeking a cotter's place.

All of these meetings had taken place around a small group of crofts in the neighborhood. But now I hurried off past both people and houses up into the deep side-valley which the river of ______ runs through. Here I boldly entered yet another crofter's cottage. The elderly cotters evoked my sympathy greatly; the wife was crippled and twisted by arthritis, the man worn-out and dulled by labor and destitution. For a long time they had had only some bog land for which they had to pay a high rent. From interest on a debt of 18 spd incurred on the purchase of grain they had to feed a young heifer, etc. Now their small standing crop of rye had been sold at auction to cover the same debt. They had accordingly little or nothing for the winter. Two small children in the house belonged to the son and daughter-in-law of the old ones, who lodged with them. The young people were away now, but they were also said to be extremely poor. I found a third party in the house: a woman with two infants. Possibly encouraged by my expressions of sympathy for the elderly, she told me how hard-hearted people in the community were. She had been begging far and wide that day but had not been given more than what would make a dish of porridge, which her children were actually at that moment eating from a wooden cup. "Are you married?" I asked. No, she should have been married, but her boyfriend had gone to the Espedal works and had had a child by a girl there, so now she did not know what would happen.

This girl was from a cotter's place nearby, and the reason why she did not live at home with her parents was this: her parents had three children as well as her—among them two adults, a son and a daughter. A couple of years ago, the son had made a girl from another parish pregnant while she was a servant at a neighboring farm here in the community. The girl went to his parents and gave birth to the child there, but she could not get along with those around her and cleared off—no one knew where—deserting both lover and child. A little later the same cotter's son had a child with another girl, a daughter of a cotter from a neighboring place, a person who not being prepared to do what was expected of her had early gone out into the world. She eventually came home from the Trondheim area with her child and now, as mentioned, had another. The other sister, the grown-up daughter of the cotter mentioned, a girl a little over 17 years of age, had been a servant at a farm in the parish but had recently come home to her parents since she had become pregnant by a boy who was a servant at the same place, a teenager who was still working for just his food and clothes. But there was too much child screaming for the old parents, so the eldest daughter, with her two children, was forced to lodge with strangers, where I now found her. While I sat and listened to these stories, the girl, who had had her last child with the cotter's son—brother to the storyteller—came into the room with the child on her back. She was not ashamed to explain that she had come from a begging tour in the neighborhood, but she nevertheless did not tell what I later heard at other places, that after her return from the Trondheim area she had caroused at military drill grounds and at auctions, and that things had come to such a pass that she had had to go among the farms to beg for infants' clothes. Shortly after, the opportunity to use them was lost. It was not known exactly why.

I was in still another cotter's place and there met the married son of the elderly cotter folk, who complained that he would not be permitted to keep his father's place, contrary to expectations, on the old terms and that as a result he did not know where to turn.

So that is what I have to report of my dealings with every single member of the cotter class that chance brought me in touch with, during the course of that one day.

I will not make a point of describing the impression that the sight of such conditions must make on a mind that has any sense whatsoever of the place of virtue in human happiness. The situation speaks for itself. But I do now realize that the careful reader is likely to make the following observation: "It is rather odd to provide such an example in order to throw light on the condition of the country, since it might well have been a coincidence that during one day so much unpleasantness was revealed. Is it intended that one should conclude from a single day in one community that this is the usual situation and that it will help us to understand conditions in all Norway?"

I will, therefore, explain myself a little further. It was not only during just one day and in one community, but frequently and in several places, especially in Hedemark during that same summer that I had similarly deplorable experiences with regard to moral conditions in the countryside. What I saw and heard has astonished and appalled me, and the questions that forced themselves upon me were: What has given rise to these conditions? How long has it been this way? Is it reasonable to suppose that society can thrive and even survive when family life exhibits such depravity? In the hope of finding answers to these mysteries, the next year, 1852, I journeyed to Gudbrandsdal and lived in the parishes of Vaage and Lom, directly north of Fron, from which the above illustration was taken. For weeks on end these conditions were the object of my inquiries and reflections. Much became clearer to me than before, but new oddities were revealed which I did not know how to explain. Therefore I went again in 1854 to Vaage and Lom and continued my singular investigations. Were I to recount in detail what I experienced and learned, it would be evident that for each new insight gained, a new question arose, demanding to be answered. It is as if the work of the mind can be likened to the unfolding, one day, of a leaf or two. Then suddenly one discovers in the middle of the two grown leaves a new shoot, struggling forth which needs to be given time to grow. In the meantime, one sets aside questions of cause and effect and sticks to the matter in hand: How did I find conditions in the two particular parishes? In regard to this question, I recall the experiences I had among the cotter class, among whom conditions were worse than among the farmer class. I remember how I often involuntarily came to use the everyday phrase "things are as bad as they could be" and I remember how I continually came to compare the conditions with the situation in Fron, which by chance had stamped itself on my memory. And even though it is always questionable to point to a single case as illustrative of conditions in a district, I do believe that what I have experienced I dare to argue that the impression provided by Fron approximates to what one can observe in cotters' families, neighborhood by neighborhood, in the two adjoining parishes of Vaage and Lom. There are, of course, some differences, and particularly in Lom the conditions are not as bad as in Vaage, but the differences are not great.

But perhaps the immorality in Fron, Vaage, and Lom is but a deplorable exception to what prevails in rural districts throughout the rest of the country? Here one must make comparisons, and this must be carried out with the assistance of numbers and statistics. These statistics must embrace the entire population and not merely that one part of it, namely, the working class, which has been given the most attention in the foregoing.

Now the reader will know how one usually calculates the frequency of illegitimate births, by counting both the legitimate and illegitimate births and then combining the two totals. It was a method of calculation which I tried in the beginning of this essay. For several reasons I shall however use another method, namely, as follows: First I count the illegitimate births, and then I bear in mind the parents of these same children. Now it follows that for all the children born in one year, there are as many sets of parents (the slight difference caused by the birth of twins will have little effect either way). I find it therefore both more informative and suggestive to compare the total of these sets of parents with the total of those couples who enter into regular marriage. That is why I compare the number of illigitimate births with the number of marriages in the same year (for a fuller explanation see appendix A).

This matter can best be illustrated with an example from the same three parishes—Fron, Vaage, and Lom. Here, during the twenty-year period from 1831 to 1850, there were 1,422 illegitimate births and 2,115 marriages. (Only live births, since I do not have the number of illegitimate stillbirths.) In reality the conditions are somewhat worse.

According to this method, I can now calculate that for every 100 couples who married, the number of couples who bore children outside of marriage was no less than 67; thus the relationship of the former to the latter was 100 to 67.

This last number, 67, I now use as a measure of the frequency of illegitimate births, as an index of the degree or extent to which this kind of evil has prevailed in these communities during this period. If one could, year after year, have traveled from house to house in these same communities, then one could have seen and observed the phenomenon itself, but now this reality is encapsulated by the number 67. Had the conditions been still worse, the number would have been still higher; if on the contrary conditions had been better in the communities concerned, the counts and calculations would have resulted in a lower figure. If I now find the same or a larger or a smaller number in another community, I conclude that the conditions there must in reality be the same as in Fron-Vaage-Lom or worse or better, entirely as revealed by the numbers. This, then, is my method of drawing the comparisons.

STATISTICAL REVIEW OF NORWAY

First I investigate the case for the entire Kingdom of Norway during the period from 1831 to 1850, and I find that the relationship between marriages and illegitimate births (excluding stillbirths) is 100 to 30.8. This ratio is certainly less than that for Fron-Vaage-Lom. The conditions in these particular communities must accordingly have been much worse than in the country generally.

From the official printed tables I can find further data for each of the five dioceses and thereafter calculate that from 1831 to 1850 the relationship of marriages to illegitimate births was as follows:

Christiania diocese	100 : 34.5
Christiansand diocese	100 : 11.8
Bergen diocese	100 : 20.0
Trondheim diocese	100 : 48.5
Tromsø diocese	100 : 39.6

These figures do present a most serious situation, particularly for the diocese of Trondheim. Still we do not find even for this diocese as unfavorable a figure as for Fron-Lom.

Is it then possible that the three parishes do in fact present a deplorable exception? It seems reasonable to speculate, however, that when we learn of the conditions for the smaller areas into which each of the five dioceses are divided, perhaps we shall find among them even greater differences and equally unfortunate deviations from the usual, as we have already observed in the communities in Gudbrandsdal. I have therefore made use of the original documents on which the official tables are based, and, going beyond them have made the same calculations for each of the 53 deaneries for the period 1831–1850. (I do not wish to present the results of my calculations without also presenting the figures on which they are based—so that the reader can check the correctness of the calculations—and since it occurs to me that it has not been easy to assemble the figures, I have put the totals for the country, dioceses, and deaneries in appendixes B and C.)

These calculations regarding illegitimate births are to be found in table 1.1. Here the deaneries are listed from east to west and from south to north. I suggest that the reader examine this table with some care. In a couple of recently published studies of the population conditions (*About Mortality in Norway,* chapters 12 and 13, together with *On Marriage in Norway*), I have permitted myself to present to the public several such tables, notably on the frequency of deaths and marriages. I have called attention to the prevailing similarities and differences between the districts. But in neither of those reports do the similarities and differences emerge so clearly as here.

One can best grasp the relative position of the districts if one imagines a map of Norway marked with lighter colors for the districts where the condition as to illegitimate births are better (and accordingly the numbers in the tables are low) but darker and darker colors for the districts where larger numbers depict a worse condition. This map will then show a contiguous very dark area which stretches from the boundary between Lower and Upper Romerike, crosses the latter and continues north over Østerdal, Hedemark, and Gudbrandsdal in the Christiania diocese then over to Romsdal, Nordmør, Fosen, and Dalerne in the Trondheim diocese. To this may be added the neighboring Christiania diocesan-deanery to the south and the adjoining Trondheim diocesan-deanery in the north. In all these districts there are about 50 or more couples with illegitimate children for every 100 married couples. The map is immediately lighter toward the south, over Lower Romerike and Borgesyslerne or Smaalenene, still lighter west of Lake Mjøsen and the Christiania fjord from Valdres to Laurvik. The area around the fjord of Skien (Bamble and Lower Telemark) appears in this context to belong to the diocese of Christiansand, since it is clearly separated, to its advantage, from the eastern districts and has much in common with the Bergen diocese except for the diocesean deanery there, which is entirely urban. In the last-named diocese, the districts around Sognefjord appear as a dark area, which unfortunately contrasts sharply with the neighboring areas, since the other Bergen deaneries are uniformly on the light side. The neighboring Romsdal, which belongs to the previously described

Table 1.1. Illegitimate births per 100 marriages, 1831–1850

Administrative District		Births
1.	Lower Borgesyssel diocesan deanery	38.1
2.	Middle Borgesyssel diocesan deanery	19.9
3.	West Borgesyssel diocesan deanery	34.5
4.	Upper Borgesyssel diocesan deanery	28.6
5.	Lower Romerike diocesan deanery	29.7
6.	Christiania diocesan deanery	58.5
7.	Upper Romerike, Odal, and Solør	52.3
8.	Østerdal	55.4
9.	Hedemark	49.0
10.	Gudbrandsdal	49.7
11.	Toten and Valders	25.6
12.	Hadeland, Ringerike, and Hallingdal	28.5
13.	Kongsberg	20.4
14.	Drammen	25.6
15.	Jarlsberg	21.9
16.	Laurvik	25.6
17.	Bamble and Lower Telemark	14.2
18.	Upper Telemark	13.9
19.	East Nedenæs	8.4
20.	West Nedenæs	12.2
21.	Robygdelag	9.5
22.	Christiansand diocesan deanery	26.4
23.	Mandal	6.6
24.	Lister	5.6
25.	Dalerne (Christiania diocese)	8.5
26.	Jæder	13.4
27.	Stavanger	15.2
28.	Karmsund	10.5
29.	Ryfylke	17.3
30.	Hardanger and Voss	12.3
31.	Søndhordland	14.3
32.	Bergen diocesan deanery	35.0
33.	Nordhordland	7.8
34.	Outer Sogn	41.4
35.	Inner Sogn	54.7
36.	Søndfjord	12.2
37.	Nordfjord	8.4
38.	Southern Søndmør	11.3
39.	Northern Søndmør	21.6
40.	Romsdal	47.3
41.	Nordmør	61.4
42.	Fosen	56.3
43.	Trondheim diocesan deanery	63.0
44.	Dalerne (Trondheim diocese)	49.0
45.	Indherred	37.0
46.	Namdal	32.9
47.	Helgeland	45.5
48.	Salten	32.2
49.	Vesteraalen and Lofoten	45.8
50.	Senjen	41.0
51.	Tromsø diocesan deanery	45.4
52.	West Finmark	25.8
53.	East Finmark	27.9

large dark areas, also emerges in sharp contrast.

If we now review the entire table in order to find the districts which reveal the worst conditions, we see that they are the Nordmør deanery (61.4 illegitimate births per 100 marriages) and the Trondheim diocesan-deanery (63 per 100). But even in these districts the situation—as judged by the figures—is not as bad as in Fron-Vaage-Lom (67 per 100). Thus one might infer that these three parishes did actually present a unique exception. But this would be too hasty a judgment. One must point out that the whole deanery of Gudbrandsdal (no. 10), of which the three parishes are a part, reveals a more favorable situation (49.7 per 100) than the same three parishes. Therefore one will infer that the conditions in Fron-Lom must be worse than those in the other parishes in the same deanerys. It would, therefore, seem reasonable that if we were to choose from other less-favored deaneries individual communities where the situation is at its worst (and as an example I believe that I could designate the three southernmost parishes of Østerdal, namely, Rendal, Aamot, and Elverum), we would find many parallels to these individual communities, in which from the beginning and quite by accident I became aware of the magnitude of the problem.

We have maps which show the country's mountain ranges and the courses of its rivers, and now I have conceived a map which should indicate the moral condition of the people. "No," one will likely say, "No, we do not want to know about it. The mountains have their designated place and the rivers have their courses. These one can draw on a map. But the moral condition of a people is subject to change, like a snowbank—something a gust of wind might shape today while a storm tomorrow may change its whole appearance. The flights of the spirit or the sudden gusts of temptation—one does not know where they come from or where they will go—could quickly transform the morals of a people, rapidly for the better, or just as rapidly for the worse. Therefore, away with the idea that there should be such fixed and permanent similarities and dissimilarities in the moral conditions of the people in the country districts."

But there is something singular which I shall now develop. By making separate calculations for the periods 1831–1840 and 1841–1850, I find that for each 100 marriages the number of illegitimate births in Fron, Vaage, and Lom was 68 for 1831–1840 and 67 for 1841–1850. In the other parishes in Gudbrandsdal the number of illegitimate births was 38 for 1831–1840 and 38 for 1841–1850.

Time after time the situation between the different parts of one and the same deanery-district have been markedly alike. Whatever were the internal and external circumstances which influenced morality and made the conditions worse in one district than in another, there was no marked change from one period to another.

Certainly one must be surprised. Or might it not be a coincidence which one is observed by chance in Gudbrandsdal? No, it is no coincidence; the stability in the moral conditions is markedly evident over the entire country. One will find this by reviewing table 1.2 with some care. In it I first presented all 53 districts, according as table 1.1 revealed a lesser or a greater frequency of illegitimate births in the period 1831–1850 as a whole, so that a district has been given no. 1 where the frequency was least. Thereafter I have ranked each district as to frequency, separately for each of the 10-year periods 1831–1840 and 1841–1850; and finally I have numbered the districts according to the situation in each of the same 10 years.

The deanery of Lister was no. 1 in the period 1831–1840 and no. 1 during 1841–1850; Jæder stands each time as no. 13; Sønderhordland remains no. 16 in both periods; Kongsberg and northern Søndmør both times are side by side at nos. 20 and 21; in both 1831–1840 and 1841–1850 we find Hadeland at no. 29; Lower Romerike, which in the first period was no. 31, also retains its place in the second. The district which is actually the neighbor of the latter, namely, Upper Romerike, in each of the 10-year periods, stands low in the rank-order, and in the last 10 years seems to have widened the difference a little more (no. 43 and 46). Østerdal is at first no. 49 and then no. 50, a rather small shift, and both times it is on the list quite near Fosen, no. 48 and 52, though it is in fact a long way away from there. In short, among the majority of districts the conditions are markedly similar from one period to the other.

Naturally they are not wholly without change. But changes occur so slowly and to such a small extent that it is possible to make such comparisons. Let an agronomist visit a farmer on his farm and accompany him to the fields to inspect individual plots of land; by observing the different kinds of plants, sand, loam, water plants, etc., he can judge the greater or lesser richness of the soil, and if you wish, rate it accordingly; let him then return in 10 years, and to the extent that the farmer has not in the meantime made any changes through ditch digging and mixing of soil, etc., he will find the same plants and thereafter conclude that the plots of land have the same characteristics as before.

The people in the country are also a field where the seeds that bring forth virtue should grow, a vineyard where the noble senses should thrive and mature like grapes. How does the unevenness between strips in the fields occur, these variations yield from different plots in the garden? What reasons can there be for the persistence of these differences,

Table 1.2. Illegitimate births per 100 marriages

Number and Reference to Table 1.1	Districts' Rank According to Conditions in 1831–1850 as in Table 1.1	Conditions During the Years 1831–1840	Conditions During the Years 1841–1850	Rank Order 1831–1840	Rank Order 1841–1850
1 (24)	Lister	4.8	6.4	1	1
2 (23)	Mandal	5.1	7.9	2	3
3 (33)	Nordhordland	8.1	7.7	5	2
4 (37)	Nordfjord	8.9	8.1	7	4
5 (19)	Eastern Nedenæs	8.0	8.7	6	5
6 (25)	Dalerne (Christiania diocese)	7.7	9.2	4	6
7 (21)	Robygdelag	7.4	11.4	3	7
8 (28)	Karmsund	11.4	10.0	11	8
9 (38)	Southern Søndmør	10.6	12.0	8	9
10 (36)	Søndfjord	10.9	13.4	10	11
11 (20)	Western Nedenæs	11.7	12.6	12	10
12 (30)	Hardanger and Voss	10.6	13.7	9	12
13 (26)	Jæder	12.5	14.0	13	13
14 (18)	Upper Telemark	13.0	14.6	15	15
15 (17)	Lower Telemark	13.8	14.5	17	14
16 (31)	Søndhordland	13.8	14.8	16	16
17 (27)	Stavanger	12.9	16.9	14	17
18 (29)	Ryfylke	17.0	17.6	19	18
19 (2)	Middle Borgesyssel	16.4	22.9	18	22
20 (13)	Kongsberg	18.4	22.0	20	20
21 (39)	Northern Søndmør	20.2	22.8	21	21
22 (15)	Jarlsberg	22.6	21.4	22	19
23 (16)	Laurvik	25.8	25.5	24	25
24 (11)	Toten and Valders	24.5	26.4	23	27
25 (14)	Drammen	26.1	25.3	25	23
26 (52)	West Finmark	26.3	25.4	26	24
27 (22)	Christiansand	26.8	26.0	28	26
28 (53)	East Finmark	28.1	27.7	30	28
29 (12)	Hadeland	27.5	29.4	29	29
30 (4)	Upper Borgesyssel	26.7	30.2	27	30
31 (5)	Lower Romerike	28.1	30.9	31	31
32 (48)	Salten	30.7	33.5	32	33
33 (46)	Namdal	33.3	32.6	34	32
34 (3)	Western Borgesyssel	30.8	37.4	33	35
35 (32)	Bergen	35.2	34.7	36	34
36 (45)	Indherred	34.7	39.0	35	37
37 (1)	Lower Borgesyssel	37.2	38.8	38	36
38 (50)	Senjen	42.0	40.3	41	38
39 (34)	Outer Sogn	37.1	45.2	37	42
40 (51)	Tromsø	50.4	41.8	47	39
41 (47)	Helgeland	46.1	45.1	42	41
42 (49)	Vesteraalen and Lofoten	48.6	43.8	45	40
43 (40)	Romsdal	40.6	53.3	39	45
44 (44)	Dalerne (Trondheim diocese)	40.8	57.3	40	49
45 (9)	Hedemark	47.9	49.8	44	43
46 (10)	Gudbrandsdal	49.0	50.2	46	44
47 (7)	Upper Romerike	47.1	55.9	43	46

Table 1.2. (Continued)

Number and Reference to Table 1.1	Districts' Rank According to Conditions in 1831–1850 as in Table 1.1	Conditions During the Years 1831–1840	1841–1850	Rank Order 1831–1840	1841–1850
48 (35)	Inner Sogn	53.3	56.2	50	48
49 (8)	Østerdal	52.5	57.8	49	50
50 (42)	Fosen	51.9	59.9	48	52
51 (6)	Christiana	62.5	56.1	52	47
52 (41)	Nordmør	54.3	67.3	51	53
53 (43)	Trondheim	69.1	58.3	53	51
	District				
1	Christiansand	10.8	12.6	1	1
2	Bergen	19.4	20.5	2	2
3	Christiania	32.8	35.9	3	3
4	Tromsø	40.6	39.0	4	4
5	Trondheim	43.9	52.4	5	5
	Kingdom	29.1	32.2		1

more or less unchanged? Weeds we certainly see all over, but there is this difference, that in some places they are thicker than in others, as if they were on the way to dominate here and there; and why is this? The world "lieth in wickedness" and sensuality and brutality are the soil in which the seeds of sin thrust upward and thrive all too well; but certain special factors must in some places have checked that evil growth which we have before our eyes, or encouraged it in other places.

Lower Romerike and Upper Romerike are two communities which lie side by side and which are more or less alike as to natural resources, employment, and housing. But the conditions are worse in the latter district than in the former. Who can explain this oddity? Upper Romerike is inland and Romsdal and Nordmør are coastal districts where all the external conditions which influence people's lives are completely different, and yet the similarities in the lives of the people with regard to the matter we are discussing are remarkably great. Who can tell us why this is so? Inner Sogn is a district whose people reside in that narrow strip between the steep mountains and the deep fjord that penetrates them, and likewise Hardanger is situated around Hardangerfjord's innermost branches; but while the moral conditions according to the figures presented, is especially good in the latter district, it is still extremely bad in the former. So what does this tell us of the causes?

If there were a field or meadow whose fertility, good or bad, had attracted our attention, then surely many could give a satisfactory explanation. For science has worked a long time on fields and meadows. Botany has had its researchers, who generation after generation have communicated their observations to each other. The current researchers in chemistry stand on the shoulders of their forebears, and the men who now guide our farmers have sat at the feet of remarkable teachers. But have the curiosities in the lives of the people, which I have named, been the objects of such prolonged investigation? But it is absolutely essential that what has not been done so far must be done in the future. A small contribution to our understanding of conditions today can lead to greater insight tomorrow. I would like to think that with continuing research we will succeed little by little in finding the connection between causes and effect, the relationship between the wickedness of the people described here and certain other circumstances in the lives of people, which until now were unknown or little noticed, so that later generations with greater knowledge than now can say, see, this is the cause, or, this is one of the major reasons why people's lives in this particular situation have turned out so disastrously here or here. Thus such an understanding of conditions should be important for science, which with great effort contemplates the nature of the human condition, and statesmen and legislators should draw benefit from this knowledge in their struggle to govern and administer for the good of all.

What do I say? Scientists and statesmen? Yes, for we are so used to thinking that a few men administer and govern and direct the thoughts and lives of the masses, and in part this is actually the case. But there are people who have a cleaner knowledge of and are closer to failures and sorry lives, that is the mass of the people themselves. I would regard a year of my life well spent if I could write a book on the *people,* a book which 10 of the best men in the country could approve and have some use for; but I would gladly give 10 years if I could write *for* the people and *to* the people about the *serious matters* in their lives, so that the masses of the people could say: "Yes, it is true, what he said. We already know this after a fashion but now it is clearer to us. This we must think about from now on."

Nowadays printers can print at speeds for everybody, and everybody can certainly read the printed word. And here is one thing which I would at once give the young people of Gudbrandsdal, of Hedemark, or of Upper Romerike to think about: According to the information which appears in the figures given above, it can be said with certainty that insofar as young people are now growing up in these communities no better than their forebears, so they will accumulate for themselves such a mass of remorse and pain, that is much, much greater than that encountered by their contemporaries in most corners of the land. It must be assumed that hithertoo special factors have caused bad conditions for so long in the same communities. Certainly there is something mysterious and distressing in this, which perhaps the sharpest intellects could hardly master, and which those who govern the country could not possibly control. But this much we know for certain, that these same factors are really not so coercive and irresistible, that those individuals, who together make up the enormous mass of happy or unhappy people, dare not deny their belief that they could master and govern themselves.

Added Later: Relations between Town and Country

In the comparisons this chapter has drawn between the different areas, there is one drawback—that *town* and *country* are treated as one. In the towns the situation regarding illegitimate births is usually worse than in the adjoining country districts, and when, besides, a deanery-district as well as some country parishes which include one or several towns is compared with another deanery district, in which there are no towns, then one is not comparing like to like.

During the years 1851–1854 there were 37,872 marriages and 14,121 illegitimate live births in rural districts; in town districts there were 6,618 marriages and 2,866 illegitimate live births. The ratio was thus: in rural districts for every 100 marriages there were 37.3 illegitimate live births, and in town districts for every 100 marriages there were 43.3 illegitimate live births. (The ratios are a good deal higher for 1851–1854 than those previously recorded in this chapter for 1831–1850, but one should not conclude therefrom that the conditions worsened so much; in this connection see appendix A regarding the years 1851–1855.)

These ratios show, as has just been noted, that conditions are usually worse in towns than in the country districts. They confirm the fact that those of the 53 deanery-districts in table 1.1 which consist either entirely, or for the most part, of urban areas are less favorabley situated, with regard to illegitimate births, than do those deanery districts which are adjacent to them and which consist almost entirely of rural areas. This is the situation with deanery district no. 6, the Christiania diocesan deanery (i.e., the capital and the rural parish of Aker); no. 22, Christiansand; no. 32, Bergen; and no. 43, the diocesean-deanery of Trondheim (i.e., the seats of the dioceses of the same name).

Lower Borgesyssel, or deanery no. 1 in the same table, includes the towns of Fredrikshald and Fredrikstad, and Western Borgesyssel, or no. 3, likewise includes Moss and the recently established Sarpsborg. One might consider this to be the reason why both of these deaneries show up much less favorably than Middle and Upper Borgesyssel. And it is further possible that if we could isolate the towns in those deaneries and investigate the situation for the rural districts alone, there would not be such a difference.

This deficiency in the tables in this chapter could no doubt be corrected. With the help of the lists that are preserved by the pastors, it would have been possible from each of the relevant deaneries to add up the totals of both marriages and illegitimate births for each of the years from 1831 to 1850 for those parishes, which for the most part consist of urban districts, and by removing these be left with those which relate to parishes with rural districts only. But this task would have been a very tedious one and in any case would not have been practicable for me. It is then the case that only in recent years has the statistical office produced for official publication a calculation that has taken account of the urban and rural differences. That is why I have only been able to present figures for the entire kingdom's urban and rural districts for 1851 to 1854.

One is often inclined to imagine the conditions in the towns as worse than they actually are; especially misleading would be the view that the towns, particularly the larger ones, are to be seen as the source from which immorality spreads throughout the rural districts. In this connection I can give an unusual fact from Denmark. In the Danish statistical tables on population in 1840, the situation with regard to illegitimate births is recorded separately for urban and rural in each individual diocese, and the calculation shows how many legitimate live births there were for each illegitimate one (table 1.3).

According to this method of calculation, the larger numbers denote a better condition and the smaller numbers on the other hand a worse one (the opposite of the method of calculation used in my table 1.1). But the foregoing figures show that in those dioceses where the entire area, urban and rural together, is bad, then it is usually bad both in the urban and in the rural areas. Something similar is to be found in Norway:

Table 1.3. Illegitimate births in Denmark, 1840

Diocese	Town	Country	Total
Sjælland without Copenhagen	1: 8.17	1: 14.82	1: 13.69
Fyen	1: 5.37	1: 5.98	1: 5.88
Lolland-Falster	1: 9.41	1: 13.12	1: 12.51
Aalborg	1: 5.42	1: 8.32	1: 7.87
Viborg	1: 4.98	1: 9.74	1: 9.22
Aarhus	1: 5.95	1: 11.10	1: 10.16
Ribe	1: 11.27	1: 15.77	1: 15.16

the Christiania and Trondheim diocesan deaneries, that is to say the dioceses' largest towns, reveal a very unfavorable situation and they are surrounded by rural districts where the situation is likewise unfavorable. On the other hand, the Bergen, and still more the Christiansand, diocesan deaneries (i.e., the diocesan seats) are surrounded by rural areas with better conditions and whilst they themselves are no doubt worse than the rural districts but they are still a good deal better than the other diocese seats mentioned.

Would it now be right to conclude that the evil comes from the towns, so that it is the fault of the towns when conditions are shown as bad in the adjoining rural districts? Or might one be permitted to turn matters on their head thus: If the moral condition is at the onset bad in the rural areas, it is to be expected that it would be still worse in the towns within those same districts, as a result of the pernicious influence stemming from the rural areas, which combines with particular moral dangers associated with town life.

The reason for this last reflection on the matter could be that the towns generally receive a steady stream of young people from the country who naturally bring with them the concepts and life styles which so to speak belong to their home districts. This situation is found particularly in Christiania: a very large proportion of the servant and working classes there consists of migrants from Upper Romerike and Hedemark, where, as my table shows, the situation regarding illegitimate births is very bad. Were one to assert that this destruction of morality emanated from Christiania (with people who returned home, etc.), then it is rather odd that the capital city should extend its ruinous influence way up to Østerdal and Gudbrandsdal, but to a far lesser degree to the neighboring Romerike or Ringerike.

2

Rural Dwellings

THE parish of Lom lies in Gudbrandsdal. In North Berget, its remotest hamlet, lies the old farm of Løkre. I have seen a dwelling on this farm which is quite remarkable because of the old-fashioned style in which it is built. The ground floor forms a longish rectangle, at least 24 feet wide and 30 feet long. A cross wall between the two longer walls divides the room. On one side is a living room, which takes up the largest part: on the other a small chamber. The roof extends some 4 to 6 feet outwards from one of the long walls. Supported by posts and clad with wood panelling this now forms a small covered vestibule. The entrance to the living room is about halfway along this same long wall. And from the living room a door leads into the small chamber. At each end of the vestibule

Fig. 2.1. The Ramloft dwelling on the farm of Løkre in Lom. The drawings are taken from a later work in which Sundt returned to the farmhouse that he describes here.

are closets in which tools and other possessions are stored. That part of the house which forms the actual living room consists of only one floor. Above it a ridgepole, which extends the entire length of the building, bears the sod- and grass-covered roof. As this also forms the ceiling of the living room, one can see right up to the ridgepole. But this is not true of that part of the house containing the chamber. For there is another floor, or loft, above this. Though, like the chamber this is narrow, it is as long as the house is wide, since its outer wall is that of the house itself. The gables on each of the smaller ends of the loft face in the opposite direction to those of the living room and the ridgepole, which bears

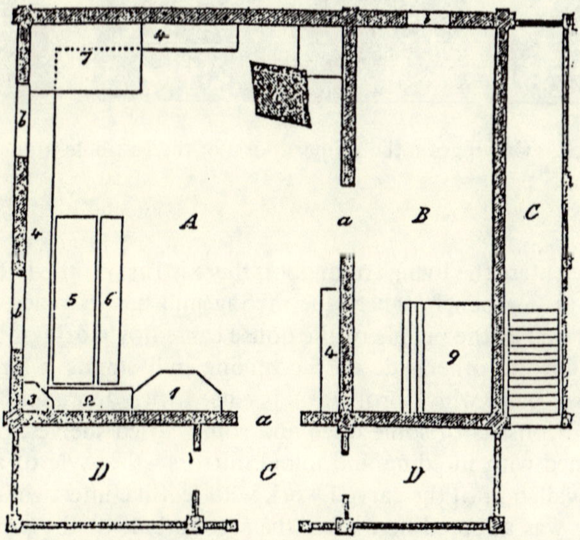

Fig. 2.2. Ground floor plan of the Løkre dwelling. Here we have the living room (*A*) and the chamber under the Ramloft (*B*); two vestibules (*C C*), at each end of the longer of which are small closets (*D D*); the doors into the living room and the chamber (*a a*) and the windows (*b b b*). To the left of the outer door (*a*) is a large dresser (1), the so-called *fremskab;* then the seat of honor (2), which is fixed to the floor; a smaller cupboard (3); in front of the cross wall is a fixed bench (4); there is a long table (5) in front of this with another long bench (6). On the long wall facing the entrance is the bed belonging to the master of the house (7) and another fixed bench (4). On the inner cross wall is the fireplace (8) together with yet another fixed bench on the other side of the door leading into the chamber. Finally within the chamber itself is a bed (9) with a couple of steps leading up to it.

these gables, is not only high above that of the living room, but lies at right angles to it. If one stands in front of the longer side of the building, one sees that the greater part, that is to say the longest section with its sod roof facing one, is lower than the smaller part, this being one floor higher. The gable of the latter looks like a small tower. The picturesqueness of the whole is heightened still further by the vestiblue which, with the remarkable carvings on its supporting posts together with the apertures in the wood panelling, runs along the entire front of the building. Steps lead from the lower part of this vestibule up to the entrance of the sleeping loft above.

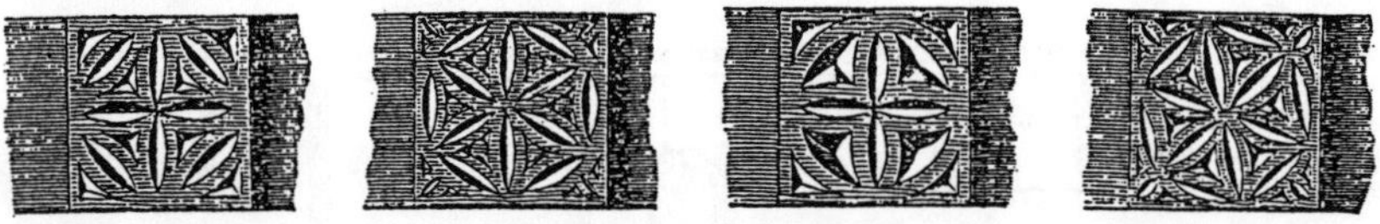

Fig. 2.3. Carvings on the support posts of the vestibule to the Løkre dwelling.

If one enters the living room door, there is first on the left-hand side a stool or a low bench, where the mixing mill has its place and where visitors as well as the people of the house can enjoy a drink of a mixture of whey. On the other side of the mixing mill stands a large cabinet whose lower part, which protrudes, is closed with doors and whose upper section consists of some open and some closed shelves; overall it is well adorned with molding and inlaid mirrors—the style of adornment which prevailed until the carved work with leaflike intertwining or curls that likely was adopted here after the second half of the previous century. Lom and a few other communities in Gudbrandsdal later became famous for this type of woodcarving.

On the other side of the cabinet is the high seat, with its own small and uniquely adorned high seat cabinet in the corner. In the next wall there are two small windows placed in lead frames and thereunder a permanent bench with a long table before it, which also has one end turned toward the high seat. By the third wall, which is at the entrance, there is in the corner against the window-wall the master of the household's bed, and in the corner against the vestibule is the stove, a neatly cut out soapstone block shaped as a fireplace. On the fourth wall, on the right of the entrance, is the door to the vestibule, a room whose single, little leaded window yields only a dim light, and in whose innermost corner a large bed is built into the walls.

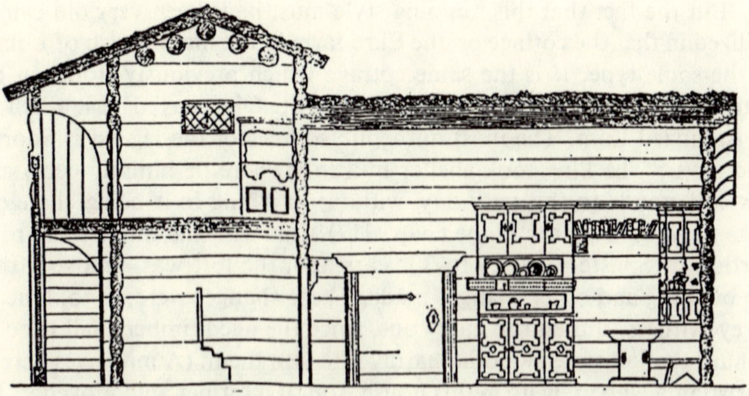

Fig. 2.4. Interior of the Løkre dwelling with entrance door.

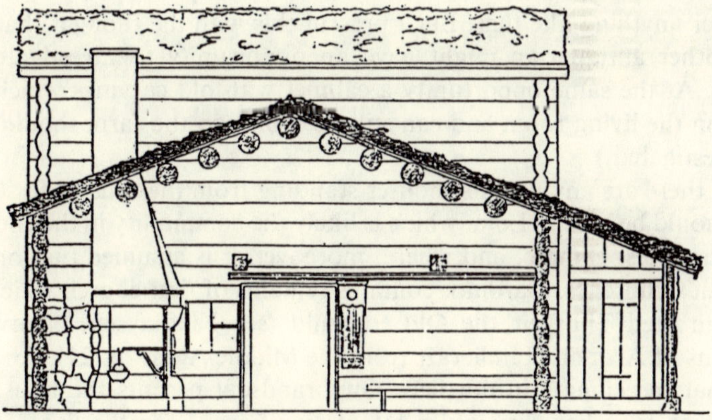

Fig. 2.5. Interior of the Løkre dwelling with door to chamber.

This is what one old gabled cottage looked like. But the one at Løkre, whose ridgepole bears the year 1769, is likely one of the youngest, and there are not many of its counterparts remaining. On the farm Elgsæter, at the foot of Galdhøen in Bæverdal in Lom, there stands a gabled cottage from 1640, but it has been torn down and rebuilt and thereby has suffered some changes. And while both of these buildings are aging and unoccupied, there are two small cottages of the building style in Bæverdal (Slettet and Holen) which are still occupied, but they are sagging and ramshackle.

But the fact that this building style must have been very old can be realized in that the cottage on the Ekre farm in the main parish of Lom is of the same type. It is the same cottage which previously stood on the Sønste-Næs farm, and legend has it that St. Olaf stayed in it when he christianized Lom. The most authentic source for the legend is Snorre, who says: "The king took shelter in a loft where he himself slept, and this still stands to this very day, without anything in it being changed" (*The Saga of Olaf the Holy,* chap. 117). But with the move to Ekre (a portion of Sønste-Næs) 20 to 30 years ago, the loft was removed from the building and other changes made. These changes were, as told me by an eyewitness, difficult to carry out, since the aged timbers had become so hard that ax and saw could hardly bite into them. (A man lives here in Christiania who grew up in this house, son of a farmer who moved it. He says that he well remembers how the ridgepoles are inscribed with carved-in letters of a strange shape which no one could read. When I was in the house I was not yet aware that the ridgepole usually has on it the year and writing, and since it was late in the day and dim, I did not discover anything like that. But I present this with the thought that one or another antiquarian might have an opportunity to investigate the matter. At the same opportunity a cabinet with old carvings which has stood in the living room and can still be found on the farm should also be investigated.)

If there are any wooden houses standing from the time of St. Olaf, they should be here in Lom, which is likely the community in the country with the driest climate, and where, moreover, it is assumed that one of the annex churches, Gardmo, contains remains of that church which St. Olaf directed Thorgeir the Old to build (see Nikolaysen, "Norway's Remains of Art and Handicraft from the Middle Ages," p. 21). And the fact that the climate in northern Gudbrandsdal permits the houses to survive so long has certainly a lot of significance for the lives of the people and the culture. It is often said that common people of Gudbrandsdal, like those in Hedemark and Romerike, indeed reveal a hanging-on to the old, certainly a conservative character in custom and belief. But perhaps this old-fashioned characteristic has its basis in part in the simple surroundings, in that so many generations lived in succession in one and same house, so that each new family had to accommodate itself to directives and furnishings which were adapted to the original customs of grandparents and great-grandparents.

But I have already nevertheless suggested a change in the building styles in Lom also; the old furnishings along with lofts were eliminated and a new building form became the dominant custom. This new form nevertheless is not introduced with any foreign style; in fact, in Lom one can see clearly how the later building style has evolved from the earlier, about the way a flower whose petals begin to fall off is a continuation of the [flower] which recently had stood in full splendor. The houses which left off the gabled living rooms did not have the gabled towerlike height, nor so many prominent vestibules, and the posts in the vestibule, which still in some houses protected the entrance, lacked the earlier remarkable carved adornments. Otherwise the basic form of the wooden building continued to be the same arrangement of the high seat and the cabinet and the bed and so forth; the long and narrow bedroom at the panel wall was merely cut in two, a bed-closet (in the part of the building where the fireplace for the living room is located) and a handy closet where the housewife kept her water buckets and curdled milk. To these two rooms there are two small doors in one wall of the living room, which are a part of the wall panel and painted; then there is the middle space between these two doors; here hang towels for holiday purposes, the long and narrow towels decorated on the ends with knotted fringes, which hang smoothly spread over a roller at a proper height; and above this is the "throw in," a little cabinet in which one can toss one's mittens or other small things. Such a living room one can see, for example, in Kvaale in Bæverdal; this also resembles the little loft there, in that a person in the living room can see all the way up to the ridgepole, which shows the year 1752. From one long wall to the other there is a large loft beam (the crown), and from it run two cross-beams (cross crowns) over to the wall which divides the living room and the closets. Should the farmer dry his raw lumber, he puts them there, but he might also lay some loose boards over the cross-beams so that a half loft (a loft of loose boards) is formed, where, for example, the hired man sleeps in winter. The farmer's bed, as noted, stands in a particular corner of the living room and the bed-loft is a guest room.

Little by little the large empty room under the roof was found to be inappropriate; it is dark up there and the living room was cold in the winter on account of the heat rushing up. Therefore the idea was thought up to lay a paneled ceiling or loft above the living room as previously. Sometimes, as in the living room of 1761 in Glymsdal in Bæverdal, where in former times there lived rich and powerful people, this paneled ceiling was built in a sort of arch under the roof, but mostly, and commonly in later times, it was laid pure and simple on beams. It can also be noted that as glass became easier to obtain, the windows increased in size so that for the most part they admitted adequate light into the living room.

In order to have a name in contrast to the older loft rooms I will call them small bedrooms. Their common characteristic is that they are wooden, built in a longish rectangle; in one end is a small bedroom which often is divided by a panel; at the other end is an almost square room whose cabinet, high seat, bed, and fireplace stand in the same place as explained previously, such that on entering one becomes familiar with them all and at first glance sees that the room serves simultaneously as kitchen, sleeping room, and living room; again there is a cabinet of remarkable facade adorned with molding and inlaid mirrors, and a vestibule stands before the long wall where the entrance is.

This building style must have been very common in the country. Since I first became aware of its peculiarities, I have regularly found traces of the same in older buildings everywhere I have traveled in the parish of Christiania. It must have been a standing custom to build houses in this manner, and the customs have had such an influence over the people that it did not easily occur to a man to build his house any other way. The oldest house of this kind which I have had occasion to see stands in Onserud in Ullensaker in Romerike; it is from 1628. Until a score of years ago, it served as a dwelling; now it is moved and somewhat rebuilt and used as a washhouse; the cabinet, which has the aforementioned special shape but is more simply put together than those from later times, has on the edge of the three shelves this inscription in raised letters:

> My hope to God alone, year 1628,
> and Jesus who died for me and rose again.
> ora et labora. pray and labor. Jesus name

Here in Romerike in Nannestad, Ullensaker, and Gjerdrum, where one finds several quite well maintained buildings of this kind, the walls in back of the high seat were decorated with a painted board of paneling or linen cloth, with Bible verses; instead, in Lom one used to hang, and still does in part during holiday festivities, a tapestry on the wall of the kind called Upstad tapestry, which is not woven but in a manner interlaced and decorated with biblical figures and sayings or inscriptions—an art which is now completely forgotten in the area and recognized only in the few inherited pieces which are owned.

Since vaulted ceilings or lofts were made over a living room, meantime in southern areas calculations were made to heighten the wooden walls with a couple of beams so that there could be a roomier dark loft above. These beams were allowed to project out over the lower long wall and form the roof for the vestibule, where the stairs to the loft were placed. A rather large cotter's cottage is exactly in this style at the place Duenæs ved Ødemarks-sjøen. It is from the year 1754, and the old widow of the cotter who this winter lived in it told me that when she was a child all houses in the parish were like that; in the arrangement of the living room there was the peculiarity, which has been unique to this area, that the fireplace did not stand in one of the corners but between two doors which led into the two bedrooms, or small rooms, as they were called; and since it stood in this place, it had a roundlike protrusion on the floor with a similar bricked-up vault on top, unlike the Gudbrandsdal type of fireplace which stands in the corner and protrudes at an angle.

This living room interested me because, like the two cotters' living rooms of the old loft form, it exemplified how cotter folk in the furnishing of their small houses strove to emulate the style of the large farm-estates. These small cotters' houses were built of thinner boards and therefore rotted faster; but such examples as they revealed—let us assume that if we could have visited the grandparents of the current cotters' families during the previous century, we would likely in the better places have found house furnishings like those of the farm-estate people, only less elaborate.

There are many who maintain that in all ways the old characteristics were the best. For their sake I will share a small glimpse of the older farm generation's home conditions. In one cotter's "north of good manners" living room in Lom, in one of the houses which could still provide the opportunity to use the designation "folk customs from north of good manners," [Norwegian idiom—implies that manners are crude in the far north] I became aware of the special furnishing. It was a long narrow tray with a handle in one end, charred and black, so that it looked most like a so-called baking board which the bakers use to give a surface to the bread before baking, but it was bored through with many small holes and had its place at the inside edge of the bed, where it lay up to the wall. "What is this?" I asked. "A bedbug board," was the reply. "But what kind of equipment is this?" I had to continue to ask. "To catch bedbugs with—because they are a kind of small animal which are so named." Finally I got the following explanation: These same small animals have the habit, at night and as long as it is dark, to walk around, but with the first light they see, they become somewhat confused and hurry into cracks and holes. Now when the man of the house wakes up at night and notices that they are about, he gets up and lights a fire in the fireplace; this chases many of the small ones into the holes in the board mentioned, and skillfully and stealthily the man takes it and sets it in the middle of the fire—this is why it is burned so black. Now this was a cotter *nora* folk custom, and I honored him for the discovery, since necessity motivated the solution. But in a conversation with an old cotter in Næs in Romerike, I had the occasion to test him by telling him about this trick. "Yes," he said, "it was likewise done on the farm where I was a hired hand in my youth (one of the larger farms in the community). The old man lay in the old-room (one of the bedrooms) and there he had such a board by his bed. One of the girls each morning had to take and carry it out to the ash heap; it was exactly one of the old bedbug boards." And later a farmer, who now lives in Skedsmo but otherwise is from Aker, related that he had seen the same kind of board in use here, where it was named virgin-board. But after these examples it seemed that the object had likely been nationwide and was a necessary requirement for the bedrooms.

In another glimpse of the simplicity of the old days associated with the simple building style I saw in Lom, the board had been quite common and to some extent is still used to bake flat bread at the fire, which for the preparation of the mash for the animals is set up in the cattle barn. To see food preparation in such a house becomes doubly unpleasant, since the animal quarters here are both small and very dark. I might tell more about how the animal quarters had to serve as living quarters for people. But since I tell about bread baking, I am reminded of when I both laughed and wept when I once peeked into a drying room in Lom, while the farmer sat there in smoke and steam to bake oven bread, or the remarkable "Lom cakes." In the bedrooms there are no baking ovens, and the work in the smoky drying room is so exhausting that womenfolk could not endure it. Instead the man sat there and baked cake-bread for his daughter's wedding, while the wife brewed beer in the living room. This hardly resembled a brewery because three tailors sat at the table and sewed holiday clothes. Here I had a good opportunity to observe how extremely difficult the life of a farm family can be, since for three days there raged such bad weather that it was impossible to leave the farm, and I could not shut myself in the bedroom as it was without a heating stove, and a snowdrift almost covered my window if it was not pushed away every second. This was, you see, in Brotene, high up under the Bergen mountains.

It can be remarked that this method of heating a large room with the help of a fireplace is by no means pleasant. I had to find this out during the winter when I intended to sit by the fire and read—where it is too hot—or by the window during the day to write—where it is too cold. This is not so in the summer, but then the one not used to it is bothered by a custom which is still often seen both in Lom and other places in

Gudbrandsdal—that the container of bark with all its strong-smelling hides is placed under the table.

Therefore the desire for roomier and more comfortable buildings has been felt for a long time, and one has striven to furnish them better. Particularly in the last half century there has been a lot of building, and even in Gudbrandsdal it is now very difficult to again find the original simple form of the small bedroom. Sometimes a new bedroom cottage has been placed at the side of the old, and the two could be connected with a hall or something similar, but they do not fit together perfectly; the new house is maybe built of narrower lumber but has higher doors and bigger windows. More often, either at the beginning or during repairs, people built another floor over the first and furnished a bedroom and clothes closet, or an unmatching house near the farm house itself, for such extra convenience. There is no particular early rule or custom for all this, and on the larger farms there is also some duplication of storehouses and animal quarters and, in addition, all kinds of sheds for pigs, sheep, etc. The total cluster of buildings presents a completely remarkable picture. The thousands of artistic woodcarvers during the last generations have created even more confusion with their curlicue carvings. When I saw last year the drawings in the picture magazines from Krim of the cities of the Tartar chiefs and palaces with the many bay windows and towers, they made me think of such farm-estates as Haakenstad or Tolfstad in Vaage, with the many large and small houses, extensions and annexes, hallways and stairs, corners and covers. In Hedemark and farther south, in particular perhaps in Næs, Urskoug, and Høland in the course of this century, there has been a complete break with all these characteristics, and houses have been built which remind one of the houses in towns, with a special kitchen and a day living room and a large living room, ballroom, guest rooms, paneled and painted. The building clusters in Gudbrandsdal began at a time when it was a definite custom which all had to observe, and they have developed according to no plans in the other communities named. The houses show some evidence of a time when the expression, "So many heads, so many minds" was valid, so that without hindrance one tried to furnish oneself according to one's comfort, since style had not made any great demands yet. I was still entertained often by finding in the somewhat impressive buildings in Næs a remnant of the past: a ceiling with grills and carvings held up by a couple of posts over the main entrance—a small decoration in the house from the old vestibule.

HOW THE TENANTS LIVE

Quite commonly up to half a century ago, the leading farmers in Næs and Høland sat in their high seats [a chair was reserved for the head of the household] in the old-fashioned living rooms and ate the mid-morning meal with their cotters and hired hands, who sat on benches at the same table; the table board was the common plate for them all; the farmer's wooden spoon in common frugality lay together with those of the others in the drawer, and even with the eating of the smoked herring no one was so persnickety as to miss a fork. But this picture of early times is regarded with nostalgia by the cotters in the communities. Since the farmer acquired a separate kitchen and bedroom and a living room, etc., the "people" ate by themselves in the old manner, and the housewife set the family table in the living room. "And there is so much paint and finery that a simple workman does not know if he dares to go in and talk with the farmer of the house about this or that, as might be appropriate." "Well and good," I replied to the cotter from whom I heard these remarks. "Well and good that there are some proper houses so that you and others could learn how proper folk should live. You look at me with astonishment. I naturally can understand enough to realize that a cotter cannot afford to build so large and fine a house as that of the farmer himself, but a good fellow could quite certainly arrange it so that he could live a little more like that than is now usual among the working class in the country."

Greater comfort and cheer in dwellings are surely one of the best indicators of a rising culture. But precisely in the aforementioned communities, in contrast with the farm classes, I became aware how little progress in this regard was evident in the working class. I will not assert that no progress can be seen in this class also, but I dare say it has been very small.

One winter I visited a cotter family in Høland, the man and wife about 35 or 40 years of age, with a beautiful bunch of children. I found everything in good order; yes, I learned to know an unusually tidy cotter family. Only one matter disturbed me. I seated myself at the table to eat an egg pancake (it was a rare occasion, observed the wife, that she had a guest just on the day when the hen had laid the first egg, and she thereby took the opportunity to offer it to me), and at the same time I noticed that the floor sank under my feet and the cold draft blew in. It was nothing new for me to see a floor with loose boards which are not sealed together but only laid side by side—such floors are likely the most common in the living rooms of cotters; time and again I have seen cotters' living rooms look so thin and open that it was impossible to keep out the winter cold. And this observation has never pained me as much as here. Have I all along been blinded by the thought that simple folk, that coarse people, as they are often called, are from the beginning created for a hard life so that they are able to endure cold in this country? I would express myself very badly if I said about the aforementioned wife that there was anything ladylike in her being, but already her fine regular features and her beautiful, secure bearing made me aware of, and even the naive directness in her speech made me so much sooner recognize in her, a deep and gentle spirit which truly would grace the most noble woman. But now such a woman in an open house in our Norwegian winter—and for her entire life! When such a family can be discovered to live in this way, does one need to know more to imagine how it is with the masses?

In the parish of Næs, there was a conversation between a farmer and me which ended with my requesting him to name one of the most shipshape and orderly cotter families he knew of in this area, and he mentioned one of his own cotters. Here I found also a particularly able and hardworking man and a very good housekeeper of a woman, with whom I had both the benefit and the pleasure to talk and therefore often visited. Once our conversation was interrupted when a visitor arrived, a woman who brought a little pig. How happy the children became, four little girls! They all had to kiss and pat the pig. It was also a joy to the house because it had been born so early in the year (it was in March last year) and thereby could become so large by fall. Therefore the woman guest had to be served, and there was set forth porridge and milk for her at the little table before the window. But at the same time the family itself should have their dinner. The four little girls stood on their knees or hunched around a chair where their porridge bowl was placed; the woman stood beside them and ate from the same bowl, but the man sat on a box in which the pig was already sleeping, and he ate out of the kettle which had been removed from the cookstove. But during the changes which took place in the living room, I had to move around carefully from place to place, since the space which was not occupied by people was overoccupied by three beds (since there were in all five children in the house) and by the fireplace, cooking stove, kitchen cabinet, and a carpenter's bench with all kinds of saws for the cooper work which the man was tinkering with that day. This living room was the family's only room for living; there was no other room. And in addition this house was to a great extent leaky and rotted, so that I could stick my knife in the wood right to the handle. A storage building belonged to the cottage, which must also have served as a dressing room, and the woman here is better off than the neighbor woman, who did not have a room and had to make use of a dark loft as a storage room and climb a shaky outside ladder to it. I was up in this dark loft; with some difficulty I got in through a low opening. I was not able to stand upright inside, and truly I had to be careful to find the first rung on the ladder when I was to go down again.

For a couple of days in the parish of Ullensaker, I walked among a group of cotters' places and spent an evening with the most attractive man and in the most attractive place that I could find. The man was both sensible and impressive, and I spent a satisfying evening. When I was already sitting on the edge of the bed before sleeping, one thing occurred to me. The occupants of the house were: the older man and woman, two grown sons—the one a shoemaker, the other a tailor, both of whom were away (which made it possible to have an extra overnight place for me)—plus a grown daughter and a small indigent boy who was fostered out for pay—and I saw only two beds. I asked the man how there were beds for all. "Well, I sleep here with my wife and the little boy, and the shoemaker sleeps there, and the tailor, who is smaller, has a little bed in the small bedchamber."—"But your daughter, Gurine, where does she sleep?"—"Well, tonight she sleeps in the small bedchamber, but otherwise, when everyone is at home, she shares the bed with her brother the shoemaker." And all of this was told as if there were nothing unusual about it.

In another parish in Romerike, I visited a place last fall where I was pleased to find what might be called a well-established house. The building itself was larger than usual in that the roomy living room had a beautiful bedroom as well. I remember the family, and in particular the head of the household, fully, both by conversation and through others. The somewhat young man had a wife and one child; he was an artisan and was engaged by the farm to be responsible for the work required. His mother lived as a pensioner with him, and she had with her a mentally retarded daughter plus another grown daughter with an illegitimate child. The cottage was orderly and attractive, and three beds stood along the wall. "Tell me," I asked the old woman, "how do you arrange for beds here, for I see no cradle in the house?" Well, she herself and her frail daughter slept in one bed, the other daughter with her baby in the other bed, and "themselves" with their baby in the third. "And the hired man?"—"He sleeps on the farm."—"The farm?"—"Yes, when he works there, but that is not all the time; today he is at home and cuts wood."—"Where will he sleep tonight?"—"Well, when he is at home he sleeps together with 'themselves,'" was the answer. This last example shows clearly that the whole nature of dwellings and living is something that is related to the stage of the culture. It is not always the means and will which are lacking but very often the perception to desire something better, since this perception usually stimulates serious effort, and this effort can generate the necessary resources.

3

Sleeping Quarters in Barns

THE foregoing chapter ended with the remark that the cause of the deplorable conditions we see in the working class in the rural areas, the cause of the inexcusable dwellings and the indecent life styles in part must be sought in the low level of better standards of culture of those concerned. Yes, the low level of culture, here there are many who would quickly agree. Precisely in these times we hear so many, in part in a very inconsiderate manner, make remarks about the many coarse misdeeds in the working class—apathy, recklessness, drunkenness, and more. As a sort of reaction to this, once in a while a "poor man's friend" in the newspapers or other places describes the sufferings of the working class and urges the other social classes to help with humane arrangements of various kinds. But I do not like this compassion, which does not see a hope in the helpless and irresponsible wretches, nor can I make the judgment that working-class people find their pleasure in wallowing in all kinds of coarseness, so that one without hesitation regards them as all bad.

If we constructed a weighing scale so that we could weigh the status of one class compared with the other, we would probably find that the sums of true virtues or flaws, of real happiness or unhappiness, are nearly alike for the different statuses and classes, the higher and the lower. But even without such a scale, I assert that we can recognize this: that the cultural condition which at the moment is found in a single class—the working class or the cotter class—has evolved partly through the common influence of the personal conditions of its members and partly through the influence of all the others, as we say, higher-up people, as these two classes have lived together in the country. There is a certain relationship between the separate classes' morality and circumstances and between the degree of enlightenment and morality which has evolved within the whole of the total population.

This interrelatedness can naturally only be perceived in fragments, but the following presentation attempts to be a contribution to it.

I imagine myself again in the cottages of cotters in a few areas of our country, the eastern parts of the diocese of Christiania, and I notice that people not only live in miserable conditions but seem not to realize it themselves. Seem? I absolutely know that when I have talked with cotters about their expenses (naturally a favorite problem for conversation) and they make comparisons between the various places in the area, they recall precisely how much (or how little) grain can be grown, how many cattle and sheep can be fed, what access there is to wood and pasture—but whether or not there is a proper house in the place or a rotted, ramshackle cabin, for the most part they do not consider. Only when I deliberately ask about this do I learn that in such and such a house two of the bottom boards are rotted, and the roof is leaking, etc., and on such and such a place there is a truly nice house, built last year, with quite a large bedroom next to the house.

But why is there this apathy regarding a matter which to so great an extent has to do with health, morals, and daily comfort?

Has there been from the beginning an accommodation so that the man of the family is a poor man and has no outlook other than to be a poor man all his life, so that he can think of nothing else than the struggle to satisfy the immediate demands of food for the many mouths and rags for the naked? But such awful conditions are nevertheless not the usual situation. There can be quite orderly, hardworking people who with care and thought have arranged it so that they eventually have arrived at a tolerable situation, which is common in the working class; but even with such people I have often deplored the strange lack of appreciation for a healthful and comfortable dwelling. Why is this?

A great deal is due to upbringing. And here it must be recalled that the upbringing of the man of the house and his wife falls into two time periods, first, the childhood years, when they grew up in their father's and mother's plain cabin, and then the years of their youth, when they—like almost all children of cotters in these parts—lived as servants of farm owners.

This last period of upbringing is not the least important one. It is part of how the master and mistress of the house become a model for the servants. From this they learn what is good enough for them, and years of habit give them a certain idea what demands on life it is possible for them to make, what goal they can set for themselves in the future.

In many of our rural communities it is good enough for the servant folk to have their sleeping accommodations in the animal barns.

While on a stay in Hedemark in 1851, I became aware of this custom. For me, who had grown up in the western part of the country, this custom was completely foreign, and it struck me as disgusting. "You then regard it as unhealthy?" a farm wife remarked. "But it is harmful," I answered in a strong voice. And later experience has taught me to make a stronger judgment, since during my subsequent trips I have constantly watched out for this thing.

In Gudbrandsdal I visited a farm owner on a large and beautiful farm. We strolled together over the land, and I enjoyed the new fields as much as the excellent view of the valley. But then I became aware of a newly built, expensive animal barn. This I had to look at, and he was naturally willing to show me around in there. There was a large and orderly row of stalls and bins. But in one corner I discovered a curious furnishing: a large arrangement of double beds, one below and one above, each one big enough for three or four persons. "What—do you have eight milkmaids?" No, it was intended that the girls should lie below and the boys above. I looked at him and he continued: "I meant that this arrangement should be best—for so can one party control the other."

A few days later I walked around among some cotter places up in another little part of the Gudbrandsdal community, and here I was taken aback by a house which was oddly small. It stood on a bare piece of ground without an animal barn or hayloft, even without an enclosure around the small black piece of earth, which had been a potato field but which had not even been planted that summer. I went in. An alert young man was in a strange situation. He had a screaming one-year-old child on his lap to feed, and he was occupied with preparing the food as well; and, lacking a kettle, he had a frying pan tilted over the fire. I saw near the rim of it that a couple of spoonfuls of water gruel were being boiled. This he had to do because the wife was away, since she with the two older children had gone to the neighboring farm "to get some milk." The general condition in the house was completely deplorable, and I struck up a conversation in order to get at the cause; questions and answers were exchanged at length. "So," I eventually concluded, "you had children before you were married?"—"Yes, that is the custom now."—"Custom? You call that custom?"—"Yes, poor folks do not come together unless it is so."—"So, a poor people's custom! It is then worse than evil. But tell me: you were servants together, and she likely slept in the animal barn, but you, where did you have your bed?"—"Oh, we were in the same animal barn, because that is the custom."

I do not condemn all sleeping in the animal barn. On October 14, 1844, a cotter in Lom placed the ridgepole in the first house on a spot which he had begun to furnish, and a few days thereafter he moved in with his wife and his small animal herd—the house was an animal barn. But I can well imagine that the newlyweds had a happy winter, since they must be fond of the animals. I had actually heard a long story about the cow and about each of the sheep and goats, and I know that it had cost a great deal of difficulty and worry to nurture and protect them until the day when the man and wife could have them under one roof. They must have been fond of each other, since he had been a beggar and on public welfare and a goatherd and a servant boy, and she was the daughter of a farmer. But thanks to his honest heart and ability and to Dean Hiltberg's good instructions for confirmation, he won her trust. When he was certain that in spite of the opposition of her relatives she was devoted and trusting, he turned his few small animals, which he already as a servant boy had collected, over to his father's use and care and went to Romsdal. During that time the economic conditions were favorable, so he became a servant there, worked at odd jobs, tried business, was deathly sick for a while but recovered, lost some money because of the unreliability of others but regained the loss, and could return, after an absence of five years, in the spring of 1843, with 42 daler together with tolerably good clothes, a picture Bible edited by Winthers, a rather large piece of leather for a pair of boots, and a lot more useful things, so now the girl's relatives could no longer oppose her joining with him. He was, of course, not yet a farmer, but he had made a place for himself with such standards that he would not be a worker. Besides, the girl's mother must realize how she already on the boy's confirmation day had harbored a favorable regard for him. Although the boy was only a welfare recipient, the minister had placed him in the next-to-the-highest position on the church floor, right between farmers' sons from the best farms, as if he were a son from a respected farm where he was placed for care, and the mistress of the farm, being pleased with him, had made a whole set of new and good clothes for him. And what happened? At the same day of the ceremony, his future mother-in-law was fortuitously present on the farm and was the first one to meet him returning home from church and greeted him with these words: "I hear that you have earned the room on the farm—you must be an able boy."

Now they still lived in the animal barn over the winter and lived both well and good; it certainly became a trying time when the wife in 1845 gave birth to their first and still only child and was ill a long time thereafter, but she nevertheless came through it. But what judgment should we make about the home life and the overall condition of these people when we hear that again in the next winter they remained in the animal barn? Now I am not offended by it, for I know how the man had to devote all his time and resources to break his land, a small fertile woodland. It had not been possible for him to build a house, which after the animal barn was the greatest need, namely, a hayloft which first came into being in 1846. It was well enough that the father-in-law helped him with the carpentering of this building and took no pay; there should still have been quite a bit of outlay. They therefore had to live in the animal barn a third winter, but this also became the last. During the same time the man had to work for strangers in order to make money, since his own field and pasture did not yield enough to support his family and animals, he also had to continue to clear the place which would be his family's livelihood, and alongside all this he succeeded in constructing a dwelling during the summer of 1847—and that a quite satisfactory building, better than many of his neighbors'.

And even less could this example of life in the animal barn offend me, who knew that in the area where they grew up. There—even in the circle of people to which the wife, the daughter of the farm owner, belonged—one lives in such an intimate manner with domestic animals that the houses where these are kept appear almost like one of the rooms of the house, where the people who lived there have moved out as if the rooms had not been comfortable enough. I remember at any rate examples on farms where the sister of the farmer, or the mother of the farmer's wife, or some of the grown sons and daughters always slept in the animal barn in the winter. Yes, in the same community I have, as told in the foregoing, seen bread baking take place here.

Perhaps when the black death swept over the country and the survivors had to use all their efforts to maintain their means of sustenance so that they could hold on to life, perhaps then it came about that most of the farm families adjusted to such an intimate way of living, since when there was not enough strength both to fetch wood from the forest to warm the house and moss from the mountains—or to carry leaves to stretch the fodder for the animals—so the last had to be done before the first, and thus the animal barn became the warmest and best room on the farm. And while it was customary for a hundred to two hundred years in Gudbrandsdal or Hedemark that the farmers themselves on the better farms let their grown sons and daughters sleep in the animal barn, one cannot complain if they put the beds for the servants there.

OFFENSIVE AND DANGEROUS CUSTOMS FOR SERVANTS

But the situation is very much otherwise when the farmer's own people are repelled by the dirty animal barns and still the father of the house directs his servants and indigent folk and cotter men to sleep there. It was so in the parish of Næs in Upper Romerike. Here a farmer placed a cooking oven beside the fireplace in the kitchen and from it placed a pipe through an attractively furnished upper room, which method without any expense maintained an even warmth. "This room should be a girl's room," I said. "No, I have it for a guest room because it is so nice to have a warm room when visitors arrive late in the evening," the man answered. "So let me see how the girls have it in the animal barn," I continued, and what an arrangement I got to see! Animals in two rows with heads to the wall; between the rows a dirty passageway, and innermost in the passageway the girls' bed: splashes and odors of the worst sort could reach those who slept in it. At the other end of the animal barn was a pigpen where the two beasts grunted and stank, and wall-to-wall and back of the pen stood the beds for the servant boys and the boarded-out man, arranged so that one had to go through the sheep bin to get to them. "It seems to me that there is a danger that the beautiful small lambs there in the bin might be stepped on and killed when people with their heavy boots have to fumble their way through here in the dark."—"Oh, they must be careful," the farmer remarked. "But do you know what, the whole setup is terrible."—"Yes, but," the farmer continued, "is it not remarkable anyway? Of the three girls, only two sleep in the animal barn and the third we have in the kitchen in order to have her nearby, but they change over because none of them wants to sleep inside."—"Well, yes, for there is precisely something bad about this matter which all farmers should be aware of. Here in the animal barn girls and boys could well have free play at night, but they certainly do not have permission to." I chose precisely this example in order to show the conditions—not to anger the farmer from whose farm the example is taken but to emphasize that when such a situation can be found with so fine a man (yes, zealous about morals, as I learned from becoming acquainted with this farmer), there is thus no wonder that the old custom exists in so many other places.

But one must keep one's eyes open for what kind of a custom this is. Once—it was in the same parish—I was engaged in a very confidential conversation with a cotter. "Listen, Ole," I said, "I have a suspicion that certain girls, such as those who have an illegitimate child or two, sometimes in a devious way hang around young boys in order to marry them;

what do you think of that?"—"Oh yes, I know too much about such—because that is what happened to me."—"To you? It would never occur to me because I have been so pleased to find that you are happily married to a fine wife."—"No, it was another one with whom I had a child, just the kind you talked about."—"And were you probably only a youngster then?"—"I was 17 years."—"17 years? How in the world—?" I am unable to report the man's frank and detailed explanation, but it should be told that he and this troll girl served together and had been shown to the animal barn as their sleeping quarters, the two alone. I was upset. "Oh yes," he said when he noticed my feeling about the barn idea, "they [the farmers] could readily be rid of this custom, because they do not gain much from it but harm."—"Harm? That we hear enough of, but how can you talk about harm only to the farmers?"—"Yes, the bedding; it rots much sooner in the animal barn than in the other houses because in the animal barn they are likely to be damp."—"You show remarkable innocence, here with your memories of your own experience to have the mind to think of the farmers' miserable bedding." The man otherwise had, however, revealed his sense of honesty. He told me that this woman, shortly after the child was born, was in jail for theft and then went to Christiania, after which he had not asked about her. He first got his parents to bring up the child and later, as a married man, he took the child in his own house and looked after it well in all ways.

Here I must explain that in Næs, and likewise as I later will show in other places, the custom has decreased somewhat. And there are likely two reasons: in part, the basis for the change might be with the farm owners, who have come to feel more responsible for the servant folk; in part, the reason might lie with the servant folk, who now and then—I heard it in Næs—express their dissatisfaction with the old ways, namely the men, who often take off their wet clothes at night and then in the damp animal barn must put them on equally wet in the morning. But the change continues mostly in that a separate servants' quarters is set up only for menfolk, so that the girls still must occupy the animal barn. And when I struggled hard for a greater change for the sake of the girls also, I encountered the following reasons: (1) where there is a heater in the animal barn (to warm the animals' water, namely in Gudbrandsdal), it is necessary that people be present at night to watch over the fire; (2) the animals might break loose and butt each other; and (3) it might go badly with the cows during calving when there are no people present.

But a farmer explained his [differing] opinion thus: as for no. 1, he was more afraid of the matches and candle stumps which the suitors of the girls of the animal barn ran around with; as for no. 2, one can tie the animals with iron chains instead of with bands; and as for no. 3, when he has his girls lying in the kitchen next to his own bedroom, he can wake one of them to send out at intervals, and then the cow is safer, for a dairymaid can sleep too soundly out there in the animal barn. And to all these counterarguments, I add the ordinary observation that there are many communities in our country where there are large animal barns and many animals, and where the old customs are now unknown, there are no apparent disadvantages therefrom.

One part of the more often mentioned Næs parish is on the west part of Vormen and reaches up to a part of Ullensaker which is called Kisa. Here, on the farm Onsrud, I attended a funeral for an old man and there had a conversation with many of the men of the community. Among other things, I heard a story of a boy from the same area who had hired out to a farm in that part of Næs but remained there only one year because he could not get himself to sleep in the animal barn; this he was not used to, since this custom is not common in Kisa, also not in all of Ullensaker, where only one farm was named as an exception. There can also be a remarkably clear boundary between individual communities regarding various customs. The above custom is prevalent more or less evenly from Næs and toward the north, but it stops at Næs; when one reaches Ullensaker and the other parishes in Upper Romerike, or when in Lower Romerike or in Smaalenene one asks a boy or a girl if they know about sleeping in the animal barn, the reply is not only a simple "No," but more likely an ardent "Of course not!"

STATISTICAL OVERVIEW OF THE CUSTOM

In many respects it would be interesting to have an exact knowledge about the distribution of this animal-barn custom in the country. A careful explanation about it now in the middle of the century should moreover put those who are living at the end of the century in a position to compare what followed, what progress the culture is capable of making in the period of a generation.

As of April 25, 1853, I wrote to parish pastors in the dioceses of Christiania and Christiansand (except the archdiocese) with the request to report to me some information which would serve to clarify the condition of casual marriages and illegitimate births. A portion of the reports obtained gave me the material for chapter 11 in the monograph *On Marriage in Norway*; the remainder will cover a substantial part of the content of the current writing, and I permit myself hope that for the honored clerics who showed the interest to acknowledge my request, my use of their reports should be evidence that I acknowledged them.

Among the many questions which I requested the pastors to answer, there are two which are pertinent, namely: "Is it (1) common, or (2) somewhat common, or (3) exceptional that grown children or servant folk on the farms in the country in winter sleep in the animal barn or stable?" and "Has there been any evidence that this custom has decreased during the last 10 years?" As is seen, these questions concerned only the country parishes, and I have received answers from 148 of them. These answers are naturally opinions, and they could be ranged somewhat differently according to the understanding of the informant or knowledge of the matter, so possibly one would have said the custom was common while another might have said it prevails partly, or the opposite. But with all this, one still might dare to assume that the opinions which several pastors together have found to report for a larger district might be comparable to those which other pastors have reported for another district; and therefore I combine the many responses for certain large districts where I find the two dioceses shared them.

One will understand this division by glancing at table 1.2 in chapter 1, which contains an overview of the frequency of illegitimate births in the parish districts; each of my larger regions includes a group of deanery-districts as follows:

Christiania diocesan deanery-districts	
Group 1	deaneries nos. 1 to 5
Group 2	deaneries nos. 7 to 10
Group 3	deaneries nos. 11 to 13
Group 4	deaneries nos. 14 to 17
Christiansand diocesan deanery-districts	
Group 5	deaneries nos. 18 to 21
Group 6	deaneries nos. 23 to 25
Group 7	deaneries nos. 26 to 29

Table 3.1 gives an overview of the situation.

Herewith it must be remembered that the study does not cover all of the country parishes in the two dioceses, although certainly the great majority. Still, I must explain since the question was so general (grown children and servant folk). The pastors have likely noted that when they called the custom common, it was for the servant folk alone and not for the grown children, and a few pastors have added that for the most part

Table 3.1. The custom of sleeping in the animal barns

Deanery-Districts	Country Parishes Where the Custom of Sleeping in Animal Barns Prevails: Common	Somewhat Common	Exceptional	None	Total Parishes
Group 1	...	...	5	23	28
Group 2	20	4	2	1	27
Group 3	2	5	5	5	17
Group 4	1	1	5	19	26
Group 5	1	3	3	14	21
Group 6	...	...	...	13	13
Group 7	2	...	2	12	16
Dioceses					
Christiania	23	10	17	48	98
Christiansand	3	3	5	39	50
Both	26	13	22	87	148

it applied largely to girls only, or sometimes only to the girls who had responsibility for the animals. In this way the tables are deficient in giving us complete and accurate knowledge of the condition.

In the totals of these same parishes shown in table 3.2, the decrease in the custom for the last 10 years can be traced. The table gives us a complete and accurate knowledge of the condition.

Table 3.2. Decreases in the custom of sleeping in animal barns

Deanery-Districts	Country Parishes Where There Is Evidence That the Custom Has Decreased During the Last 10 Years: Common	Somewhat Common	Exceptional
Group 1	...	...	1
Group 2	5	3	1
Group 3	...	2	3
Group 4	...	...	2
Group 5	...	3	2
Group 6	...	...	...
Group 7	...	...	...
Dioceses			
Christiania	5	5	7
Christiansand	...	3	2
Both	5	8	9

It is also likely that the tables by and large gives us an accurate idea about the differences between different districts. And now I will let the reader make a comparison. The animal-barn custom is seen to be more prevalent in the diocese of Christiania than in Christiansand, and in table 1.1 in chapter 1 we learned this: that the immorality—as judged by the frequency of illegitimate births—is greater in the former diocese than in the latter. Moreover, in group 2 (Upper Romerike, Odal, and Solør, Østerdal, Hedemark, and Gudbrandsdal), the animal-barn custom is most common; in group 6, in contrast (Mandal, Lister, and Dalerne), it seems not to be present at all; the former deanery-districts unfortunately divided themselves from the others in the parishes with many illegitimate births, and the latter were prominent in this respect ahead of all the other areas of the country to their advantage.

A pastor has told me the following: he became aware that from two farms in his parish, illegitimate births were reported very often; in order to investigate the reason, he found out that while it was not otherwise the custom in the community to let the servant folk sleep in the animal barn, it was the custom at these two farms, and he was convinced that this house-custom was at least a major influential reason for the harm. With one of the two families, he knew personally, it was useless to talk about morality. With the other family, on the other hand, he urged adoption of a better custom, and that helped. The observation that the pastor made in the individual instances, tables 1.1 and 3.1 have permitted us to make in general, and the observation contains the strongest exhortation to all who are receptive to reject the old custom where it now prevails and to adopt a better one.

The last one, table 3.2, also shows that there really are people in the country who can benefit from being talked to about such things. There are, of course, quite a few communities where in the last 10 years the decrease in the custom has been noticed. If we could have continued the comparison over a longer period of time, we should likely have found changes to the better earlier; we would have found the custom prevalent in quite a few communities which are now in the classification "None." At least I find in the examination of Hole parish in Ringerike that the custom was found in part for 50 years, that later it has only been the exception, and during the last 10 years it has hardly been known. One can well understand that this coarse custom has caused coarseness in the moral condition within the servant and working class, and so this bad custom will not be soon discarded or accompanied by more tidiness and respectability, but little by little the results will certainly end.

OTHER COMMON SLEEPING QUARTERS

Until now the talk has been about the servant folk sleeping in the animal barn. This can well also be simply the nature of old-fashioned ways. But there are still also many simple old-fashioned ways in many of the communities where this custom is not prevalent. In Ullensaker and Gjerdrum, for example, where many farmers live quite simply, one can quite often find an arrangement in which beside the farmer's own bed there is a cabinet bed with two levels for servant folk, a cabinet bed with a door attached; in the upper level the servant boy has his room, and underneath the servant girls sleep. On the larger farms, the farm owner has a bedroom for himself, and the servant folk are thus alone in the cabinet bed in the kitchen. At other places here and in Lower Romerike, sleeping quarters for both sexes are found in the room for the hired men. In a similar simple manner, it has also been customary in Smaalenene, where still in later times, according to what a knowledgeable man explained to me, there has been an effort among the farmers to arrange things so that there are separate rooms for each sex, for girls in the kitchen and for boys in the room for the hired men. Even as close to the capital as the parish of Asker, the joint sleeping room for both sexes has been much too common, and farther west the pastors, particularly in Jæder and Ryfylke, have asserted the same is conceivable. A pastor here on Østland has provided his servant folk of both sexes sleeping quarters in the room for hired men. He thought that when there were so many together, it was really unthinkable that there could be improper behavior among them. I also view the possibility that the children of the cotters who serve in the same parish will not be either helped or harmed by these conditions, to which they are certainly well accustomed already. But I also believe that in this manner the farm owners do not contribute to the improvement of the people's standards and do not bring up their subordinates to a tidier life. In that the pastor agreed with me.

But the story is not over yet. Whether or not the servant folk sleep in the animal barn or other places, it is very common, yes, it takes place with few exceptions, that they, as soon as summer comes, take their sheepskins and quilts with them and make nests like chickens and barn swallows in haylofts, one here and one there and sometimes two together. I would very much doubt that proper people allow their own children to follow this bird-custom, but I have never heard here in Østland that it is censured when servant folk do so. Yet possibly I expressed myself too hastily. I remember a farmer in Næs in Romerike who told me that he would not want to know about this custom on his farm; that same farmer also showed a praiseworthy concern for his people, and in particular he did not let any of his servants sleep in the animal barn, although it was customary in his community, but provided them proper sleeping quarters, each sex by themselves; he and I were in full agreement in that matter.

In Vestland, in Jæder, and in Ryfylke, there appears to be another method. In their investigations concerning this matter, a few pastors have mentioned it as a custom (or more correctly, a bad custom, because they tell about it reluctantly) that young people in the summer "when some hay has been stored" move into the haylofts and sleep in the hay. In Østland one moves out immediately when it is spring, as soon as there is some warmth in the air so that one can sleep outside and avoid the company of lice; in Vestland it seems more that they seek each other's company.

After everything I have allowed myself to present, yes, I can say after the many things I have dared to tell, I am convinced that a considerable part of society would agree that this part of the domestic life in our country must become more orderly and better, or at least more proper; that the change to the better, which can already be noticed, must be accelerated in all possible ways. In all possible ways, since we must be practical and not expect to change everything in a day. There clearly were quite a few farm owners who already today or tomorrow *could* remove the objectionable and satisfy the expectations of civilized behavior, but often changes in domestic life cannot be made until there are resources and the ability to pay for new houses or considerable rehabilitation of the old, since the farm owners themselves live in humble circumstances on many farms.

In spite of the expensive times in which we city folk must live, we are sincerely happy about news of improved conditions for the men on the land, the country's most numerous class. If the conditions become better—as there is, in fact, reason to expect—then one can be certain that the rational farming to come will result in new and more comfortable stables and animal barns for improved breeds of horses and cows. Given this possibility, one must remember to set up good buildings for people on the farms, for the benefit of the servant class! Perhaps the farm owners in a few years would be happy to see themselves surrounded by more respectable and moral worker families, by a more spirited and able worker stock.

4

Night Courting

A Pastor in the upper part of the diocese of Christiania told me the following: There was a farm family in his parish who had once been in better circumstances which had now ended, requiring that they get support from welfare. This had lasted a few years. But during a meeting of the welfare commission, one of the members finally said that as much as he felt sorry for the family, he nevertheless found that when the family became poor they should know enough to accommodate themselves like other people in the same condition, and it was not right that two grown daughters remained at home instead of being sent out to be servants. This talk seemed reasonable to the group, and action was taken to cut off the support which the family had received up to now, when the pastor requested a delay in the decision because he would be pleased to talk with the wife first. Not long after he had her see him and reported how the matter stood. The wife could not make any objection to what the men had said. "But," she added, "we have to manage as we can, but to send out my daughters I feel is completely impossible. I know now they are two good girls that I, with God's help, have brought up. Should I let them go, it would be like losing them altogether, for I could not expect to enjoy them anymore, because father well knows how it is with servant folk in the community."—"I understand," answered the pastor. "Unfortunately I understand you, my good woman, and from me you will not hear any more criticism on this matter."

So—a barbaric situation which a mother fears and which a pastor must regretfully recognize?

We are sorry when we see that wildness and drunkenness do not allow the young trees to grow in peace which are planted along the way for decoration and pleasure. But what kind of barbarism is there which attacks the honor of young girls and disturbs the peace of the family?

It is the immorality of night courting. Immorality? Others call it a *custom*. "Here we must not," I hear a pastor say, "tread too heavily; it is quite necessary to tread with care, since here we have to do with an existing custom, possibly a custom peculiar to Norwegians, and in any case, inherited from the oldest times and deeply rooted in the morality and ideas of the people." And from the established men, one can hear the matter being explained almost similarly: "Oh, it is surely a custom; this custom has existed as long as the world has been here, and I believe it can well be found wherever people live."

A custom? Something which, accordingly, respectable people do, and which everybody has permission to participate in?

When I first came to Hedemark, Gudbrandsdal, and Østerdal and there saw and was horrified by the amount of immorality, which I had not thought possible in our rural communities and which truly often brought me to regard all domestic life of the rural society with repugnance, so this talk and idea of a custom served to calm me down. It is obvious that the more this night courting and night running around bore the signs and marks of being a custom, the more could the many false steps and falls into which it certainly leads folks appear in a softer light. So that one does not judge so harshly the failing and falling of individual persons but rather forgives them and feels sorry for their ill fortune, since they observed the custom in the manner of proper folk. A custom is like a highway which was built long ago and which the present generation travels over. Imagine a road built over a steep cliff, and imagine that, year in and year out, one constantly hears of awful events when in the rock-strewn slope below the high wall of the road people are found lying with crushed skulls and with broken liquor bottles and liquor kegs all around. At first glance this could be looked at as a sad sign of a greater degree of drunkenness in this area than in other places in the country. This looks less painful when, after some thought, one discovers that in part it is the fault of the road, which the old road engineer built so dangerous and steep and which the authorities of the community had not yet been able to alter or at any rate provide with a railing.

In one of the parishes of Gudbrandsdal, I walked a few days around a cluster of homes of cotters and there found a really unbelievable number of examples of immoral behavior. I went from house to house, and almost everywhere it was such that the man in the house, or the wife, or one of the relatives living with them, or one or several of their grown children were infected with this kind of immorality. It was an exception when any grown person was free of it, and almost without exception, people talked about the matter in the most casual manner. Fathers and mothers talked about their daughter's disgrace as if they had no idea what was meant by a woman's honor and modesty, or when they did express themselves reluctantly, it was mostly about the domestic troubles that a girl who had been a servant came home with, causing a ruckus in the house because of the screaming child. On the other hand, I could not fail to note a great many attractive examples of tidiness and order among these fellow citizens of mine. I became completely perplexed how I should regard and judge the moral condition among these people. But it helped me to reconcile the contentious judgments and regard the harm with pity when a pastor, in whose knowledge of people and sensitivity I have a great deal of faith, told me of a single example: In the vicinity of the parsonage in the same parish lived an elderly woman of the cotter class who as a girl was a mother of two children of different fathers. The pastor made the judgment that, not only now but in her early days, she did not have a deep and truly Christian spirit but had always been what is known as a good person, because he knew how she had become involved in this unlikely situation. When quite young, she became a servant at one of the larger farms, and the eldest son on the farm fell in love with her and she with him. His father opposed the relationship and made him marry somebody else, but he showed his true feeling by keeping the child he had with this girl and bringing it up as his own. The girl went away in the meantime, and when she was scorned she did not look for a rich boy anymore but came to an understanding with the son of a cotter. The parents of the son preferred another girl as daughter-in-law. The boy would not go along with this, but in order not to lose the opportunity to keep his parents' status after they died he did not marry the one he desired, who accordingly was left again with an illegitimate child and was "scorned." When the story was told, the circumstances were such that the son of the cotter had taken over the deceased parents' cotter acreage; and again, by getting a pension for it, he had turned it over to the son he and the girl had had 20 years ago, and the mother lived again with the son; thus, the two previous lovers in their elderly days in a fashion became united and came to live together.

And how often have I myself not found during my continuous travels through the communities similar examples: fallen women who told me in confidence all the circumstances, so that I did not want to add stones to the burden with the slightest remarks.

Besides, the woman who is scorned could have behaved in quite the same way as the one who was uplifted to the status of the true wife: without placing blame on anybody, and therefore without distinguishing between the proper and the improper, both could have engaged in the custom of night courting.

HOW NIGHT COURTING CAME ABOUT

Night courting was called "the morals and ideas of a people deeply rooted in custom." Deeply rooted? It must then have deep soil in which to stand, and there must be a long time since the seed was sown. What comes to mind is the depth of feeling given us by the saga stories about the testing of our earliest ancestors, and so numerous that we are inclined to regard them as peculiar to the nature of the northerner—deeply felt. Where feeling can be ignited, yes, passion can burn, but controlled by the understanding and self-control of the calm exterior, so that the inner does not dare show itself to the world. It is quite certain that a great deal of this peculiar nature exists today among our common people; I think of the truly odd customary behavior in the country—that while proper city people without offending the presence of friends and acquaintances could express their regard for each other with a kiss or touch, I have never seen or heard of such examples among the common people. One can thus conclude that when the prevailing ideas about proper and good ways of living demanded such emotion and self-control of the married, the same rule applied even more strictly to the unmarried during the passionate years of the young. During the day when the sun shone on them or when they were seen by other people, self-control had to conceal each visible sign of inner emotion.

This is consistent with the authority which parents in the olden days exercised over their children regarding marriage arrangements. The experience and soberness of the older people had to control the passions of the young. This is illustrated by one of the most superb sagas about the Icelandic chief, Nial. "I have," he says to his son Helge, "arrived at a marriage for you, if you will follow my advice."—"That I certainly will," Helge answered, "since I know that you will and can advise me well." The father really could only guide the son with his advice; over the daughter, on the other hand, he had complete authority. The same saga tells about Osvif and his son Thorvald. Thorvald wanted Halgerd, Høskuld's daughter. So "the father and son made a courting trip to Høskuldstad and were well received. They explained their intention to Høskuld and proposed courtship. Høskuld answered, "I know of your favorable circumstances; while you yourself can see my daughter's appearance and courteousness, I do not want to conceal from you that she is strong-willed." But Thorvald answered, "Do not set any conditions since her nature will be no hindrance to our negotiations." They reached an agreement, and Høskuld did not ask the daughter for her opinion since he had decided to give her away, and they had settled all matters.

Thereupon Thorvald settled for Halgerd and rode home. Høskuld told Halgerd about the negotiations. She said, "Now I have experienced what I have long feared, that you did not grant me as much as you seemed to since you did not find it worthwhile to discuss this matter with me before. This marriage agreement by no means seems as favorable as what you had promised me." And it was apparent to all that she felt she had been married off badly. Høskuld answered, "I pay no attention to your arrogance so much that it stands in the way of my negotiations, and I shall decide, not you, when we disagree." Høskuld had the right insofar as laid down by the laws of pagan times. When this event took place, such authority was justified for the father.

This excessive authority of the father the Christian laws began to counteract, so that finally marriage laws were decreed illegal, as clearly opposed by women in the presence of witnesses. But it is certain that in real life the old way of thinking and custom has, despite the law, persisted a long time, even up to the current era. What—next to plowing and harvesting and other daily needs—has occupied the lives of the common people these last centuries? Possibly military enterprises, by which ambitious objectives can be attained? No. Possibly war and politics, by which the drive for power can be satisfied? No. But those who had the power, the older ones, the patriarchs and landowners, busied themselves with an everlasting repetition of many small upward steps by negotiating and quarreling over marriages, whereby the audacious and the cleverest dreamt about taking over several farms and glories. This same way of thinking, by which the older ones sought to direct marriage matters to their own advantage, also influenced the young. It became a manner of speaking that to marry was the same as to improve your lot. Once upon a time, it was said in the aforementioned saga, two brothers, Høskuld and Rut went to the Thing, and then Høskuld talked with Rut as follows: "I really wish, brother, that you would improve your lot and find yourself a wife." Rut answered: "I have had it on my mind a long time but have been uncertain; now I will nevertheless do as you suggest. But where should we try?" And then there is a detailed description how it went with a man by the name of Mørrd and his announcement for his daughter Unne. The girl's father, who promised a large dowry, required a big gift on the part of the courter, but Høskuld, as Rut's representative to convey the message, took it upon himself to be responsible for everything, and thus Rut came into a favorable settlement. This story also occurred to me during a conversation with a farmer who last spring gave me a ride of six miles in Høland. He also during this life had engaged in such negotiations. In one case a father and son had agreed on going to a rich farmer to ask for the daughter for the son. The bargaining took a long time, and the father of the son, in order to get the matter arranged, turned over the ownership of the farm to his son at a low price; thereby the other children were certainly deprived of their full share, but it nevertheless resulted in a gain for the family that a rich man's daughter was acquired with a splendid dowry and large inheritance.

This is one side of folk custom and perception. But it is always so that when one plate on the weighing scale sinks, the other ascends, or when a branch on a tree shoots out vigorously on one side, another branch usually becomes a counterweight on the other side. So it also is in society. When the values and concepts and morals in society evolve strongly in one direction, it is natural that certain opposite tendencies and drives take place. When a patriarchal authority is on the way toward tyranny, and when calculating scheming is close to getting control over society, for the protection of family life and the spontaneity of society it is well and good that the natural generosity and liveliness and sense of freedom, which are still usually characteristic of youth, increase, even though it might happen that the young little by little take over and are allowed certain habits and customs which are defiant and aggressive.

Night courting is such a custom which overshadows wise and objective counsel, whereby fathers sit and bargain over inheritance and goods and over the hearts and hands of sons and daughters—fathers who have forgotten the meaning of love and heartfelt joy.

If I have guessed right, night courting is then not, as is sometimes heard, a direct remnant of the morals and customs of olden days but has come into being as an antagonism to the strict customs of the past. (In olden days when the authority of the father was so great and the father stipulated elaborate conditions for the daughter's marriage, when the representative of the suitor came to convey his wish it is very unlikely that it occurred to the boy to call on the girl at night. In the sagas no trace is found of such night courting, and we dare to conclude that it did not exist, at least in the better families.) The marriages which were mentioned in the sagas, and which were begun by bargaining or purchase, as it was called, and also regarded only as family contracts, ended very unhappily for both parties, and likely this happened often to marriages for the same reason in our country! It can well be assumed that if the old custom had continued in its one-sidedness it would have ended with smothering all spontaneity and poetry in the country; and the more frequently sad results of the forced and unhappy marriages became evident, the sooner one or the other and finally the majority of the people would wink at the young people seeking each other out secretly where they could freely indulge in their hearts' desire. Most of us nevertheless regarded the freedom of the youngsters as too great, but most of us also thought that the strictness in matters of the heart was much too great. The two extremes collide, and as long as the strictness of this custom was dominant, the one of freedom was in some way right.

I am still not able, with historical certainty, to establish the many transformations of the ideas and conventions about the condition between the old and young regarding the relationship and union in marriage. But a full knowledge of this would be highly important to understand society as a whole, and I shall therefore collect some facts drawn from today which could give some idea about the custom of night courting.

All day long, a good and industrious son of a farmer works on the farm together with his father and servants. But now comes Saturday night. The labor of the week has ended, the day is over, and the evening meal eaten. It is said that the day belongs to the farm owner but night is free for everybody. So the boy puts on his best clothes and goes out. It is said that he will meet one or another companion, and he also looks for one of the sons on the neighboring farm, but the objective is to play around with the farmer's daughters. In the night these girls lie fully clothed. Now there is a slow tap on the windowpane. It is known folk who want to come in, and the doors open. Naturally this pleasure is not available to all, since only a minority of the girls have their rooms separate from the parents. They sit on stools and benches. The boys have brought tobacco pipes; a fire is made in the fireplace or the heating stove, and the conversation is carried on according to the ability and wit of the young people. In such visits, sometimes at one farm and sometimes at another, acquaintances are established and lead to liking each other, and little by little it can turn out that a boy prefers to seek out a certain girl and that she prefers to see him come alone. But that Ole is "going with" Anne is soon observed by others. The boy is teased by his comrades, who from now on have fun in disturbing these heart-to-heart meetings. But it is more important that the girl's mother is wideawake and also is aware of the situation, and also that the father begins to know about it. Quite a few hints and guarded remarks from the parents' side let the daughter soon realize that they are in the know. These hints can be such that the girl finds it wise to pull back, and the boy also has that thought in mind. If so, the relationship is over. But it can also happen that the girl finds the parents' hints less unfavorable, or maybe favorable. This the boy soon learns, who now with some assurance devotes himself to his heart's desire. At last, when he has secured his parents' approval and support, one fine day he screws up his courage and, if he is well-known in the house, he himself arrives unexpectedly and presents himself to the parents of the girl, or if he is less sure in this matter, he has an older relative as a representative carry out his purpose, or as it is called, deliver the message.

The representative must be well informed about the suitor's possessions and must be well-spoken in order to recommend the one he represents, and here good manners are required so that all sides until this day appear to have been completely ignorant of each other's intentions. The representative, with a Russian egg or a silver spoon as a suitor's gift to the girl, greets the parents from the party, so the gift is accepted and thereby the affair is open and shut. Later the suitor comes himself to greet his father-in-law-to-be, and he is very shy and awkward and does not even venture to look at his dearest and hardly talks to her. No one should be able to see that they have been lovers for a long time. But this settles down, and from now on he can come to the house at any time; he shares the mealtimes with the house, and when the other people in the house go to bed, he also lies down in the arms of his sweetheart—although both are in their clothes. The two youngsters must learn to like and respect each other, it is believed, and it does happen that the mother, when she is truly fond of her son-in-law, brings them coffee in bed in the morning. This arrangement can last for a year or more, until the young man has an opportunity to acquire a farm so that he can marry, and even after the actual and public engagement these visits and night intimacies are called by the old name, "courting."

This portrayal is based on examples known to me, but I particularly remember now what a somewhat elderly man in one of the communities east of Christiania told me about his own experience as a youngster. He is one of the most honorable and highly regarded farmers in his community, and he added that in his more mature years he marveled how it went with him during the dangerous courting period when he was only a little over 20 years of age. He could not claim that the fear of God had much influence on him at that time, but a high degree of natural shyness made him visit his sweetheart only seldom so that people should not believe that he lived with her as a wife, and when he lay in her arms, his great fear was that he would violate her trust in him, and thereby both his and her happy love might vanish.

There can be different side effects with the custom which at times are quite typical. As such I have heard the following story: A boy became engaged to a girl in a neighboring community. The engagement had taken place as agreed to by the parents and with the representative as intermediary, and the two young people hardly knew each other when the boy made the first formal call to her parents' house. Night came and they were to go to bed together but fully clothed—as was understood.

The girl was already lying on the bed, fully clothed, and the boy threw off his jacket and kicked off his shoes, and no more. He was following the custom of the community. But unfortunately it went against the custom in the girl's community. She was upset. "If you take off your jacket, take off your pants, too!" she shouted, and dashed out of the room. He stood miserably behind, and I do not know if they ever became reconciled. But this can be learned from the story, that by no means are there frivolous girls who have followed the night custom.

It is also clear that to the same extent that father and mother wink at the daughter's being visited nightly by unfamiliar boys, and thereby having an opportunity to establish and cultivate a trusting relationship with one or another among them, to the same extent it becomes more difficult for the parents to disapprove seriously when the suitor announces himself. The negotiations of the representative still remind one of the ancient custom of olden days, but night courting has made them merely a formality. And this formality is therefore often ignored. Things might go as follows: A boy and a girl think well of each other, and he visits her constantly in all secrecy. Little by little they are aware that secrecy has been discovered, but they are not aware of any opposition from the parents' side, and now they do not try to hide the matter. The boy comes and goes quite openly, and the girl receives him according to aforementioned friendly manner; and a year can pass without the boy's making a formal proposal for the girl to her parents or their pressing him to express his intention. At both places they understand the situation and what is wanted and intended, and thereby an agreement is arrived at but entirely on the quiet side, until it becomes so widely known that a date must be set for food for the wedding and brewing of beer and all the many things that go with a wedding. It can preferably go in this simple manner when a son of a richer farmer courts a poorer farmer's daughter; the rich boy can then assume, "If he wishes to know my purpose regarding his daughter, he might well ask," and the farmer who is poor probably thinks thus: "He should not be allowed to believe that I will simply offer my daughter, and therefore, I will not ask but appear as if I am paying no attention."

There are several reasons for the increase in the independent, intense spirit of freedom in the cotter class. Up to now I have thought mostly of the farm-owner class in the communities where the olden days' view dominates; I will now try to describe the situation in the cotter class by giving some examples.

A cotter in Ringerike was as an orphan placed out as a ward on welfare. First he was placed with an official in the military and his lot was hard. He had to run many errands and barely learned how to read. So he came to a good farmer and went to school for a year. It was really uncomfortable for a big boy to be seated with beginners, but the schoolmaster was kind to him. The boy was now old enough so that he had to report to the pastor for confirmation and took part in the instructions, but eventually he was declared too immature to be confirmed at that time. The pastor really did the right thing, he said, "but when I was walking home and began to think about what would become of me, I felt that it was also impossible; I sat down at the side of the road and bawled, and if it had not been for one of my comrades who felt sorry for me and sat waiting for me, I do not believe I would have ever gone home." Now the next year his abilities were still modest enough but he passed his confirmation. Thereafter he became a servant boy on the same farm where he had been placed out as a welfare ward. He worked first for food and clothes but later was paid wages, larger and larger, as the years went by. So a young girl came to serve on the same farm. The next year she moved to another farm. But then the boy realized how much he liked her, and the first Saturday night he went out to find her. But now she was a servant to an old, ill woman who lived on a pension provided by the farm and she had to sleep in her room, and thus he could not come to the girl. This was as amazing as it could possibly be. Later in the summer, when the lice became worse in the bedroom, the girl accordingly got permission to sleep in the kitchen, and here the boy was let in to her. Once he came when the door was closed, and it was not opened right away. Two of the farmer's daughters stood at a window and made fun of him. "Shall we help you?" they asked. "Of course."—"Yes, but what do you want?"—"I want to get in, you must know."—"Will you then admit that you are courting Anne?"—"Simply let me in—I will admit whatever you like." But what was to happen one day in the fall? When the boy came in to eat morning breakfast, everyone looked at him and smiled slyly at him, the milkmaid and the cook and everybody. Finally he learned what it was about. A gossip of a girl had come to the farm and had told that his girl was pregnant. The boy threw himself into harvesting grain and taking care of the horses more zealously than ever before, both during coffee breaks and rest periods, since what he now heard was something he had never thought about, for he was only a foolish youngster. For a month he lived in despair. Then a man came to him, a relative of the girl, saying the girl was also in despair about his having left her. He had to promise to visit the girl at an agreed-on place, and there they became reconciled so that it was between them as before.

And so it became as before, and he visited her every Saturday and thought about nothing. But then again something went wrong there, worse than before: the other servants in the house had gotten the news that the girl had given birth to a baby boy, and they told him this with giddy laughter. He did not know in which corner he would hide; it was as if he did not dare to talk to himself about it either, and he knew no better advice than to fling himself into work. But the next Saturday night the farm owner talked to him. "You, Ole," he said, "what have you thought of doing with the girl?"—"Well, I cannot think of a single thing."—"Well, yes, yes, but tomorrow you ought to go and see her." That he must promise. "But I want you to talk with me tomorrow before you go," the farm owner added. And therewith he played a mean practical joke on the boy. The boy had thought that he would get going early in the morning so as not to meet women and children who would arrive with wheat porridge boiled in cream [for a woman who has given birth], and now he had to wait at least until 8 o'clock when the farmer usually got up. As early as possible on Sunday morning, he appeared before the farmer; and what the farmer wanted was that the boy should take the girl a bundle which the wife had prepared with some bread and butter and cheese. This was likely good enough, but now things went as the boy had thought: he met both one and all of those who had been to the girl with gifts, and everyone would stop and ask him questions and he was so bashful. He made the visit itself very short. He hardly dared look at the child, and he had only a confused answer to the girl's question about whether he would want her to travel to Christiania and serve as a wet nurse; and he had no idea how things would turn out. So he talked about the horses which should be given water at home, and he left. The woman of the house, the girl's mistress, became angry with the boy for his short answer and followed him to set him straight, but he ran on, ran as hard as he could all the way to the stall, and remained there with the horses most of the day. A few weeks passed by, and again the farmer talked to him. "Ya, Ole, I believe that the boy should have your name as father, and now I am on an errand to the pastor so that I can arrange for baptism, and I wonder if it would be good to talk with him about the wedding announcement at the same time?"—"Oh my, please let me go! I am really a child and have no understanding or ability for anything." But the farmer promised to pay for the cost of the party and to arrange for paying the pastor and sexton and to provide a house with a dirt road to it, so that he could become a cotter; and the boy then again had to promise to follow the farmer's instructions. He got one of the relatives of the girl and one of his own relatives to go with him to the pastor as best man and maid of honor, and when they came home from that walk, he offered them some whiskey and sweets he bought for one mark and eight shillings, because he had exactly this many shillings laid aside. And so there was a wedding, and the young people got a house to live in, the same house where I met them as happy people.

"And I will rightly say that the farmer was good to me, for had I not followed his wishes I do not know what would have become of us, and now we have lived well and good in this house now fifteen years." Thus did the man finish his story, the one which the wife sat and listened to and elaborated with one or another addition, while I sat and wrote what they told me in my notebook.

It is my intention that this story can serve as an example of how the custom of night courting has become a wide road in the country, a road which is easy for thoughtlessness to follow and which is walked on continually, so that it does not occur to the older and experienced ones to keep the young people from it. Surely many times things have turned out well, as for this young couple, but there is not always a kind farm owner present to help them out of their difficulty.

A cotter in Romerike gave me a ride for some six miles the previous winter and told me his story. As a young person he left home and became a servant in a neighboring community. Here he met his present wife at a dance and immediately fell in love with her. Then a year passed by when they did not see each other. But they still heard about each other, and one Saturday night he looked her up on the farm where she served. His excuse was, naturally, that he wanted to talk with one of the servant boys on the farm, and he met him in the kitchen where he and the two girls slept. There was some chatting for a while and it was soon clear, you can know, what the visitor's purpose was. Slowly they went to bed, the farm boy in the upper compartment of the large cabinet bed, and one of the girls in the lower compartment. Lastly, also the suitor and his girl went to bed to sleep, although not until they had carried on a talk in whispers. "You are only making a fool of me"—in such a way she pushed his love-making away; but when early next morning he got up to go home to care for his master's horses, he still felt that she liked him in that she had permitted him to "bundle" with her.

So it went a second and a third time and a fourth time; she took him in alone, and now he could know for certain that she wanted him. And this was naturally known by the other servants, because a nice girl does not let a boy "bundle" with her several times if she does not want him. But there is also a rule that what co-servants see and hear should not be known to anyone else, because otherwise respectable folk might not want to be co-workers. At that time the boy was 22 years old and the girl 20. It might be dangerous for two people so young to get together in this manner, but they knew what they were doing; two years went by like this, and during this time they knew, as stated, that they were to have each other but had not come to the stage of commitment. Such decisions are many times not made before one can know how to manage the marriage, or before one can be sure of making a living. But after two years had passed, they went to the girl's mother, who was a widow on her place, and made an agreement with her that when she wanted to release the place, they were to get it. Then it became secure for the boy and the girl, and they became engaged to be married. Still they continued to be servants, each at their farm, and the boy visited the girl as described, and this lasted for another three years. So by summer it was agreed that they would have access to the farm in the fall, and since the time of the agreement they were no different from married people, except that they did not yet live in the same house and had not yet had a wedding ceremony.

It cannot be concluded from this example, however, that it is regarded as proper behavior among the children of cotters to reveal their relationship to parents and ask for their approval and blessing. This I learned namely with the following example.

A man in Romerike was the son of a cotter, a servant boy, but he went in for handicraft and worked at it such that after several years he was able to buy a good piece of land and build up and clear a nice place of his own. He lives there now as a happy man, married to a splendid woman, a cotter's daughter and for many years a servant girl, but a woman with a more attractive appearance and maturity than are usual among cotter people, a breeding she had acquired in long service with a particularly noteworthy and well-bred farm-owner family. Both were people around 35 years of age, lively and sensible, so that it was a pleasure to talk with them about the cotter class in which they were born, the servant status they had experienced. The conversation also dealt with offensive, irresponsible behavior. They told me about all the women within a large radius who had had illegitimate children, and I heard a detailed explanation about their origin, upbringing, and morals besides. Just about all of them had been servant girls at the time they made the wrong step, and this gave me an opportunity to condemn vehemently the scandalous practice of night courting, which I clearly saw as the cause of this frequent calamity. "No, I am not quite sure," remarked the man. "You don't mean that? I know for sure then that your wife agrees with me. What do you say, my good woman?"—"Well, it depends on what kind of people they are," she thought. "But," I answered, "according to what we have now heard, I think that it shows what kind of people they are."—"But my wife and I," said the man, "we knew each other in this way for nine years."—"For nine years? And it went well?"—"Yes, it did not go wrong."—"Now I must be given a careful explanation about it." And that I was given.

You see, these people who had grown up in the same area had known each other since childhood, and so they became servants and grew up and he began to "hang around" with her. They soon realized that they were fond of each other, and she always let him in when he knocked on the door to the animal barn where she slept. Here there were also two servant boys in their bed in one corner of the room, and in the other bed our girl slept with another girl. But many times he knew how to sneak in so slowly that none of the others noticed, and since she fortunately had her place on the outside part of the bed, he could sleep with her until morning; but then he watched out and was on his feet and gone before the cotter came who usually woke up the farm. So it went for two years; they liked each other but had not yet admitted it to each other. The situation was somewhat secret for them still. I compared it to a rose, which seemed the most beautiful as long as it was in bud. Then the rose leapt out when one day they pledged each other's hearts and promise, but still they kept it secret from others for the following seven years. It occurred to me to ask the woman if other suitors sought her out, since they could not be sure about her engagement and had not guessed wrongly. She naturally let only her sweetheart in, but since, as I said, there were several people in the animal barn, the door must have been opened and shut on Saturday nights and another boy might strike up a conversation with her. But if such a suitor made signs to lie down with her, then she had to stand up and sit on a bench with him or on the edge of a stall and direct the conversation to trivialities. In the meantime, her real boyfriend might stand outside in rain and bad weather and wait until there was silence inside, and if the visitor stayed a long time, and if a slight hint did not help, she could tell him straight, as for instance, "No, now it must be enough for tonight; I tell you, I do not want to put up anymore with your visit—you must go now."

In the long run, the thing could not be kept very secret, despite the fact that the co-workers were not to talk about what they see and hear at night. Something always slips out, and our couple became aware that the farmer and the woman of the house knew about it. But they said nothing, and when the boy—as could happen time and again in the course of so many years—had a quick errand to his sweetheart during the day, he always knew how to find an excuse to come into the yard and get her to come behind the load of hay. If they met on the way to church or in company with others, they had to let on as if they never saw each other. "But why in the world did you insist on keeping it secret that you were engaged to a fine girl?" I asked the man. "Oh, I was not such a fool that I felt it was anything to talk about." When this explanation did not satisfy me, the woman remarked that little good came of talking about these things because when servant folk wanted to meet each other, there were so many who wanted to interfere: the boy's parents would feel that the girl is not good enough, and the girl's parents could also find something to criticize in the boy. One could well believe that when there is a boy and a girl who are both poor, one could be just as good as the other, but it is strange that it does not happen this way. It might be, for example, that the girl's parents have promised a cow or two sheep as a sort of dowry, and therefore they want the boy to be at least as good. Our couple had experienced something similar themselves. The mother who has some concern for her children always knows how to provide for them. Once in a while, for example, she can invite a servant girl from one of the farms for a cup of coffee, and she knows how to question her in a nice way about which boys are visiting such and such a girl at night, which girls such and such a boy dances with most at the district potluck parties, etc. As might be expected, our boy's mother had learned of his understanding with the girl and wanted them to part. "Oh, be quiet, mother—I will be careful, don't worry"; with such expressions, which sound more hostile than is intended, he could try to assure her or spare her from continuing quarrels about this matter. To keep the secret or (since complete secrecy cannot be observed) to avoid confession, is for the young people the same as protecting their independence in a matter in which eventually the heart should rule and not the account of a cow or two sheep.

In this situation, the young people whose story we have had to be in their posts almost to the end of nine years. It must have happened that during all this time the girl met her mother-in-law-to-be at times, even in her own living room, but they greeted each other as strangers. But as the boy during the last half-year of his engagement bought his land and began to collect kitchen utensils, so that the parents realized that he now intended to be serious about the matter, his mother then sent one of her daughters to the girl and invited her home for a cup of coffee. An excuse was found for this kind of courtesy, but it was obvious that it was the beginning of an understanding. The boy, who knew about this preparation, took care to be far away that day, but the mother-in-law and the daughter-in-law did not come to any particular understanding. While they were having coffee, the elder pointed to a new pot which stood by the cooking stove and which the boy had brought home from town. "Do you see that pot? I wonder if that will become your porridge pot?"—"It is not easy to see that from looking at the pot."—"That pot is not very attractive." Such hints were made, but nothing was talked about outright. This first took place a few days before the announcement of the marriage bans from the pulpit, when the boy presented his intended to his parents. When this boy was engaged (or began to "go with" the girl seriously) he was 20 or 21 years old; when he was married he was 29 or 30 years old; she was the same age.

I am inclined to believe that within the cotter class it is a widespread view that they could, all the way to the end, keep their love for each other to themselves so that the parents and relatives could not stick their noses in it. And I can well believe that there could have been some reason for the young people among the cotters to behave this way. If farm owners, in their decision regarding their children's marriage, had too much concern about goods and inheritance, it is conceivable that the cotter folk would have felt likewise. It is unlikely that they would have much to bargain with—no large farms with expensive possessions—but if the same sentiment exists, they would busy themselves with the same intensity with very small things. It could well be that a hardworking cotter, who has not had more to work with than the feeding of one cow and one heifer, would gladly be an in-law of one who is so well-off that he feeds three cows, and therefore the first would want his son to court that daughter. And when the children of farm owners in the dead of night and on the hidden paths could already in part avoid the supervision and guidance of parents, it made it so much easier for the children of cotters. These for the most part left the home of their father and mother to become servants and work their way in the world; and it makes it easy to believe that one who succeeds in the world should also be permitted to decide for himself.

Here I have collected the footprints and signs of the ancients found mostly in my wanderings in the diocese of Christiania in the people's morality and concepts rooted deeply in custom. I believe I understand how people have actually come to tolerate and permit and approve night courting so that it became the natural and open custom of love in contrast to the stricter and colder point of view in olden times, which mostly made marriage into a useful contract for the sake of livelihood. Those who are most aware of the enormous extent of immorality associated with the custom today perhaps will object that such serious and sober people as our Norwegian masses could never have been able to approve its looseness and stamp its practice as custom. But that night courting *can* pass as good morality is found in interesting evidence from Østre Dalerne in Sweden. The custom is described as follows (Carl Säve, "Dissertation About the Morals and Language of the People in the Valley," *Journal of Literature* 5, 1852): When a valley fellow wants a sweetheart for a wife, he begins as often as possible to visit her at night in order to chat with her for a while. If the girl is known to have a kind heart and has means, it often happens that there are found to be several visitors at the same time, without its usually resulting in envy and fighting . . . these visits never take place on the sly but are very open and known to parents and everyone else, whether the girl sleeps in a small room in the house or has her bed in the animal barn. At times the girl lets her devoted admirers wait long and well before she decides which one she might prefer. The one who finally discovers his fortune then goes to the parents to show he is serious, that is, to court. Here either he is entirely rejected and then all is over, or he gets a yes, naturally after preliminary, detailed, critical examinations from the standpoints of both parties on the suitability of their coming together. (Here one is directed to the unusual dividing up of land in Dalerne. Each child inherits a part of the piece of land which the father owned, and thereby in time the land is divided into numberless small pieces 20–24 feet long and 6–8 feet wide. When a boy can expect to inherit a score of such pieces on one side and the girl a few pieces on the other side, the farm becomes unsuitable, and the girl's father then says no to the suitor.) During the often long engagement period, the suitor continues to visit even more ardently, and now for the most part without anybody else butting in. In Dalerne such night visits are called courting, and they might continue one or several years; yes, I talked with one who had courted his present wife all of ten years. Since olden times this practice has been the country custom and not regarded as in the least shocking, either for modesty or decency. It is correct not to view it as immodest or improper because it is not. All dependable witnesses agree that it attracts no more attention than is seen: two dressed young persons in conversation and innocent rest and sleep beside each other. And as evidence, the author presents the number of marriages and births for each parish, which shows that during the ten years 1832–1842, there were for 100 legitimate births, 2.4 illegitimate, and for 100 marriages, there were 8.7 illegitimate births. But these figures indicate a particularly favorable situation, as can be found by comparing it with any parish in our country.

CURRENT CONDITIONS OF NIGHT COURTING

But why? Do I want to defend night courting as a custom which respectable folk should also practice? No, I have struggled only to understand how it has come about, that the *barbaric condition,* which I regard night courting as being today, has been able to get into and succeed in common usage among our masses.

It may be that morals and styles of thinking and the situation in the country in the previous centuries were such that the custom of night courting could be tolerated and permitted. Nowadays it is very different. Many great events have taken place in our country during the last fifty years, and the changes in morals can be noted particularly. Parents do not think about supervising their children with such authority and do not direct their loved ones in such great detail as in times gone by, so that the children do not need to seek each other in secret. And if this still happens, too often the old custom is used as an excuse to hide indecent behavior. The enormous frequency of illegitimate births, especially among the cotter class in Upper Romerike, Hedemark, and Gudbrandsdal, is for me evidence of the profligacy of night courting. And it is not enough that there are many known servant girls who fall; the inner person can also become soiled by the darkness of night courting. I became conscious of this by hearing from a now highly regarded and honorable farmer confessions of his youth, confessions which were scorched by remorse and smelled of sin. (It was, among other things, shameful for farm owners to seek out servant girls at night, but in contrast, it was chivalrous when they visited the daughters of farm owners. It is not possible to repeat the man's descriptions of these visits, but he told how he himself was close to falling under the demoralizing influence of this immorality. He was not capable of working, uninterested in life, plagued by a profound inner restlessness, and a constant buzzing in his ears "as if he were standing in a waterfall." There were not as many unfortunate illegitimate births among the farm-owner class as among cotters, but immorality was in reality just as great.)

The nightly get-togethers of the young have for the most part turned into night running around and night swarming with riot and revel, with noise and racket. The lone night courting is the road to seduction. The secret engagements are much too often the broken promises of faithfulness. It is unfortunate that while the old custom has gradually become a bad custom which should not be tolerated a day longer, it has still kept the *name* of the custom. Hereby good custom and bad custom are mixed in the people's opinion, so that respectable young people with no further thought become mixed up with the disreputable; indeed, a good conscience much too lightly accommodates to the temptations of sin. Everything considered, whether one feels this is the most immediate and topical need and this country's demoralizing affliction, or whether one has the sense and awareness of the soul-searing indignation, I do know that in Upper Romerike, Hedemark, and in Østerdal, not to mention several areas of our country, this barbarism of today must fill the friend of humankind with more concern than the custom of olden days.

There are many who believe that in order to find innocence and clean morality one should travel far from the cities and look into the most remote communities. I also thought that in order to find unique customs, which we deal with here, in their original state and purity, I had to devote myself to one or another hidden side valley. I thus traveled to innermost Gudbrandsdal, to Lom, to innermost Lom, and to Nordherredsmark. But here in Brotene, the most innermost branch, I found something else. Here lives an unusually sensible and serious farmer with an equally sensible and endearing wife; moreover, they are very ordinary farm people of poor means (and with due respect I give his name), Ole Olsen Braek and Inge Olsdatter. They had no son who could inherit the farm; their eldest daughter was "the farm's girl" who would become the custodian of the parents when age bade them to give up farming. No suitor had dared to approach this house, although this place was an ordinary one in the community. But one fine day a boy came from one of the neighboring farms with a representative and asked the father for the hand of his eldest daughter. The father's answer was that inasmuch as he thought well of the boy, and inasmuch as he knew of his daughter's high regard for him, he didn't mind seeing him as a son-in-law. He had two conditions: as long as they were not married they should not sleep with each other, and likewise that the house had heretofore been welcoming to the "kind ones" (visiting God-fearing people, members of the Haugean sect) and would continue to be so when the son-in-law took over the running of the house. The conditions were immediately accepted. But the matter created a stir in the community; a few outsiders tried to get the first condition rejected, and an old grandmother from the previous century expressed her dissatisfaction with the new practice; "she could not understand what kind of love there could be between the two unfortunate young people." But all this talk did not abridge the good decision, and when I was a guest in the house exactly during the preparation for the dear daughter's wedding, I felt that everything was in good order.

Day after day the newspapers reported by name men who went out and got drunk and died miserably on the road—would it not be better to name respectable people who set a good example? Day after day we see the farmer praised who has found a way to cultivate his land in a new and better method, or who has gained by digging out a dangerous swamp—and might it not likewise be right to point out with respect and gratitude a respectable family who have begun to adopt a finer value and banish an old and damnable custom? As stated, there are some very solid people in the large masses, but for that very reason they are more familiar with the life of the masses than others of us are; and when such people denounce the old custom, it will be doomed.

Ever since I left Ole Braek's house in Brotene, it was my wistful hope to see this old custom (or better, bad custom) little by little disappear and be replaced by a new and better life style. Wistful hope—since it is like a deep ditch dug out in a swamp, and the water has been let out, and the rushes and sedges and moss plants die little by little, and a blade of grass here and clover leaf there appear to improve the soil: one's wish is seen in each small sign of improved growth, but one becomes saddened to see how many fine seeds do not survive the still-infertile base.

It is likely that in some of our communities night courting has never been tolerated by a few respectable farm-owner families. I do not know this for sure, but I am willing to believe it. However, I have gradually become acquainted with quite a few farm-owner families whose fathers and mothers had themselves during their youth practiced the usual custom but now denounce it and bring up their children to think likewise. There are people who in their more mature age are seized by a bad conscience and therewith have been taken by a religious aversion to the custom, a view easily supported by the commandment, "Lead us not into temptation." There are farm-owner families (probably the most numerous) who have relatives who in one way or another have connections with city people or families of the civil service class, and by this means they have learned to regard this old rural custom as indecent and crude. In Hedemark and Romerike, for example, there are not so few farm-owner families who are called by the cotters and small farm owners "upper-class farmers"—well-off people who now and then take their wives and children to the city or visit relatives in the neighboring communities, who engage home teachers or female teachers for their children, who let their daughters embroider and crochet, and play the piano, and appear at balls in flowery gowns so that pastors' wives felt it had gone a little too far. I am sure that among some such families, and among others I believe it to be true, they would regard it as an insult if some suitor would misunderstand the extent to which the style had changed if he visited the daughters in the old way.

Also in the cotter class and among servants, changes for the better can be noted. There was a constant noise of gatherings at night when a few years ago they flocked together to dally with the girls and thereby enjoy all kinds of mischief, but for the most part this racket has been stilled. This agrees with what can be observed, that the youth of the country masses have become a little better in behavior and conduct. The plank haulers in Romerike, who previously were rumored to be the crudest of people one could meet on the road in recent years before the railroad ended their era, are hardly as wild as earlier. A young fellow of the plank-hauler kind expressed himself about this as follows: "Oh no, there is not as much spirit in people now compared to former times." It should quickly be explained that (thanks to temperance societies and liquor laws), a he-man can no longer drink and steer, and we also dare believe that each new generation that has grown up (thanks to the overworked schoolteachers and pastors) has adopted finer ideas and a more decent style of life. In any case, it has been explained to me in practically all the communities in Østland that there is less racket and uproar from night running-around compared to 10 to 20 years ago.

But how is it within the servant class with the individual night courting and secret betrothals? Has any decrease been noted in this? A servant girl of Inge Braek had a lover, and when the mistress of the house noticed one night that he visited her in the animal barn, she went there and surprised them and pointed out that it was not the "way," not the God-fearing way. I also remember a couple of cotter people in Romerike who told how they were servants of God-fearing people of the Haugean sect and had learned to reject this courting custom. I am presently thinking of a worthy farm-owner family—a highly respected man (one of the pastor's assistants), a thoughtful, cultured woman (daughter of our most highly regarded Member of Parliament farmer)—who I know feel very completely responsible for their servant people and quite certainly admonish them against the dangers of night courting. Yes, I also remember some other families whom I must believe to be the same. On the other hand, I must confess to being very confused to observe how fathers and mothers of the house appear to be casual about this situation of the servants, although for the sake of their children, they want to banish night courting from the house. Certainly in almost every community one can hear stories about farm owners who, in the middle of the night, have gotten out of bed and with a stick and scolding words have driven the night suitors off the place, and once in a while, in addition, reported them to the local police to suffer the punishment established by law. But the young people do not allow themselves to be influenced this way, and such proceedings have only been attempted when night running-around has been accompanied by too much racket and uproar, or when they have made the farmer anxious about the matches and candle stumps which they sometimes had with them to make light in the animal barn. On the other hand, if an individual suitor comes unobtrusively to the girl, usually nothing is said to him about it; not that it is not known. Now and then the servant girl's suitor may feel so at home that he is bold enough to stay all night and far into the next day, and the mistress of the house can be so kind as to give him food in the morning like the other people in the house. But a few think, "Oh well, it must be their problem how they look after themselves," or the conclusion is, "The servants do not like to hear commands, and thus it is best to be silent, when saying anything serves no purpose."

The farm owners who have followed the custom themselves in their youth dislike admonishing their subordinates; and if they allow their own children to continue in the old way, they can hardly think of controlling their own servants. It may well have come so far that masters and mistresses of the house, more than they themselves realize, let themselves be influenced by such thoughts with regard to the servants: "Oh well, they are only the children of cotters and thus it does not matter so much." But while in recent years, as presented, quite a few farm-owner families for various motives have rejected the old custom for their own children's welfare, there are still communities in which it can hardly be shown that a single married couple of the cotter class has not become acquainted and come together without the dangerous intimacy of night courting. It can surely be expected that gradually, as improved behavior is adopted by the better farm-owner families, the same would spread to the servant class, who little by little copy the example of the higher class in one way or another. I must also add that the majority of the people in the cotter class I have talked with about this matter, both unmarried and married, have been quick to admit that the old custom "should not exist." And it seems to me that since I have more often heard this admission among the younger generation, I can then assume that a change to a better way of thinking and morality is underway. But how slow it has been so far!

It is necessary to stand on my own with my writing on this matter. But a pastor writes to me from one of the highly regarded parishes in the upper part of the Christiania diocese in 1853 as follows: "Courting takes place even among the families of the most well-to-do and well-bred farm owners' families only during the night, and among the working classes running-around at night is found to be usual, especially the nights before and after holidays. No change can be observed in this for the last 10 years. Night courting and running around must surely be regarded as one of the most important and immediate causes of many of the immoral offenses in this area; somehow there would not be so frequent opportunities if such animal behavior and so little Christian and spiritual attitudes were not so prevalent, which must be regarded as the deeper reason for the immorality. How difficult it is to tear up and be rid of this root with its fruits—night courting, running-around at night, and resulting immoral offenses. I have seen this as a result of 12 years of experience. Although in all these years I have forgiven pastor's assistants who came to me because they had committed this immoral offense after their first communion so that I could absolve them of their bad conscience before they were ordained, I have striven to do this as aggressively as possible by admonishing them to consider God's wrath and the blasphemy which they can be blamed for when they pray in the Lord's prayer 'Lead us not into temptation!' and to not lead themselves and others into temptation by night courting and running around at night. To that extent the number of illegitimate births may have decreased. Before a higher sense of behavior and a more Christian outlook becomes more widespread and influential among the numerous, less well bred class of people, the efforts of institutions to root out bad practices and prevailing immorality will be fruitless. The chief means against them will be that the better-bred and higher-status people maintain a sound human and Christian development which does not weaken their strength and desire to influence their less-educated and lower-status fellow humans, but, on the contrary, strengthens and sharpens them so that they really become the spiritual salt which revives and protects the human spirit from animal-like love-making; and the world of light will shine on the good deeds of others so that they can learn to regard, love, and emulate them, and thereby be in harmony in the praise of their heavenly Father."

And a pastor in Romerike writes among other things: "When I have said that some decrease in night courting has possibly taken place, this observation is supported by the fact that there has been two girls—of the working class—that by diligent school attendance have become more than usually well informed and have achieved a self-regard so as not to be willing to accept night suitors, which clearly almost all the daughters of the better farming class would not wish to reject because they might remain unmarried: a fact which proves that it is *only* a forward-looking and Christian instruction which can be expected to improve anything, but hardly by any decree. The mentioned girls have become engaged and married, as good a result as could be expected of their status."

These remarks are taken from the previous chapter, from the reports mentioned from pastors of the dioceses of Christiania and Christiansand, reports as responses to the following questions from me: "Is it (1) common or (2) to some extent or only occasionally that there is night courting or night running-around?" Also, "Has there been any evidence of a decrease during the last 10 years?"

As with the question about the servants having their sleeping quarters in the animal barn, the answers to the other questions could also only be estimated. In the meantime, I have an overview using the same method as with the figures for the other custom, such that I have seven larger areas or groups of deanery-districts. This overview is reported in table 4.1.

In the lower part of the table, it can be seen that in the parish where two girls had rejected the custom, a decrease has been noted. Also, the count has been made carefully. But it is quite possible that there has been a rapid decrease in other areas, and this is the reason that so many parishes in the first part of the table now appear to be quite or almost free of the custom. Or is it possible that there has been this difference in the communities since olden times? A careful study of this might lead to particularly worthwhile information about the many strange differences between the various areas of our country.

An example of such differences can be seen in the following explanation from the parish of Kleps in Jæder: Night courting, or night running-around as in Østland, where the young men often go in groups in the community to the girls, is not found here. As noted in the forego-

Table 4.1. Night roaming and night courting

	Country Parishes Where the Custom Prevails				
Deanery-Districts	Common	Somewhat Common	Exceptional	None	Total Parishes
Group 1	7	10	9	2	28
Group 2	24	3	...	...	27
Group 3	14	3	...	...	17
Group 4	10	6	9	1	26
Group 5	7	4	2	8	21
Group 6	...	3	3	7	13
Group 7	5	4	6	1	16
Dioceses					
Christiania	55	22	18	3	98
Christiansand	12	11	11	16	50
Both	67	33	29	19	148
	The Same Parishes Where There Are Signs of Decrease in the Custom During the Last 10 Years				
Group 1	3	5	3		
Group 2	3	2	...		
Group 3	2	2	...		
Group 4	5	6	3		
Group 5	2	2	2		
Group 6	...	1	...		
Group 7	1	2	3		
Dioceses					
Christiania	13	15	6		
Christiansand	3	5	5		
Both	16	20	11		

ing, it might well happen that young men and girls on the same farm or from the same house take advantage of the opportunity to sleep together in the same haylofts; for that matter, it is not uncommon that servants of both sexes, although separately, have their beds in the same loft. The more frivolous youth have come together here and there Saturday and Sunday nights by themselves, but this custom has in recent times almost been stopped, in part because of the closer watch of pastors and their helpers, in part because of an agreement last year among a large portion of parents to close the doors to the household people who during those nights were not home by 10 o'clock.

NIGHT COURTING AND THE EVILS OF ILLEGITIMATE BIRTHS

The first part of the table permits us also to reveal a comparison between two things: the dominance of night courting and the evils of illegitimate births in the various areas.

To make the comparison easier I say this: Insofar as the custom of night courting encourages immorality, it can then be assumed that where it prevails usually, it is twice as bad as where it only prevails somewhat, and here also twice as bad as where it is the exception. According to this calculation, I find that in group 1 the condition is such as if the custom prevailed usually in 51 percent of the parishes, and this figure of 51 is then in a sense a measure of the prevalence of the custom there. I find the measure of the frequency of illegitimate births with the help of the pastors' reports for the two years 1851 and 1852, which show me that in the same group 1, there were 39 illegitimate births per 100 marriages. In this manner I put together the comparisons in table 4.2.

Table 4.2. Prevalence of night courting and illegitimate births per 100 marriages, 1851–1852

Deanery-Districts	Night Courting	Illegitimate Births
Group 1	51	39
Group 2	94	66
Group 3	91	36
Group 4	59	26
Group 5	45	16
Group 6	17	12
Group 7	53	20
Dioceses		
Christiania	72	42
Christiansand	41	16
Both	61	35

The smaller figures show a better condition; the larger, on the other hand, worse. And now look at the relationships. In group 1, both night courting and illegitimate births are fewer than in group 2; in the latter, both are more frequent than in group 3; here both are more frequent than in group 4; in both respects, it is still worse here than in group 5; even here the condition is worse for both one and the other than in group 6; but in this group, both night courting and illegitimate births are less frequent than in group 7. The observed relationship does not hold precisely overall: In group 1, night courting takes place more seldom than in group 3, and still the illegitimate births are more frequent. But the reports about night courting are only from the country districts and not from all of them; reports of the illegitimate births are, on the other hand, from the total parishes, the towns included. Such reports cannot result in precise comparisons. But still, the outcome of the comparisons is impressive and reveals undeniably that we have found in the various distributions among the areas one of the principal causes for the remarkable differences regarding illegitimate births which I have noted in chapter 1.

Accordingly, night courting and irresponsibility follows; so we must then conclude with examples from the two dioceses. There has been some thought and talk given to this relationship, and I will remark that the more realistic insight which has now been achieved must be understood and acted upon. When the authorities in the communities—the chairmen, welfare commissioners, and associates—think and complain about the prevailing immorality and the burden and problems of the many mothers and their children, they should not take to talking about the matter in a vacuum and not immediately speculate about new laws to punish and jail the few who on occasion find themselves in the unfortunate circumstances; but rather they should first look at the main causes of these unfortunate happenings, the "deeply rooted custom" of night courting, and seriously and in agreement work to eliminate it.

Who can work on the elimination of the custom? First and foremost, masters and mistresses of the households. In the country there are likely more servants in the homes than in the towns, and the servants are in closer and intimate relationship to the farm owners so that the duty of the master and mistress is doubly important regarding the moral condition of the numerous working class. This is evident precisely in the item: "Yes, but what could we do?" I hear the farm owners object. "If necessary, we can counsel our own children, but with servants it is completely impossible; for one thing, they keep the courting rage to themselves, and the other thing is that if we wanted to forbid them, we would not be able to keep the people, particularly in these times; they are so bold about this that one hardly dares to admonish them."

Courting is secret? Yes, it is certainly called that, but listen to an example how it is. I became aware of a nice, quiet, young 22-year-old girl on one of the larger farms. She was weaving. "Beautiful weaving, my girl! You enjoy it, it seems?"—"Yes, it is such a peaceful activity."—"And while you are weaving the cloth, perhaps your thoughts and wishes are woven together like warp and woof in a still finer weaving for your inner spirit. I will give you a thought to think about, so you must listen carefully. I know how the girls in this community have it. Have you ever taken in a suitor at night?"—"Oh, there has not been much of that."—"But perhaps some?"—"Yes, I will not deny it."—"Are you perhaps engaged?"—"Oh, I have no knowledge of that."—"Does a girl of 22 years know whether she is engaged or not?"—"Well, I suppose so."—"So it is likely that you are engaged?" She admitted it. "May I know who your sweetheart is?" She named a servant in the community. "He, maybe I know him. There are two boys on that farm and they are very different from each other. The one I know does not have good holiday clothes, but the other is well dressed and wears boots and a topcoat and has about 30 daler in the bank. Which of them is it?"—"Oh yes, it is the last one."

"Now I wish you good luck as you are engaged to one of the most highly regarded servant boys in the parish. Tell me, have you told the master and mistress of the farm about it?" No, she had not. "Or have you told the parents and obtained their approval?" Not that either. "Listen, I request that when the boy visits you the next time that you beg him to let you talk to the fathers and mothers and to the people of the farm and let the engagement be witnessed by God and people and then never come together as before. Believe me, it will be better for the conscience, and when childish people have fooled around and harassed you for 14 days, all sensible and good people will praise you as good and attractive young people. Would you not promise me this?" Oh yes, she promised me. The boy, with whom I talked the day after, also promised me. And I still think of the trustful and hopeful couple, whose trust was so easy to win.

And how did the other objection sound? That a master or mistress of the house dare not forbid their subordinates to behave immorally on the farm? Now certainly the forbidding can be carried out harshly and angrily and therefore in a provocative manner, but if subordinates realize that they are seriously being counseled out of concern for their own good, one can be secure in so doing. A father still does not lose the regard of his own children because he uses his fatherly authority with love, and you, dear master of the house, let your servants see and note that their welfare, happiness, and advantage is of heartfelt concern to you, and you shall win them. On the other hand, should there be individual boys or girls among the servants who are so corrupted that they will not listen to the warnings for their well-being and piety, I then do not believe that such are useful servants who deserve their keep and pay.

I have presented my conviction and requests to masters and mistresses of the house as follows: Do not allow night courting in your house! Strive, you mistress of the house, first, to influence each girl to greater modesty and regard for herself! If you notice that any of them is engaged, then approach her with the certainty of goodwill and obtain her admission. Tell her that her sweetheart will be welcome to the house during respectable hours, but when he comes sneaking in at night he will not be welcome! Let her know that word has gone out over the country that the old custom cannot be called a good custom and is not appropriate for honorable girls. By this let it be known in the community that you will finally keep your house free of the abomination! And you, master of the house, if you continue to observe strange boys visiting the sleeping quarters of your servant girls, go there and grab one of them so that you will see who he is, and the day after, go to the farm where the boy likely works, talk to his master and call the boy forth and thus punish him orally in the presence of the master! It would be a remarkably callous young man who would not find such treatment reasonable. And a single such example, gently but seriously on the master's part, should be sufficient for the future to teach all the boys of the neighborhood to honor his wish and judgment. On the other hand, should you still find one who oversteps, so can you, master of the house, confidently seek the support of the police and the law. At the present time a fine or bread-and-water punishment does not look promising for a deed which has been regarded as permissible in the community, but the man who first wishes to do the right thing need not fear objections when he is forced to fight the evil of immorality. I therefore plead, master of the house, do so, and you will do a good deed, first for your own people in the house, and truly for the community where God has put you to live and work.

5

The Working Class

LATE in the fall of 1855, I was at a cotter's place in one of Upper Romerike's parishes and found attractive and sensible people with whom I wanted to get better acquainted. I had an opportunity to do so a couple of days later, a Saturday evening, when I arrived at the same place. Since it was late in the evening, lights were out in several of the houses I passed by, but here the light shone through the windows, and I entered. Kari, the elderly wife, sat by the fireplace, and if I am not mistaken, she had a small chalk pipe in her mouth. I greeted her and sat down beside her. The cotter, Ole, a tall and handsome man of 65 years, had cut wood for Sunday and was carrying it in; he soon finished this chore, cast off his cap, and sat down, and I had to tell him where I had been since the last time.

Finally my turn came to say something else.

"It becomes dark in the evenings now."

"Yes, so it does!"

"And there is drizzly weather at night and muddy roads!"

Here the cotter agreed with me. "And how is it? Is it not over six miles from here to the Kløften railroad station where you have a room?" he confirmed.

"But as for that, my dear Ole, I do not wish to walk tonight."

This he found to be reasonable; on the farm below which the place lay good accommodations were available, and he offered to take me there.

"Tell me, you have a son who is a shoemaker and one who is a tailor, and they live with you. Are you expecting them home tonight?"

"Oh no, they will stay on the farm where they have work this week, for they push my boys hard and stay up way into the night."

"Where the sleeping quarters for these two usually are, could one of them stay for a single night?" I asked.

"Yes, but it is best that you go to the farm."

"You do not really wish to offer me a place to sleep," I said jokingly. "Will you say no even when I ask you so nicely?"

"Oh no, of course I want to," the old one answered very warmly, "but I do not know if the women are prepared to accept a stranger." With this he looked at Gurine, the grown daughter who had just finished washing the kettles and had generally started to do something desired by the frail mother.

"We have to ask," he said. "You, Gurine, you certainly do not want me to fumble in the dark again. Would you mind getting a bed ready for a visitor? Say yes."

But Gurine clearly became embarrassed and did not answer immediately.

"Do you see," I turned to the father, "your daughter does not answer no, and therefore she means a definite yes."

The father laughed and Gurine had to laugh too, and no outward expression of the mother's thinking was evident. The matter was sealed and delivered. I hung up my travel clothes. As for Gurine, I saw both confusion and satisfaction when she immediately plunged into the job which the unexpected visit needed. As I again sat down on the stool with my full pipe, the old woman had gotten the fireplace to flame up better, and Ole held a lighted stick ready for the pipe.

Gurine's first task was to make one of the two beds in the room ready for me. Its original makeup was straw, and over that was a sheet of burlap and a head pillow stuffed with stripped rags, together with a sheepskin blanket. Then a couple of clean sheets were put on, which were not quite long enough. The sheepskin blanket was taken to the small room where Gurine fixed up her place to sleep for that night, and a good down quilt with a beautiful cover was put in place of the sheepskin.

This down quilt in the course of the evening gave the opportunity for an explanation which pleased me.

"In earlier times it was customary that when a girl had served for a few years she would have accumulated bedding, pots, baking equipment, and such which might be useful when she had a house to run or, as an old woman, might be by herself; but nowadays it is not likely that the girls are so prudent, for now the young people run around too much with frills and foolishness."

Thus have wives of farmers complained to me at least a hundred times. Therefore I have become even more satisfied when I have been in the houses of cotters themselves, from which the servants have gone out and to which they gladly return, and have seen examples which show that the young people are not so badly off, and I found such an example in how the down quilt had come to the house. It was Gurine's possession. The girl was now 34 years old; she had been at home for the last two or three years to help the mother but had previously been a servant. Following the almost completely fixed standard for this community, she had the following wage: alternating every other year, 6 feet of homespun cloth and 12 feet of canvas cloth, or 12 feet of homespun cloth and 6 feet of canvas cloth; plus each year, 24 feet of burlap, one 12-pound blended linen, 3 pairs of shoes, 2 merker wool for stockings, 2 daler in cash (the only money wage), ½ daler allowance, plus fodder for a sheep and its lamb.

With this income Gurine had not only kept herself in clothes for the 12 years she had served, but she also owned good dresses (which she had in part exchanged for homespun, in part made of the linen she got and of the wool she sheared from the sheep belonging to the servant) and, in addition, several pairs of shoes and other items of clothing, the down quilt mentioned and other bedding, table cloths, towels, and a number of good things.

"When the farmers' wives severely criticize the love of finery and preening, I shall remember the down quilt with the lovely cotton and wool cover," I said to myself, when late in the evening I went to sleep under it.

Getting the bed ready was soon finished, and the serving of the evening meal did not take a long time either. The waffles for Sunday were already baked, you see, and for some of them a portion of freshly churned butter (Saturday is churning day) and a cup of freshly strained milk—all of this set on a cloth-covered table looked good in the cottage of a cotter. And as an added sign of a well-ordered house finally, Gurine could produce a rather thick homemade candle put in a candlestick. Candles and candlesticks are rarely found in all cottages of cotters. Sometimes there is a long wick of burlap yarn, which is only soaked in tallow and wound up in the form of a wax heap, but more likely in these communities so-called sticks are used, finely split wood whose dim light can hardly light up a living room in which the walls are blackened by the fireplace and the smoke of these same sticks. Because of the light in the candlestick I was now better able to look around in the room. This room, which had once served as a kitchen and workroom and sleeping quarters, had a very ordinary appearance, the floor for the most part covered by the fireplace, heating stove, beds, table, cabinet, benches and stools, pots, kettles, water tub, and chopping block. The walls are customarily fixed up to hang clothes and kitchen utensils, and the cracks in the logs are covered with scythes and knives and wooden spoons. On a beam (a crosspiece under the beams of the loft) toward the fireplace, clothes and stockings were hung to dry, and on a roost farthest into the corner sat a rooster with his two or three hens.

"Oh, such disorder!" many will say, but here there is no other way for the many things a family needs. As for the nook, or the room off the living room (this house is, you see, like most of the older rooms in this area, a six-loft building in which there is an end-wall dividing a four-cornered room and a narrow room)—this room is filled with any number of things: spinning wheel, a flour chest, clothes chests, etc. I am also considering how these good folk first made me aware of their frugal life so that I wanted to thank them for my opportunity, and Gurine's apologizing for the food and service when she at last invited me to the table was completely natural, even though my good appetite quickly showed that her apologies on my account were unnecessary.

But I return to the place in my story, when with my pipe lit I sat together with the elderly cotters by the cheerful fire in the fireplace. The whole experience led to talk, and to spend one or two quiet evening hours of conversation with these people was precisely the objective of my visit, which was not as fortuitous as it appeared to be. While enjoying the pleasant rest, I turned to my hosts to let them have their say, and it did not take long before Ole straightened up, cleared his throat a little and came out with the first question:

"But explain to me, why are you traveling around as you are and looking over the cotters' places?"

"You are not the first one who has asked me this question, Ole. I do not do it for bad reasons; it should be for good ones."

"No, I also did not mean that it could not be for bad reasons," Ole answered agreeably.

"I mean," I continued, "that I must tell you how it went with an old wife of a cotter over in Næs parish just 14 days ago. I came to her just as she was trimming a portion of butter she had churned. We struck up a conversation and she told me in great detail how she had had it in her life, and how her children had made out and were married and settled all around—for the woman was an old grandmother. So she seated herself to spin, and the spinning wheel put an end to conversation, but I picked up my notebook and set to writing. Now you can well understand that most of what such a dear old woman talks about I leave out of my memoir, but some of her talk I wanted to remember, and I wrote it up. But when the woman saw that I was writing, she stopped the spinning wheel and stared at me. I continued to write and at last I was finished and I closed the notebook. But she asked:

"That writing—will it go to the administrative officer of the district?"

"No, if it is to go to anyone it should go to the king," I answered. Her eyes opened wide, but I explained to her that the king wanted information on how it was with poor people in the nation, and other people who had to govern and run the country wanted information so as to govern and administer the country well, and so they had sent me out to find out how it is with people and thereafter to report as accurately as I knew how.

This explanation the woman felt she could understand, and when her husband arrived in a little while, she told him in such manner that he and I soon became good friends. That the powerful ones in the nation wanted information on how poor people lived, they called that good.

"Yes, I must also say it is good," Ole said, and his wife listened to the conversation.

"But," I continued, "you are such a sensible man that you understand that it is not the intent to tell and describe everything that I hear from bright and stupid people. There must be a selection of certain main themes. One theme is that there is a great deal of complaint from the poor out in the country, cotter people and such. They say that farm owners and other high-up people are so hard on them. Another theme is that there are complaints about the poor also in that they have brought on their own deprivation and needs by drunkenness and other misdeeds. You see, it would be good to have some understanding of these two themes."

"I now understand why you walk among the places. And you walk among the farm owners as well?"

"Correct. But a cotter whom I talked with the other day in one of the parishes was discontent. He was quite heated up and voiced strong grievances against the farm owners. 'Are you completely serious about this?' I asked when he finished, and he stuck to his guns. 'Very well, now I will go to the local police,' I said, 'to get his views about these same things.' 'To the local police?' said the cotter. 'Then you will hear something else, because he is one of the powerful.' 'And you, I suppose, belong to the powerless,' I retorted, 'and it is therefore well that you have talked as I have now heard. It has been useful that I have two ears to hear with, one on the right side and one on the left.' "

"Yes, you will certainly hear a great deal," my host remarked.

"That might well be, Ole! You likely know that at times people travel over the country and carefully examine all kinds of stones and plants and animals, the people we call naturalists. They get to see so much and they formulate their own ideas as to order in nature, and once in a while they make mistakes in their observations; at the same time, the stones or plants or animals do not appear resentful. But what would happen to me if I presented mistaken explanations about people in the country? Would they possibly remain silent? And were I so fortunate as to understand everything correctly and to be dispassionate about all things and thus to present my true explanations about the condition of people, still I might be badly mistaken, for many people are so constituted that they do not want to hear the truth. Therefore many times I have thought it would be wise of me to return home and take up something else. But then I have again thought that the task I set, I set honestly for myself, and in the name of God I must continue until I see it finished. Yes, I still have reason to be traveling around. But I can probably explain this better later. I have talked so much that you may have become tired of listening to me."

"No, it is very interesting to talk with such a man. So you are then not one of the Thrane fellows [Thrane was a labor agitator] who traveled over the country some time ago?"

"You might well realize this," the wife broke in. "But you are going around in the same manner, wishing to learn about the condition of poor people. Is it true that a cotter is not to be permitted to remain in peace on his place?"

"I do not understand what you mean, my dear woman."

"Look, we have been in this place since we were married, but now I am old and no good, and Ole is going on in years so that he will not be able to work on the farm, and then they would like to have us off the place."

"There you have mentioned one thing, my good woman, which I have really thought about so much these days and talked about with quite a few people. I really wish that good cotter people should be permitted to remain on the place until they die. Sometimes it is quite impractical for the farm owner to show much goodwill, for a farm owner can also be poor and not able to help his old cotters. But if it is not at all possible and even would be difficult for the farm owner, it would in many ways be better for all parties that the old people should be placed out on welfare at one farm or another. And I have as much as said so to those who complain about the welfare tax in this community."

"Yes, I can believe that it is begrudged bread one gets who needs to go in the community," the wife said with great feeling.

"No, this is not true. If there are scoundrels among people who have persisted in being a burden and for that reason need the bread for the poor, that would be harmful, but there are truly many who of right heart need the help they get—you must not say or mean otherwise. When I think of the good people, who I regard you as being, then I must call it praiseworthy that an orderly arrangement for the poor exists in this country, something we must thank both God and the authorities for. But even more I could not begrudge you the help of the community should you need it; and especially, you should not have to leave the old cottage and seek a place with others as welfare boarders."

"Oh no, no," the woman continued, "the one who has to go to eat at the table of a stranger does not have it too good and does not know if he dares go to the stove to warm himself, for always he hears that he is in everybody's way."

"Yes, even if he does not hear this," Ole added, "he can still think his own thoughts, and it is this which is so painful."

"Your observations, Ole, show sensitivity and understanding. But how is it? This place is possibly one of the best in this area. When I compare your house with quite a few of your neighbors' I must call it well-off; to me you appear to be both an understanding and honest man who has done his duty, bar none. You also have the right to the place because the farm owner could not without further ado dismiss you, since you are not on an annual-contract basis; then tell me, why should you not be able to live on your place secure in your old age? If you are afraid that you might go on welfare, then certainly all the cotter families in the parish must have the same fear. But this is a problem which I truly want to understand completely. That you will eventually be unable to do the work of a cotter is reasonable, but when there is a good understanding between people, one of the cotter's sons usually takes over the work so that he cares for his parents in their old age and later takes their place. And now you do have two grown sons; might not one of them arrange to be a cotter here?"

But here it was explained to me that the farmer who owned the place wanted to turn it over to the ownership of one of his sons as soon as it became available, and therefore none of the sons of the cotter could expect to get the place after the deaths of their parents. So none of the sons of the cotter found it wise to take over the place; they might well devote their best years on it and thus have a double loss when it would be taken from them.

"And this is justice that the owner should take the place back, certainly half of which we have improved during our time?" the woman asked somewhat questioningly.

"He has on his side," I answered, "the law and truly also the natural right. He is the owner of the land, and he of course wishes to see his own children provided for. We must be reasonable, my dear woman; there is no other way. But is there still no other way? Your sons, Ole, are laborers and might well undertake to be occasional workers on the place. And I remember numerous examples of a boy who has married one of the cotter's daughters and has made a living in this way by living together with the elderly as long as they lived. The daughter is here in the house—maybe the son-in-law is far away? You, Gurine, come and sit with us; I would be pleased to hear how it is with you."

And Gurine sat down with us and waited for the questions to continue. She joined willingly in the conversation. I heard her story, and in this way I got an explanation of her long-range plans as a servant girl. That she was 34 years old and still unmarried disturbed me, and I could not rid myself of this but to make a direct question. But I have often had the experience that when there is a frank participation in the question, the conversation can range widely without offense; and I was gratified to hear that this girl had not incurred the shame and bad luck which I have had to repeat so many examples of among daughters of cotters and servant girls. Gurine also confirmed further that she and the daughter of the farm owner where she served had not participated in the custom which previous chapters have dealt with. Here it was important to find out if perhaps that was why she was still unmarried. But I got the information that it was not because of lack of suitors who had turned to both the girl herself and the father. They were rejected because "it was not wise to get married into such wretchedness." In particular, in considering such an offer, it was decided that it could not lead to anything if the daughter married in circumstances under which she and the son-in-law would use the place together with the elderly, since it would be difficult for the place to feed two families and when the old ones died that would be the end of the livelihood for the young ones. On the whole, it seemed to me that these people were more prudent and careful than is usual in the families of cotters, and when I first became aware I actually learned that both the man and wife were descendants of farm owners, but true enough, from poor people. Finally I sought the last alternative for the elderly to stay on the place and in the house during their lifetime, namely, that they should engage a servant man and have him do the necessary work on the farm, while they themselves cared for the cotter land. Earlier they were able to assume the burden of bringing up the children; now they were free of this and should be able to hire a manservant.

But this was met with many difficulties, particularly those that the wife brought forth. The wages for servants were so high now; the place could not support enough sheep for wool for the servant clothes; there couldn't be much left over for sale from the place in that the fields were bare sand, the pastureland a dry moor so that water had to be carried to the animals in the summer, and this water had to be fetched from the stream far down the hill, a difficulty from which the woman right now felt the pain of worn-out limbs; the place had no woodlot, so that each stick had to be bought, and nowadays hiring woodcutters was so expensive, yes, wood could hardly be bought for money; a couple of weeks ago, one of the sons had gone around to bargain for fuel for the winter, but everyone had answered no.

"They were willing to have poor people freeze to death. But is this right?"

"No, insofar as they wish it, far from it. But listen here, my dear woman. When one goes to town and you send with him a 12-pound butter to sell, and when the price on the market is 12 marks, would you wish him to sell it for 11?"

"Oh no, with the kind of pasture here I am not able to sell butter."

"I see that you keep chickens, my woman, and you certainly send eggs to town. Now I hear sometimes from my wife that eggs have become so expensive, like everything else recently, but do you mean that you will sell them for one mark a score when the others get half?"

"Oh, there are not enough eggs with which I can buy wood," the woman persisted with her objections to my examples which had to do with buying and selling of wood like other goods.

"I shall not quarrel with you any longer, old one, but I will tell you what I think. Let us hope that there will be people living in this community after you are gone, your children and also your grandchildren, and it would be unfortunate if they would not be able to find lumber to build houses or sticks of wood to warm the houses. And therefore I look favorably at the people who now own a little timber and manage it prudently and reluctantly sell it for cutting. But thereby the wood becomes expensive, and I can well understand this becomes difficult for you, old one! When you were young there were no difficulties with wood, and now it must be bought and is expensive, and you do not have much to buy with. So at last I have no other hope than that you and your husband have brought up your sons so well that they know what they owe their parents and have the heart to show their love. I myself have an old mother alive, still older than you, old one. I know how she has struggled for her children for these many years, and now she owns nothing in the world other than her sons and daughters, but now when it is her time to rest it is our turn to comfort and make her happy. I have heard the saying among cotter people, a father can feed 10 sons but 10 sons cannot feed one father. It is probably an old saying, but it is not a good one. It is unpleasant talk which must be avoided hereafter. None of your sons wants to be a cotter here temporarily, and you cannot afford to pay any servant fellow to take over the work and maintain the place; accordingly, your children must help toward a servant fellow's wages. In one way or another, as you, my dear woman, have told me about your sons, I dare to believe that they are good boys; and you, Gurine, greet your brothers from me and tell them that if I had met them personally, we would have agreed that they in time and for God's sake must help and comfort and make their parents happy in many ways."

The wife was silent now, and the conversation led to considerations which transcended daily problems. Little by little, the fire in the fireplace went out, and late in the evening we rose and bade each other good night. But when I already lay under the down quilt (Ole lay on the adjoining bed, Gurine had gone to rest in the small room, and the old woman was the last who fussed in the house), the latter came to me and still appeared to be distressed.

"You told about something going on about a new law about poor people; is it then to be expected that there is going to be some kind of improvement?"

"I can certainly answer you, my good woman, for I am one of them who is working to create this law. Yes, it is intended that there will be improvement—yes. But the law cannot do everything; it depends more on the people themselves. Listen to me carefully, my good woman, and you listen to me also, Ole; you might then understand what I meant when I earlier this evening told of another mission in the communities here to get some knowledge of the conditions of poor people. See, you are old now, and I mean that it does no good to think any more about some new law simply for your sake: you have likely not many more years to live, so in the name of God, fold your hands and hope that He who helped you bring up your children well shall also help your children so that they can provide you comfort and support. The need and sorrow of other parents are greater. When the daughter of the cotter has to leave her servant position and seek refuge with her parents with the child which her frivolity gave her, when the son was a night carouser and time after time since has been summoned and dunned for support of his illegitimate child, when the son or the daughter lived promiscuously and, in order to conceal this shameful living, has since had to get married at an early age and must now live in poverty—thus such children could not help and make the old parents happy. And how often this happens! I have found it so in many communities. I have also noticed it in this community and this neighborhood. And it may be that the leading men of the community—because of great burden and trouble with the many poor girls who should be helped, and with the many illegitimate children who should be cared for, and with the many young married people who complain about their need—that the men of the community on this account could become tired and finally no longer have the feeling to provide the worthy poor all the desirable help; and so the latter complain about the hard-heartedness of the rich and talk about begrudged bread. Not true, dear people! Is not this the way it is? But now I will stop. As long as I am able to talk, I wish to say a good word for the poor to the rich, that is one thing; but the other is that as long as I am able I will remind and admonish poor people first and foremost to work hard to take care of themselves, which means that the poor young people must reject the awful behavior which I have mentioned, and more than heretofore behave in an orderly and seemly manner. I call this my mission; I have devoted myself to this so far, when as now I have engaged in conversation with poor people in their houses; and now because I have heard your problems, old one, I vow that I will continue this mission and in the most practical manner. My aspiration exists only in words, but God can bless it. And with that we should go to sleep."

The report of this visit and of this conversation should really have been placed at the beginning of this book. Because of the words "in the most practical manner" in my promise to the worried old one, it lay and ground away in my soul until I set aside all thoughts and decided to write this book. This book is also a possible method to work against evil. I have visited many such houses and have exchanged many such words in conversations with poor people. But it so happened that this conversation made a greater impression on my mind than many others, and the expressed vow reminded me of the duty I have for the many whose need I have seen and whose troubles I have heard. During and after the conversation, I experienced a certain mood—I do not know why—and it became clear to me what I had many times thought of before, that if poor people should have good or bad conditions in the world, it depends principally on their own mutual relationships or on the family life; but here I again pictured the terrible destruction of peaceful family life and happiness which is brought about precisely by the all-pervasive immoral behavior of the poor. It became my sincere duty to talk to people on that subject seriously and thoroughly, and also in writing.

I have gone around the country so long scouting and observing that I dare believe that I have gotten a view of something, and if I briefly name the part of people's lives which most often attracted my attention and evoked my worry, I say this: I do not know anything which corrupts people's morals and worsens their condition more than the prevailing immorality.

STATISTICAL EVIDENCE OF IMMORALITY AMONG THE WORKING CLASS

Probably licentiousness and sensuality can be more deliberate and detestable among some of the higher classes, but it is certain that in the working class and among poor people, thoughtless coarseness and animal-like immorality are much more widespread. This is a severe judgment. But I need to present what I, with painstaking investigation, have found to be the truth.

According to the annual reports of the pastors to the government in the dioceses of Christiania and Christiansand, except for both deaneries of the diocese, there were for the period 1851–1852, 11,310 married couples and 3,955 live-born illegitimate children. By correspondence with the pastors I obtained quite a few particular [but unofficial] pieces of information about most of these, namely that there were 8,590 married couples and 2,868 live-born illegitimate children.

As I did earlier, I divided the two dioceses into seven larger areas or groups of parish districts, and with the help of the recorded figures I calculated the frequency of illegitimate births, both according to the first officially reported and according to the last unofficially reported numbers. The result of the calculation is shown in table 5.1.

The larger the number in the table, the larger the frequency of illegitimate births. The frequency is accordingly greatest in group 2, smallest in group 6, and otherwise there is the same internal condition between each of the 7 groups both in the official and unofficial reports.

This agreement shows that we can be quite sure to be able to depend on the unofficial reports. They are incomplete because there were a few

Table 5.1. Frequency of illegitimate births, 1851–1852

Deanery-Districts	Number of Illegitimate Births per 100 Marriages: According to Official Reports	According to Unofficial Reports
Group 1	39.4	37.4
Group 2	66.3	65.3
Group 3	36.0	33.5
Group 4	25.7	25.4
Group 5	16.3	14.1
Group 6	11.6	11.4
Group 7	20.2	17.4
Dioceses		
Christiania	42.2	39.7
Christiansand	16.5	14.5
Both	35.0	33.4

pastors here and there who did not send me the desired information, but after having seen these [numerical] agreements we can assume that the information which I have obtained from most of the pastors or for most of the parishes is appropriate to give us an approximate idea of the situation on the whole.

We can expand on this. The unofficial reports which were sent to me personally from the pastors contained, as I said, more information than the official reports which the pastors send to the government. At my request, the pastors have counted how many of the married men and women, plus how many of the fathers and mothers of illegitimate children, belonged to each of the major classes during the years 1851–1852; I believe all people are classified in the owner class (class I) and the working class (class II). Included in class I are farm owners, merchants, skilled workers, etc.; in class II are cotters, day laborers, and servants. Now I will try to compare the number of bridegrooms and fathers plus the number of brides and mothers for each of the two classes, and in this way I get an idea of how much the illegitimate births are more frequent in one class than in the other. This is presented in table 5.2.

In the frequently mentioned book *On Marriage in Norway,* in the last chapter, I was able in a few parallel tables to report quite a bit of information about differences in the two classes regarding marriages. Here I show the differences regarding illegitimate births. This kind of information on the differences between the higher and lower classes is always difficult to produce, and therefore they appear only sparingly even in foreign reports about these conditions. So for this reason I ask the reader to look at this table with some care.

Table 5.2. Illegitimate births in the owner and working classes, 1851–1852[a]

Deanery-Districts	Number of Fathers for Each 100 Bridegrooms		Number of Mothers for Each 100 Brides	
	Class I	Class II	Class I	Class II
Group 1	21	45	9	52
Group 2	26	85	12	92
Group 3	19	42	12	46
Group 4	12	32	4	35
Group 5	10	17	4	21
Group 6	6	20	4	23
Group 7	11	23	5	28
Dioceses				
Christiania	19	50	9	55
Christiansand	9	20	4	24
Both	16	44	8	49

[a] The numbers on which the calculations are based here, plus those in table 5.1, are found, together with the necessary explanation, in appendix D.

In group 2, the number 26 is found in the first column of the table. It means that when there are 100 men in class I (property folk) who are married, there are at the same time 26 men of the same class who became fathers of illegitimate children. This relationship persists, so a larger number in the table gives a worse condition and a smaller number, on the contrary, a better condition. And with this situation before us, we can generalize from the table.

Differences among Groups

In the groups where conditions appear worse in one of the classes, they are for the most part [also] worse in the other class. There is, however, a significant exception in group 6. If we look at the conditions for both classes together (see table 5.1), this group [6] reveals the best condition; if we on the other hand (according to table 5.2) look especially at the working class, it is group 5 which reveals the best condition.

Differences between the Sexes

In each of the seven groups, the conditions are better for the women than for the men in the property class. But in the working class it is the opposite, the conditions are worse for the women. All the way through in each of the seven groups and in each of the two sexes, the conditions are worse in the working class than in the property class. In group 2, for example, among 100 women [in class I] who were brides, 12 had illegitimate children, but in class II there were 100 brides and 92 who gave birth to illegitimate children. Let us note these figures and carefully try to get some insight into the conditions: let us assume an area where in the course of a year pastors marry 100 women of the working class, mostly daughters of cotters. There are then 92 unmarried but fallen women of the same class, women who are called mothers but do not have the honor of being wives—at the same time and during the same year.

I have been in communities which belong to group 2, Romerike, Østerdal, Hedemark, Gudbrandsdal, in almost all the parishes; I have walked through the communities and gone in and out of the houses and found in the cotter class so many examples of this sort that I often came to doubt that I saw and heard correctly. Therefore, in order to get evidence about the matter, I collected these statistics and worked up these calculations and found the numbers presented, and this was so horrifying that again I came to doubt if I actually had counted accurately. But when I again went into the communities and looked around, I saw the same, and when I again and again tested my calculations, I got the same result.

So there is no mistake, and I have sufficiently assured myself that while immorality on the whole is more generally distributed in the working class than in the owner class, it is particularly common in the named communities in the working class to an extreme degree.

REAL-LIFE EXAMPLES

For some years already I have traveled over the country with the purpose of learning particularly about the conditions and morals of the working class, and one of my first trips in 1851 was to the cotters in Hedemark. I lived among them for a month, and I heard and saw one thing more astonishing than the other. But one thing I remember especially. A cotter came to me, as he said, to get my advice about a matter. He was a foreman in a workers association (it was just then that the worker agitation was most intense) and he had received from a book dealer in Christiania a subscriber plan for Marcus Thrane's picture, and now he wanted my opinion if he should buy that picture or not. His real motive was to find out what I thought about the worker agitation, and therefore I let him give me his opinion first. In order to talk in private we went out to the road, and he reported his experiences and opinions of the oppression of cotters—all of it in the style which was so common that I knew it from memory. As an alternative, in order to get to a more specific and definite approach, I steered him to his own situation just as we were getting near his house. Thereby I by chance learned that his grown daughter, who had been a servant, had recently returned home. "Why so?" I asked. "Well, because she is with child."—"So? But tell me, I suppose it is expected that she will marry the child's father?"—"Oh no, I do not know how that can come about."—"Cannot you, who are the girl's father, know anything about it?"—"Well, I do not know that it will be any good for her to marry this fellow, for he now has five 'seduction' children."—"What are you saying? Five? Explain this!"—"Well, he is from (here the boy's home community is named) and he first had a child there; then he became a servant in this community and had one here also; when he went home for a while, he had one more with the first girl; when another time he came to this community as a day laborer, he first had a child by another girl, and [then] fornicated with my daughter."

The story was told me at my suggestion, but I became disturbed by the casual manner in which the father told of his daughter's misfortune and shame. And now I gave my view of the worker agitation, which only blames others for the suffering of the working class but pays no attention to the shame and damage which the working class endures because of the immorality of its own members; I expressed my view so clearly that he began to understand it. But I went down to his house with him and talked with the mentioned daughter and her mother and could not get over my astonishment at the thoughtless indifference pervading their outlook. But now, after a few years, I believe I can understand the whole thing, now that I realize that these events are a definite part of the order of things in these circles of society. Evil produces evil. The evil is that so many young people lose their opportunities and throw away their happiness; it is evil upon worse evil, because thereby the good in people is dulled and relaxed. The many shameful acts create a mountain of shamelessness which destroys all desire to improve people's morals.

There is no doubt that if we could examine the conditions it would be clear that the basis for the zeal by which the working class in many of our communities went for worker agitation in 1850 and 1851 in large part lay in the suffering which had its roots in the widespread immorality. Think of the servant boy who is alleged to be the father of an illegitimate child! Shortly he will be made to contribute annually to the support of the child, most often six daler, which is one-half of the wages a grown man received a few years ago. If he gets another child, there goes the whole annual income, and this to go on until the child becomes 15 years old. This boy is no longer able to look forward to improving his lot in the world, and hereby he is destined to give up altogether—as likely happens—and get to blaming others for his misfortunes. On the other hand, let us think of other boys who have more regard for right and duty so that they do not abandon the girls in their misfortune but marry them. That kind of married couple, young, poor, inexperienced, then live as farm laborers in the cramped cabin of another family; for a year or two they struggle through with no steady day-work, but then it cannot be managed any longer this way. They must find a place with their own house and farmland; a place becomes available in the neighborhood, but a large and good place, and many are bidding, and they do not get it; another place becomes available, a scrubby place with a small and mean piece of land and a house about to fall down, but high-priced, and that one they must take; they must provide their own cookstove, and since they cannot afford to buy one they must rent, and for this rent they must feed a sheep which belongs to the owner of the cookstove; they must also rent a cow and bring up a calf for the owner, so they wear out the clothes they had from the servant period, and since they have no sheep to shear they cannot make new clothes, nor do they have money to buy clothes for themselves and children, which now begin to wear out; thus they are in rags both holidays and weekdays and can see no way to improve their situation. Among people who have come to such a deplorable condition, it is easy to become accustomed to the ups and downs of what is right and reasonable; and instead of thinking of one's own failures and thus learning patience, it becomes easy to believe that the farm owner set expenses of the cotter at six daler rather than at five, which it had been before; and these small matters one puts together with the others and finally concludes that "right now the farm owners in the community are so hard-hearted that it is not possible for poor folks to live, and if there is no change soon, there is no other course than to begin a people's war—yes, have the people attack them and chase them off the farms." (So said a cotter in Gudbrandsdal in 1851. I could not agree with him and he indignantly walked away from me.)

I am not discussing this to criticize poor people. In fact, in my often-quoted book *On Marriage in Norway,* I have defended the poor against mean accusations which have often been heard, that their irresponsible marriages will become worse and worse. But I also believe I have the right to talk about the deplorable conditions which are still obvious. Boys in the poor class actually enter into marriage sooner than boys in the owner class. I found in the diocese of Christiania that of 100 young fellows in the owner class, 24 are under 25 years of age; in the working class, on the other hand, the figure is 30 out of 100, accordingly 6 more. While this goes on year after year, it can easily result in too many parents who seek a cotter's place which becomes available, and thereby these are put up for auction and probably all of them become more expensive. The damage does not strike down the individual but in large part the whole class. But the greater part of these early marriages in the working class are caused by the immorality among the young people.

I talked about apathy and irresponsibility in thinking and feeling. Another evidence of this which has often troubled me is that a boy marries a woman who has dishonored herself with other men and shows off her children as living witnesses thereof. A young servant girl let herself be charmed by a married cotter who told her of wonderful dreams in which he had her believe that soon he would be a widower so that they could "have each other." She had a child by him and the dream did not come true. Then she and a servant boy were attracted to each other and she had her second child—but nothing further. Again she was a servant and in the same house lived a prisoner, a person over 50 years old, whom the farm owner had promised to take care of so that he would not have to go back to his earlier surroundings, a community in Vestland, and resume his criminal life. This girl and this man were soon seen to be together often, and the farm owner heard from the other servants that at night the girl was accustomed to go to bed with the old one. "It does not matter," thought the farmer, since the old broken-down prisoner likely talked about godly matters, and it was natural, he felt, that the girl began to believe likewise and was likely entertained by the one who was more experienced in Christianity. Little by little, however, the matter turned out to be more serious; when it became apparent, he admitted that the situation was common night courting, with the only difference that in this case it was the girl who acted as the suitor; the old one had to leave in a hurry, and the girl cried for 14 days and it was feared that she was with child. So she stopped crying and shortly thereafter came to an understanding with a young Swedish worker. I had met this person and I thought well of him; therefore I became distressed when I heard that he was the one who let himself be fooled. But the wedding announcement had already been set up with the pastor so that I could do no more than talk with the girl privately and point out what she owed this man who would now join his future with hers. But the fact that a young, promising man could let himself be captured by the depraved woman, I present as a single example among many to show the bad taste and casual morals which not seldom take place in our country.

Or what should we say of the following? I heard it from a pastor, about an event which happened to a neighboring pastor. Two bridal couples stood together before the altar, and the pastor asked the first groom if he had sought God's counsel and his own heart and had decided to have the woman who stood beside him as his wife. "No," was the answer. There must be a misunderstanding, and the question was repeated. Same answer. The question was put a third time, and the third time the answer was clearly no. The couple was then shown away from the altar, while the other couple were married. Thereupon the pastor went to this strange groom who was still in the church with his party, scolded him severely, and wanted an explanation of what this conduct was all about. The explanation was that the bride, during the secret courting when the conditions of engagement were uncertain, which I told about in the previous chapter, had accepted visits from several suitors, and the suitor who finally saw himself as the visitor over his fellow suitors, and who now should be the bridegroom, had at the last made a discovery which for a bridegroom must be the worst possible. I do not remember if the bride had given birth or would soon give birth, but it was not *his* child. "And therefore"—thus the man ended his explanation—"I wanted her to have this disgrace. But now it does not matter, and if the pastor will marry us, so—." And so they were married immediately.

There are a few old-fashioned communities where there is not much difference in living styles and morals between the owner and working classes. In such a community I became acquainted with a farm-owner family who had just been hit hard by the curse of night courting. There are four grown children, three daughters and one son. The son had an illegitimate child by a farm-owner's daughter but has since married another woman. The oldest daughter had a child by a farm-owner's son, but he has since married another woman, and she herself is now married to another man, while the child is being brought up by the mother's family. The other daughter gave birth to an illegitimate child in the month of September, and in August another farm owner's daughter in the area had an illegitimate child with the same boy, who had regarded the girl as his sweetheart but shortly thereafter became engaged to a third woman. The third daughter also has an illegitimate child with the son of a farm owner who is now married to another woman. Both of these two daughters are at their parents' home with their children. The last-named was close to being married, since while she was secretly engaged to the boy who was the father of her child, another boy came along and announced to the parents that he was the suitor, and the girl had to go along with this arrangement; the wedding was already set, and a great deal of preparation and expense put into it. Then the bridegroom became suspicious, and by one or another pretext, he demanded that the wedding be delayed. The parents of the girl would not agree but stayed with the date. The boy finally declared straight out that he would like to abandon the whole thing. Now the girl had to admit that she was with child by the first and secret sweetheart, and a friend of the family was sent to him to resume the relationship which had been broken off for a while. The boy did not deny anything, but he declared that he had lost his desire for this marriage. "I could not disagree with him about this"; thus my family friend and informant ended his story.

"Do you have a big family?" I asked a man whom I found living in a house dug into a hill. From the beginning he had dug into the hill and settled in there in a most primitive manner, but he is a shrewd fellow, and as the family grew and the demand for comfort increased, he carried out an expansion of his house and created several rooms by digging inwards. "Do you have a large family?" I do not remember how many children he named. "But him there"—here he pointed to a little boy—"I do not know what to say about him."—"Why so?" I had to ask. "Well, he was born before I married the mother, yes, the one who is now my wife. She insisted that I must be the father of the child, but I was not sure that I was, and I was on the way to the local official to disavow my paternity, but there was one who advised me not to do it, and so I thought to myself that it would be just as well to accept."

On one of my travels I became aware of an odd house. There was a window and in it stood a flower pot. There was a chimney and smoke came out of it. There was also a living room, but it was so curiously small that I had to go in and measure it. It was square and was seven feet on each side. Here was a bed, cookstove, cabinet, table, two chairs, and two old people. They were a man and wife around 70 years of age, but still spry for their age. The man sat inside, and during my long conversation a son came in to him. The old ones had previously lived in a little larger house nearby with a small field, but this splendor he had turned over to his son; then he bought an old granary, moved it here, made a strange little house out of it, and set themselves up there as poor folk. The talkative old man told me a great deal about his past and present. As for now, his circumstance was that he and his wife had "half assistance" from welfare, or "full assistance for one person," namely, 36 bpd. oat flour and 1½ spdlr. He informed he also that there would be added to the assistance 36 bpd. 2 spdlr. in cash, and that the flour he received was leftover flour after the farmers had first filled their own bowls of cooking flour. "Yes, it is so," the son observed, "and it seems the worst is good enough for poor people." "Listen, old man," I said, "I could wish you 100 bpd. good flour and many dalers in cash—but not one mark flour and not a shilling from welfare."—"Yes, but who should benefit from all that the welfare commission assesses the entire community if there were no old and worn-out people like me and my wife?"—"Yes, but who should benefit from the struggle to bring up sons and daughters if it were not the old father and mother?" I said. "Yes, it should be so," the old one answered, "but as the saying goes, one father can bring up ten children, but ten children cannot help one father. I believe it is likely that it is meant for the poor." "Yes, that is for sure," the son agreed with a short laugh. "The children also become poor, each one, in such times as now."—"Such times as now? In 1856?" I spoke out with feeling. "You are, I take it, a craftsman, and now times are better for craftsmen than at any time ever. Tell me, are you married?"—"Yes, I am now."—"How old were you when you were married?"—"I do not really remember."—"How old are you now?"—"I am now well into my 38th year."—"Good, and how many years have you been married?"—"It should now be 14 years."—"All right, so you were then a youngster of 24 years when you got married. If everyone did so, it would go badly for most of them. Was it likely that you had a child by your sweetheart?"—"No, it was not so."—"There was therefore no necessity for you to tie yourself in marriage at such a young age. But let he hear further: Do you have a big flock of children?"—"I have four."—"See, it is not of course a terribly large number."—"Yes, we have one more, a girl, but she is already out working as a servant."—"So she has gone out into the world early and has then not cost you so much. It seems to me that you and your siblings must be able to help your parents at least with something."—"Oh no, it is the fact that the young ones could need help from welfare as well as the old, because when one goes to the farms to work, one can earn only 10 to 12 shillings a day, and that is not enough to feed a family."—"And you say that as a craftsman? Come, I must go in and see how you have it in your house."—"Yes, you will see that it is meager and miserable"—and these were true words. The fields at his place were so small that they could feed neither cow nor sheep nor goat; there was only a patch of potatoes and oats with a fence around it. Some of the fenceposts were in the fireplace and maintained a weak fire. A coffeepot stood on the fire; four children between 3 and 13 years of age sat around it, and a little farther away sat the wife with a spinning wheel. The wife was sickly and listless, and the children were pale and dispirited. I held out a two-shilling piece to the three-year-old child, but instead of showing the usual fun and surprise of the very young child of a cotter, this child did not dare accept the gift but turned away; an older sister who looked after the little one then got the shilling and accepted it, with thanks, to be sure, but without a smile. My shilling did not seem to make an impression on the other children either. The situation appeared serious to me. "What have these children eaten today?" I addressed the mother and noticed the time was almost 12 noon. "Oh, they have not really eaten anything today."—"Nothing at all?"—"They have had a spot of coffee and eaten some cold potatoes from yesterday."—"What will they have for dinner [at noon]?"—"It will have to be the same."—"Do you not have any fish or meat for them? Don't you have some meal for porridge, don't you have any bread? Let me look in the food cabinet."

At this point the woman stood up and opened the cabinet door, and I examined everything carefully. There was a container with a little coffee and some potatoes in a bag, otherwise, nothing but empty cups and containers. To be sure, last fall a pig was butchered, but it was born at St. Hans time, so that one must realize it was small, and it had been eaten up a long time ago. Milk must be both begged and paid for, since everyone seems to feel they need it themselves. It is difficult for poor people to buy meal because farmers do not believe it is worth the bother to weigh it by marks, and bread is so expensive when it is bought already baked, etc. I sat on the bench and looked over the only room in the house. "Where do you have your holiday clothes?" I asked the man. "I do not own any more than I have on my body," he answered. The same was also true of the woman and the children. I took a book from the shelf and read it to the oldest child, and it was evident that extreme poverty and good bringing-up of children do not easily follow the other. In the meantime, the man had gone out and I sought him out in private. "Here is, after all," I said to him, "one of the poorest houses I have seen, and you are a young, spry man and in addition a craftsman. Explain to me how this can be! Is it possible that the desire for strong drink has taken hold of you?" No, it wasn't so, he assured me, in such manner that I had to believe him. But then he wanted to explain to me again about the difficult times (no work for anybody, everything you buy is expensive, etc.), and this explanation I was not able to understand either. I went into the room again, filled my pipe, tried to joke with the children, and started a conversation with the wife to see if it was possible to solve the puzzle. The explanation was wretched: They were poor as children and had themselves begun in poverty; poverty is to be expected in the world, etc. At this point, the woman got to talking about her four children. "But I believe you have five?" I noted. "Yes, the oldest girl is out as a servant."—"Is she a servant for pay?"—"Yes, she is a servant for pay."—"She must then be confirmed?"—"Yes, she is."—"You have been married for 14 years and have a daughter who is confirmed?"—"Oh yes, she is confirmed." I did not have the heart to press the woman further when I felt I understood that these people in their early youth had had children and therefore had married as poor people early. I could only wonder how poverty was still so extremely extensive; the poor people might want to conceal its existence, but I am accustomed to having them be very frank about telling me such things. Later I was told by others that a rich man had advised the boy to let himself be named father to the girl's child and to marry the girl as well. The marriage was established in such a manner, and now I felt I understood how there could be no blessing in this house.

In one of the larger communities of Opland, on the outskirts of the community where many people from Småland and poor woods-clearing cotters live, there were various signs, and to some extent unfortunate ones, that the atmosphere was very heated during the labor agitation of 1851. I had heard about a man who was the actual leader of the movement here, but I was not going to be able to see him while I spent a couple of days here. By accident, though, we met each other, and we walked together for three miles when he was on his way home, and I had intended to go by there and might need a guide. We talked about a great many things, at first a little cautious on both sides, but little by little freer. The first part of the time was taken up by his stories about the farm owners' superior power and callous treatment of the cotters, and to demonstrate the truth of his stories he took me into one or another house now and then where we certainly enough saw signs of poverty, bark bread, bonemeal, etc. More often, I had to be given an explanation by my guide about the families whose houses we passed. It was something quite special to walk through a poor community in this manner, and the subject began to interest me despite the lamentable and unfortunate things I had to hear. "Who lives there?" I asked, and pointed to a house up on the hill. "Oh, there live a couple of miserable old people. Yes, and there is also a daughter who has come home who was a servant but who had a 'love child.'" But I already knew of a whole series of similar family stories, and now I lost my patience with his talk about the farm owners and their oppression of poor people. "Be quiet about all your talk about the great expenses of the cotter and the meager daily wage; believe me, if you were able to make a hundred new laws, they would not improve anything unless the children of poor people learn to take care of themselves better so that they will not destroy their future prospects. If you want to complain about the farm owners, then complain that they do not use their authority to control the wildness of youth; complain that often it is not necessary to direct their young servant boys and servant girls to sleep in the animal house where their wildness has free play! Such is probably the cause of the deplorable situation which you told me about in that house." "Yes, it is quite true," he answered in a curiously ingratiating manner, "I say that also."—"You do? I have not heard that from any farmer in this area."—"No, there are really not many farmers who pay attention. But I myself am the son of a cotter and have been a servant boy; I have enough experience with how things are, and now when I am a farmer and have a boy and a girl, I now observe the custom that they each have sleeping quarters, and I have never permitted the old custom in my house." I looked at the man and continued to listen, doubly attentive. While discussing various matters, we reached his house. I went in and drank a dish of milk and went on, but he accompanied me still a bit in order to show me the way to where I was expected to stay and, in secrecy, (now, when it was late in the evening and half-dark) to tell me how the authorities had dealt with him unjustly. He had been sentenced to jail and had served his time but was completely innocent, and the reason was that the judge wanted revenge for an old quarrel. "Truly, you are lying! I have also been at the jail; for five years I have been at the jail every Sunday to talk with the prisoners, and many complained about unjust convictions, but I found that none of the complaints was justified. And your voice and the tone of your words tell me you are lying." He began to swear and curse. "Don't you swear! But since we now are talking frankly, the little boy I saw in the house, is he your child?" No, he was a stranger he had adopted. "Now, why was your wife so quiet? Is she ill, or how is it between you?"—"Oh well, I cannot say anything other than I am fond of her, but really she is not all there and is slow to understand."—"Listen to my last frank words. I do not believe you're telling me that you supervised the good behavior of your servants either." Again he wanted to curse, but in a tone which I dare believe was both deeply felt and impatient, I bade that he control himself. And then we parted. Later a farmer who claimed to know the man well gave me an extensive explanation of the jail sentence and told me as follows: The man quite rightly directed the servant girl to a separate sleeping room and prevented the boys from visiting her, but in such manner that he locked her door at night in order that he alone visited her; by one and the same servant girl he had had two children, and one of them was the boy I saw in his house!

It was, as I believe I have already related, at the beginning of 1851 that I undertook the mission, through travel and other methods, to start investigations of the conditions and morals of the lower classes. Thus I was given the opportunity to look round in the country, as is the privilege of only a few people, and full of drive and high spirits I started my first trip. But then during the first summer I encountered the last-described example of licentious and vile behavior—that man who wanted to be one of the working people's leaders and spokesmen—and this example became sort of the high point of a whole series of deplorable experiences which in the course of two months I had with regard to the moral conditions among the working class. It is difficult to explain what a strong impression it made on me, and precisely these first years of deplorable experiences have had a profound influence on my life's destiny. From Christiania I traveled to the rural communities with the thought (which I believe many others had entertained) that here I should find purer morals and gentler conditions, but instead I found the conditions so gloomy—gloomy in themselves and gloom-inspiring, for I could not grasp how such a condition could have developed or been maintained in our country, nor grasp how under such immorality family life could hold together and society survive—that I decided to try hard to seek some light here, even if it would cost me several years of my life. The attempt has cost me some of my best years, and it took a long time before I began to understood matters; it took a long time before I found a glimmer of beginning light regarding the dismal condition in the country, and I underwent mental anguish because of it. I can probably best explain by saying that my best hours during long stretches were those during which I buried myself in the many figures and calculations, after which (to the surprise and disappointment of my friends, who had likely expected something more exciting of me) I wrote a book on mortality in Norway, because I then forgot my despair over this depravity and wickedness and my own incapacity to see the beginning and the end of it.

But I continue by telling how, even though often in a depressed mood, I continued with my observations and made plans to see the coarseness and immorality in its entirety, to measure its height and plumb its depth. The last example presented filled us with aversion to the depravity of human beings; it was like a woman given to extreme indecency. I think of her now, and I am reminded of the whole class of women to which she belonged, women whose errors are not diminished because they thought of themselves as sweethearts together with their lovers, women who participated in breakups of marriages with married men and thereby not only destroyed family peace but involved their own lives in a suffering of shame and unhappiness which they themselves must have foreseen. I called this a whole class of women since their number is not small. And to this number can still be likely added women who abandon themselves to men, both living according to concepts and customs which are far from any serious thought of eventual marriage, for example, when unattractive daughters of poor cotters are taken in by the passions of lieutenants or office workers or well-off sons of farm owners. I can present the results as the basis for table 5.3.
Here one can see the great difference between the two classes, that men of the owner class are most likely to marry women of their own class, but are most likely to disgrace the women of the lower class.

If we had parallel results for women who let themselves into despicable relationships as destroyers of marriage, we should also certainly discover that for the most part they belong to the working class or the poverty-stricken part of the population. That which should offset the deprivation of the poor as compared to the advantages of the rich clearly should be their pride and virtue. But now it looks as if it is customary for poor people to show less regard for this treasure. How I have struggled to intrude myself into the innermost layers of folk life to see the basis for this seemingly unnatural and unfortunate pattern! "The basis? We do not need to ask. We all know once and for all that although there can be a few moral people among the poor as well as a few dissolute ones among the well-off classes, it has always been and will always be so, on the whole, that poverty and immorality (drunkenness, irresponsibility,

Table 5.3. Marriages and illegitimate births in the owner and working classes

Men of the owner class who married	
(a) women of the same class	2,552
(b) women of the working class	686
Total	3,238
Men of the working class who married	
(a) women of the same class	4,704
(b) women of the owner class	648
Total	5,352
Men of the owner class who became fathers of illegitimate children	
(a) by women of the same class	159
(b) by women of the working class	350
Total	509
Men of the working class who became fathers of illegitimate children	
(a) by women of the same class	2,274
(b) by women of the owner class	85
Total	2,359

thievery) will always be. There is nothing more to say about this matter." This will be the rejoinder to me. But I do not give in to this answer. Because poverty and immorality just should not be related; poverty clearly should struggle hard to keep away and really stay away from immorality. And when at the same time it is quite the opposite, there can then be a justification to inquire into the cause and open one's mind to find an answer to the question.

In a mountain community in the diocese of Christiania at a large, beautiful farm, one of the most highly respected in the community, the animals in the barn became so sick they could not stand, and all of them at the same time. Something like it took place in the same barn a year or two earlier, and a wizard was summoned. He was a person who, in addition to his wife's begging and welfare for his children, made a living from this despicable service, as the name implies. He went up into the woods and found a snake, a cattle snake, took it with him, bored a deep hole in one of the barn beams, pushed the snake alive into it, and plugged the hole. This method was supposed to ward off the harm and prevent it in the future, and therefore it impressed the people as remarkable that the misfortune returned with increased force. Now when the misfortune, as mentioned, struck the farm a second time, besides the wizard, a doctor was also summoned, a doctor so eminent that he had his own horse and sleigh. When he approached the farm, he said to the fellow who was sent to fetch him and now stood at the back of the sleigh, "I wonder if I dare take my horse into the yard? Oh yes, I believe

I dare." And thereby the fellow was assured according to the usual belief that the man really had control over the trolls—since there were trolls on the farm, it was obvious; the doctor also said so himself that the ill fortune was cast upon the animals by "envious people," and he offered to send the ill fortune back home to its instigator.

Look, I heard this story together with a whole heap of stories of the same kind, which buzzed around the community, and the matter became serious for me when I learned that in many instances particular people were designated as instigators of the sickness, which now and then struck animals or people as well. It was also said of the "doctor" that, in addition to his having a chest of bottles of medicine, he also used secret methods. "What kind?" I asked. "Oh," the answer was (and otherwise the man I talked with was very sensible), "Oh, I really believe that it is nothing but nature he uses."—"Nature?" I asked again. "Yes, the same nature we walk on—yes, there is evidence from the cemetery, to be completely frank." And in that connection the doctor told how he had come driving over the ice and a man who was walking was allowed to stand on the back [of the sleigh]; when they got to the church, the doctor got off and said to the other, "Come along!" but he did not want to, because it was late in the evening and dark; the doctor then went alone to the church door and blew into the keyhole; therewith the door opened. After having heard several of these unpleasant stories, which even the farmers, who were supposed to be enlightened Christians, believed, I looked up not only the wizard himself but also several of the people who were eyewitnesses to the occurrences; with this purpose I also went to the farm where all the animals had been stricken.

First I got to talk with the farmer himself; after a short while, his grown-up son and daughter came. It was not long before we were in the middle of the matter. Both the father and the son believed definitely in trolls. I expressed my views about the matter, but they defended theirs. "It is not only on my farm that this has happened. There have been such attacks on the cattle, and everyone wishes to believe that it is caused by evil people or by the casting of spells. It is obvious that they are very awful people who can do such things." "But you, my man, do you believe this yourself?"—"Yes, it is not easy to decide what one should believe."—"Oh yes, my friend! It seems to me that it is easy to decide what one should believe. Evil people could do harm with axes and knives and poisonous plants, that both you and I know, but a cow, they could not make a cow sick with invisible things."—"Did you see any sign that there had been strangers in the barn?" I turned to the son. "Yes, it looked like it," was the answer. "What did you see?"—"Oh, different things. There was always such commotion and noise in the barn, and the animals bellowed and threw themselves on the stalls."—"But what sign did you see that it was people who had done it?"—"Oh, it was several things."—"Yes, but it is precisely this that I want to know."—"With your permission," said the boy in a certain strange voice, "we have really not seen that man before here on this farm. Why are you asking so many questions about this?"—"For the reason I have said: I have heard talk about the doings of trolls on this farm, and that is something we ought to have full knowledge of. Therefore I still ask what sign or mark you actually have about it. Or would you, farmer, or you, my boy, rather help the trolls to keep it secret?"—"It was the bag they found," said the daughter a little eagerly when the father and brother were silent. "What kind of bag?"—"A bag with something nasty in it."—"What kind of nastiness?"—"Hair and nails and more such."—"How was it found? By the milkmaid?"—"No, it was a fellow, and he has a room next to us right now."—"I must talk with him, have him come in." And the selfsame wizard came in. "Have you found a bag in the barn with hair and nails?" I asked him severely. "Yes, it was as I had described," he answered frankly. "For it was well to realize that it must be for casting a spell, and I said immediately when I came to the farm that there really was a bag, and I decided myself to take it. And my God, it also lay in the stall of the bell cow."—"And I heard," added the farmer, "how he screamed and shouted when he found it—it was really loud, it was—he fell in a heap in the stall as if he were completely helpless."—"Yes, it was a terrible struggle," the wizard continued, "I have never had such a struggle—the bag had a strong smell."—"No, I did not sense that," the farmer noted. "Not so? Well, all the others sensed it."

I let the wizard leave with the request that I wished to talk with him afterward in private, and I continued the conversation with the farmer together with his son and daughter. "I consider it reasonable that this fellow who took the bag from the stall had put it there himself in order to be paid for the big job of picking it up again." No, they wanted to believe, all of them, that it was done to injure the evil folk; thus did the farmer hold to his view. I was close to losing my patience. "You do want to be a sensible man and your son, too. So, let us talk together sensibly. When there is frost on the fields, or people get typhoid fever, or when fire destroys a house, you yourself say that this is natural under God's domain; only when some accident takes place in the barn do you call it envy and spells and the doings of trolls, but this is really only old women's gossip. We must not be so naive and superstitious."—"Yes, but it can also happen among people, they say," the farmer objected. "People?"—"Yes, it is not longer ago than last year."—"Last year?"—"A girl was a servant on this farm."—"On this farm?"—"Yes, she became very ill and it looked like she might go under."—"How was that?"—"Well, it began in the left ear of the girl, and it came so suddenly and took over her whole body as nobody had ever seen."—"And was it a spell?"—"Yes, because it was not like any other illness."—"But how in the world did you have evidence that it was sprung upon her?"—"Everyone who has seen the girl and should know about such things believes it is so."—"Did you then see some doings of trolls which evil people have devised? Perhaps you found some such nasty bag in her bed?"—"No, in her case there was another method!"—"Yes, but I want to know about this other method."—"The girl had said herself that she had gotten it in her left ear, and it came with reading."—"With reading? With evil words which were read into her ear? You must explain this to me, good people." Here also the daughter was quicker and bolder than both the father and brother. "It was, to be sure," and she spoke up, "a fellow, who came to her."—"When did he come to her?"—"Oh, it was at night!"—"Now I understand: a night rover, a courter?"—"Yes, it was in this way he came."—"And I suppose he lay down in the bed with her as they usually do?"—"Yes, it was just like that. She lay down to sleep and he remained there." So he was supposed to be the one who blew the pain into the left ear of the girl. "I would not believe she liked this suitor after that?"—"Oh no, she did not know him; she might well have some idea of who he was but not for sure."—"But what are you saying, my girl? Should she not know that person who went into bed with her?"—"You must realize it was dark."—"And she did not ask for his name?"—"Oh no, she did not happen to do that."—"And he did not say who he was?"—"No, the guy simply went and lay down with her. Oh yes, I suppose they talked, but there was nothing more, she said."—"Now I have traveled widely but never have I had the experience of hearing about what you are telling me, my girl. It really looks like this girl did not have the faintest concept of modesty and chastity."—"Oh no, this happens quite often, and she paid no more attention to him but lay down to sleep again."

As mentioned, I talked with farm people, and on one of the best farms in a large parish; in great detail they told, as was observed, how the girl's earache came about, and the matter had evoked a great deal of attention so that people on the farm and in the neighborhood had pushed it to the most fanciful explanation of the cause and nature of the illness. But neither by word or syllable was there any acknowledgment that this behavior of the girl was disapproved of, to accept strangers into her bed. This was talked about more as something that could happen frequently, and it occurred to no one to censure!

And now I felt that I suddenly knew many things which I had previously heard about in the same community. For example, "I know your brother-in-law," I once said to a well-respected farm owner, which it had pleased me to get to know. "I know your brother-in-law, an attractive young man to look at. But from the church records I know that he has had a child by a girl. Tell me, perhaps he was fond of her and once had thought about marrying her?"—"Oh no, it was not that way. And it might well be that he has suffered some injustice there."—"How is that?"—"Well, he had been together with some other young fellows one night and on the way home he stopped at the farm where he was serving, and there she lay in the animal barn, according to the custom which you have deplored. When the girl became ill during her pregnancy, the first usual question to the midwife was who was the father of the child. And she named one, and it was not my brother-in-law. But since the labor pains lasted a somewhat long time, they told her she had better tell the truth now rather than later. So she gave another name, and an hour or so went by. But then she gave a third name, and it was my brother-in-law, and the child was born, and he was recorded, and he could hardly do anything else but accept it."

But how many girls are like this one, girls of the working class in rural areas. Oh, how many! And when self-respect and natural modesty are seldom seen, it then becomes a natural trend for a few to fall into wicked ways compared to most, so that all respect for individual self-regard seems to have vanished for them. In a community in the diocese of upper Christiania, this was revealed in a terrible way by a legal suit a few years previously in which a woman was charged who had pretended to be a midwife and had given a large number of girls means to induce abortions. And in the same community from which I related two examples of how womanly modesty had died out, I heard a farmer tell about a girl, a cotter's daughter, who was to me an even worse horror of a human being.

First, a cotter had told me the story of a betrothed girl who was a relative of his. The situation was that one day an acquaintance of the girl came and borrowed a dress for attending church. Shortly thereafter the dress was returned, but when the owner was to put it on she noticed that in one fold of the skirt, which is called *mod-folden* [reverse crease], there were three clamps. (I had recently heard of a horse which suddenly became ill, which on investigation was found to be marked in the same way: three clamps which had been clipped into the mane with a pair of scissors, so that they could not be easily discovered but easily felt. Such clamps were supposed to be a suspicious sign of an enemy who wishes you evil.) The girl became very distressed on seeing this sign on her dress because she would soon have a wedding, and especially because it was on the wedding day that the evil could be expected. The previously mentioned mysterious "doctor," who stayed nearby when he was brought to a woman who "had gotten a spell and had lost her mind," on seeing the clamps declared that it was the work of evil people and offered to get rid of the misfortune. This offer was not accepted, but a thorough investigation was started to find the culprit; and one girl was under suspicion, a girl who had a child by the boy to whom the owner of the dress was betrothed. I had heard this story and I was tempted to believe that there could really be something to this suspicion, since one time this very girl who was under suspicion came to me on her own; she said that the father of her child—the one who was now betrothed to the owner of the dress—had demanded a marriage announcement, which should have been made the previous Sunday, and there was unusually bad weather which had prevented church services, but she wanted counsel and support from me to prevent the announcement next Sunday. The boy in the presence of witnesses had agreed to pay six voger of flour annually toward the care of the child and in addition promised not to marry anybody else before he made a guarantee for the payment, which guarantee had not been provided. This gave me an opportunity for a thorough conversation with one of the respected farmers in the parish. He revealed that the evil was great with many examples on the farms round about, and that evil people and evil spirits could join in trolldom he claimed to show in many ways. It was reasonable to believe that the girl could be involved in what was afoot since the mother, a cotter's wife, had a reputation for evil, and the sister was no better. He then told the following about the sister.

A month ago she had given birth to a child in these circumstances: she had left her servant position and now was by herself, isolated at a place and engaged in day work. One day she was on a farm to bake flatbread and sat working in the house with the fire. Early in the afternoon she quit her work, giving as the reason that the fire house was so full of smoke; she went into the house and went about carding wool; in this way she wanted to work the rest of the day and go home later in the evening; then there would be moonlight, and then it was pleasant to walk. But instead of moonlight, there was a driving snow and really bad weather, and the people in the house wanted her to stay overnight on the farm. But she wanted to leave, and leave she did. The young wife on the farm and another woman were suspicious and followed her and insisted that she should turn back, since they knew that she was pregnant and was already ill. But with a dirty oath she turned them down and wanted to continue on the way. One of the women ran quickly into the house and got the old man to come out. He is rather coarse and he said straight out to the girl, "Oh, you want to do the same thing as your mother!"

(The mother, as a matter of fact, had killed her unborn child and for that had spent some time in prison.) Then the girl reacted. "Oh all right, she would be glad to go in with them, and they would see that they're only gossiping and imagining," she answered with a chilly laugh, and she entered the room with trivial vulgar talk. For the night, the young wife took the woman to bed with her in order to keep an eye on her. The girl put so much under her head that she more likely sat than lay down; she was up often and wanted to get out, but she could not since the door had been locked carefully and the key hidden. She then had to lie down again but was uncomfortable and complained about a stomachache. Finally a fire had to be made in the fireplace and some light brought into in the room, and a little later she had the child. "How you run around," she was told, but she wished to excuse herself for the small lie that she "had felt that there was something rolling around in her stomach but thought it was only gas."

So far, yes, to such an extreme can coarseness be carried.

Coarseness? This word reminds me of much talk that I have heard since childhood about the coarse common people. From childhood? Oh, precisely during recent years when I have had conversations with people about these deplorable matters, not one but many have wanted to give me the pessimistic answer: "Yes, does this really surprise you? What else can one expect of the coarse common people?"

But there ought not be something which can rightly be called the coarse common people! Truly, with regard to honor and virtue there should not be any difference, no difference at all between the daughter of a cotter and general or merchant. Am I too reasonable here? Well, let others call me so. But then I turn to the cotter whose struggles and sweat I know and for whom I am glad for the cheer and trust which obedient sons and dutiful daughters should offer their father and mother—the cotter and father shall not call it unreasonable talk to be enthusiastic about the happiness of his sons and the honor of his daughters.

Truly, if I had mostly thought of my own peace of mind, these abominable matters would not have been written in a book with my name on it. I have had to make myself suffer in order to bring myself to talk about these things. But afterward I have presented irrefutable figures which revealed a worse condition in the working class than in the owner class, and thus I have reported reality as a witness to how extremely bad the conditions can be. (And all the examples presented in this chapter are from the Christiania dioceses, which in the foregoing appeared in group 2.) And this I have done in order to support more vigorously the conclusion that—*it must not be so!*

Let whoever wishes be content with the old talk about the coarse common people, but your cotter or day laborer or servant fellow should think about how the nature of coarseness can be wiped out! It is now a common cause for the entire working class; since so many of its members wrong themselves so grossly, it might too likely happen that also the respectable working-class family is looked on as of the same kind.

You, mother, who yourself perhaps was irresponsible when young and now sit in poverty and depravity, you double your efforts to watch over the behavior of your children and admonish them kindly and pray for them constantly! You, father, who was perhaps in earlier times a rascal and now for a few years a work-slave, bent and heavy-laden, raise yourself as much as you can and use your fatherly authority to teach your children proper behavior and keep them away from the pernicious customs! You fortunate parents who a merciful God has guided through life without damage such that poverty and obstacles never smothered the growth of piety in your souls, continue your worthy efforts for the nurturing of your children and talk and think over with your neighbors about the best means to spread among the young people more obedience and virtue; yes, join with each other to use your goodwill against coarseness and corruption! And you, servant boys and itinerant workers, dairymaids and other servant girls, lift up your eyes and look around the communities and side roads where you go. Be aware of the many moral offenses and the enormous misfortunes [coarseness and corruption] cause and seek the unfailing lesson you have been taught, that help can be found against the seductiveness of sin. Believe me, I do not say this for the sake of taxes, about which the farmers complain to the welfare office because of the many children placed with families after they could not be cared for by the mothers and were deserted by their fathers. I say it because it has grieved me to remember what my eyes have seen: a much bigger tax on human happiness and peace of mind which the people in poverty themselves have paid year after year for their transgressions! And whatever you do, do not talk about or wait for the upper class, among whom one can also observe quite a bit of wickedness, that they should be the first to set a good example. Since on the one hand I have not seen immorality so common in the upper class, and on the other you are not placed to follow their example, be sure that you yourself set a good example as well as they!

6

Half-Legitimate Children

WHY is it that the poor are seldom talked about favorably? It is self-evident; if there is an able and dependable servant boy or day worker, or if one happens to ask his superior about him, he does not keep still but can speak well of him. Likewise, when I have visited a welfare officer and through him been given an inventory of the poor in his district in order to examine each one of them and determine the most frequent cause of poverty, then sometimes this tedious explanation can be interrupted by one or another more cheerful account of the great efforts of a widow and her quiet patience. But it is seldom that a person in the poverty class is noticed by people in this way without a direct question which creates the opportunity to talk about and praise him. Is it because the human virtues thrive so little on the dry heather hill, where the poor man probably has his cottage? Or is it because most of them do not take the time really to bend down to see what beautiful flowers the heather bears?

I became pleasantly aware how people in a north township in Lom talked spontaneously and often praised a young cotter there. As a young girl, his mother married an old farmer who as an old man lived on a small pension, and a few years later she became a widow with a few small children. Poverty was severe, and she was allowed to live in a seter [summer hut] where she could find some fodder for a few goats and she established herself for both summer and winter. But when I learned about her she was crippled and for 30 years had sat in one spot without moving. But her son, who was now a cotter on the seter, showed her a concern and love which was much admired.

This young man had his wedding while I was staying nearby, and I was pleased to accept his invitation to be at the celebration. In this community, it is the custom not to have the parents of the bride provide for the wedding but those of the bridegroom. The wedding did not take place, however, in the modest home of the seter nearby, for the farm owner had offered his large and spacious house for the festivities. The bridegroom, after all, did not have much to offer the guests, but nearby neighbors and relatives respected him anyway. There was not a lack of guests; older men and women were deep in conversation and young people amused themselves in their way. Also, for this couple the high-seat wall was decorated with one of these marvelous old-fashioned handwoven tapestries with multicolored Bible pictures, wall hangings which I have not seen outside of Lom and Vaage, which from olden days have been used to cover walls for festive occasions. An old and experienced master of ceremonies conducted the ceremonies, which have been observed from generation to generation and have given the rural people their festive character; and there were large, neatly carved-out buckets with sour cream porridge and sweet porridge, plus baskets of cookies and good pots of meat, etc., mostly gifts from the guests. The women began to set the table to start serving so that one could in a short time satisfy one's need for food and drink. In short, everything contributed to provide a day in the life of the wedding couple when life's heavy demands were lessened and when one could feel lighthearted and gay even in these simple circumstances. There was also both festiveness and joy when one sat on the benches around the rich table, bride and bridegroom in the high seat and the guests in long rows out from them, all according to age and position!

And how necessary such a red-letter day was for this couple! His years had been filled with poverty and struggle, and her life was in large part steeped in grief, since in her early youth she gave birth to a child (now dead) whose father had disappointed her expectations; and both had surely longed for this day since they had lived together for some time as married people and already had a baptized child. We were on benches around the table, and I occupied the place of honor next to the bride. Then an infant's cry was heard; it belonged to the bridal couple; it was brought to the mother in the high seat and she put it to her breast. Both the bride and the groom were already embarrassed by the unaccustomed honor since they were seated above and we below, but the arrival of the infant did not seem to cause embarrassment; I believed I saw that the bride felt like a happy mother, perhaps happier than ever since she had acquired the name of wife and a mother's right. The participation of relatives and neighbors was evidence that they no longer accused the bride and groom for the irregular life they had lived together, but were happy to see them as properly married and proper parents. At the same time, the master of ceremonies came with the full mug; with plain gestures, the bridegroom toasted us and likewise the bride, and the mug was given to me. I rose, and if I ever have expressed myself with feeling and sincerity in a toast, it was here, when on behalf of myself and fellow guests I drank to the welfare of the wedding couple. And my participation was not lessened when during the dining I talked with the bride and listened to both her unassuming and sensible explanation of various things.

Look, had I met this woman during her unfortunate years, had I met her in her probably shabby home at a time when the unpleasant nature of daily life dominated her and her surroundings, had I met her during an hour when my own spirit was tired of all the deplorable observations which I frequently had to make regarding the life of people in our country, and of which this contains examples, then perhaps my impressions and mood would have been quite the opposite. The sight of an infant gives us a different impression when we happen to see it with a dirty face and shabby and ragged clothes or when we see it right after a bath and dressed up. But for human beings, a celebration is like a bath where the mood is more innocent and lighthearted. Therefore I say that if one often happens to see poor people in their everyday dismal conditions, he must be sure to see them also during celebrations.

CONSIDERATIONS REGARDING JUDGMENT OF PEOPLE'S MORALS

And how many things there are which in different ways can influence our mood and thereby our judgment! Just this situation which I have used is an example, that a man and woman could live together as married folk, still without God's blessing or the sanction of the congregation to mark their relationship. It was something that I kept a sharp eye out for during this series of weeks and days and severely criticized as something I felt had become dominant in the community, so dominant that it had become very common, that it had become custom. I certainly could not have called it anything other than a coarse custom, but now, when I sat right in the circle, and since I myself involuntarily and heartily took part in the manifestations of participation and homage whereby everyone sought to honor and cheer our wedding couple, now the criticism had to be silenced; precisely because the matter was so usual, this had to be regarded as an excuse for this one couple, who sort of just followed what they had seen also among respectable folk, namely, a community custom. Yes, I have here hinted at a situation which for me, at any rate, has been of enormous significance. By research on moral conditions and by efforts to collect facts according to a definite view and judgment, one is exposed to a very strange play of contrary frames of mind. Imagine that you come as a stranger to a community and by chance encounter an example of one or another living situation which you, according to your accustomed outlook, call wrong and immoral; imagine then that shortly with another person you find an example of the same kind, and you, since you now have become aware, direct questions in that direction and in a short time find 3, 5, 9, 15, yes, innumerable examples like the first and the second. Little by little, the disturbed feeling will grow into indignation, and this indignation will make you bitter and hard toward each person you find involved in the same way. But then it can happen quickly, just as your indignation is at its height, that you feel you are being unjust; it can be that you have just encountered a person with the same offence and have already opened your mouth to let him know your aversion when you see deep in his eyes that an innocent soul shines from them, a soul who knows nothing of evil in this case—since the same person has lived and behaved according to the common custom and views of people in that community! Immediately the indignation will soften, and the severe judgment of others will turn to a humble judgment of yourself, because you suddenly remember what you have forgotten for weeks and days, that there are differences among people who do the wrong on the basis of the wrong itself; there is a difference between one who does the wrong almost without thinking about it and the one who knows the right but still does the wrong.

And the matter has two sides. I will point out a certain double method of observation with regard to weddings. A bride a year or so ago had moved from her parents' up to the bridegroom's place high up on the mountainside. Why, one will ask, did the couple not first go to church to have their relationship solemnized and properly made official?

Even though they were very poor, it seems it was possible that they could have limited themselves to a church ceremony and not assumed any cost for a lavish public wedding feast. But in this community—and likely in many others—this feast was not thought of as lavish. One can often learn from hearsay when, for example, it is said of a boy that he is thinking of "having a party" with this or that girl, i.e., to marry her. Here in Lom I learned that a couple must not only be extremely poor but also have sunk deeply in regard to a sense of honor when they limit themselves to a church ceremony, since the feast is also a celebration whereby the newly married couple establishes their worth as one of the families recognized by neighbors and relatives. A year ago our bridegroom surely could have paid the pastor and his assistant for the church arrangement, but at that time he maybe still had not had cloth woven and dyed and ironed, which he now wore in new clothes; at that time the bride had likely not been able to provide herself with the cotton and wool tweed dress which she now could appear in; at that time they probably could not afford to take as much barley from their chest which the wedding beer required. Now they invited the farmers in the neighborhood and the cotters to their feast and accepted the duty that when other houses in the neighborhood had feasts, they would be prepared to return the favor and arrive with the same gifts of party food as were now brought to them. But see, this was a duty which they reasonably could not have assumed a year earlier, when their living condition was still so modest. On the whole, one can say that the double celebration (the church ceremony and the party at home) signified that marriage is a double thing, something religious and something secular; in the very olden days, one knows that marriage was regarded only as a secular agreement which was made legitimate by a celebration in the house, and it has often occurred to me that this view, alongside the views of the church, is still true in many country communities or is even dominant.

There are many circumstances which cause the wedding celebration to be delayed so long that it can happen as told that the bride sat in the high seat with a child at her breast. "Tell me," I asked during a conversation with a farmer, in whose house the same wedding ceremony was held. "Tell me: why do most of the weddings in this community take place this time of the year, early in the spring?"—"Oh well, it is somewhat easier then."—"To me it seems that it is somewhat inconvenient right in the middle of the spring thaw and bad roads."—"Yes, but during other months it is easier, for people have more time now."—"In July the fields must be watered; in August and September the grain must be harvested and the foliage cut; then I can understand that there is not time to get together for a party. But during Christmas or in winter there must be as much free time as in March and April."—"Yes, but then there is the problem that in winter the cattle give so little milk, and milk they must have for gift-porridge and for many things." Since I did not give this problem much emphasis, he presented another reason, which struck me so unexpectedly in its nature that I kept quiet: "Yes, but in winter the days are short so that there must be many tallow candles available."

I now have the opportunity to show how by using the church records I found the number of marriages in the parish of Lom divided into 12 months of the year during the following periods (table 6.1).

Here it is remarkable enough to observe this gradual change over

Table 6.1. Marriages in Lom

Month	1733–1742	1761–1770	1821–1830	1841–1850
January	8	17	8	5
February	3	6	12	13
March	7	18	67	71
April	5	17	57	80
May	6	10	16	24
June	30	27	49	61
July	14	19	22	19
August	...	1	1	2
September	1	...	...	1
October	17	20	14	28
November	43	36	34	42
December	16	9	25	20
Total	150	180	305	366

time—that the wedding celebrations shifted from November and December to March and April. This can be seen in table 6.2, and moreover, the table shows particularly the great agreement between the two time periods, in that whether due to milk, or lights, or whatever it is, there is a somewhat certain regularity in what time of the year one prefers to have the wedding celebration, so that individuals do not go ahead and decide without much ado or just according to one's own whim.

Table 6.2. Shift in wedding celebrations

	November and December *(percent)*	March and April *(percent)*
1733–1742	39	8
1761–1770	25	19
1821–1830	19	41
1841–1850	17	41

THE WEDDING DAY AND THE BIRTHDAY OF THE FIRSTBORN IN LOM AND VAAGE

I return to the remarks about the condition which this wedding celebration exemplified and shall show the figures for the parishes of Lom and Vaage in table 6.3. This table gives us a very clear idea about morals and conditions in these communities, but first understand the table correctly! If we look at the figures for the parish of Lom for the years 1848–1853, we find that of 100 married couples there were 32 who had children before the wedding (yes, a few of these 32 couples had several children, which however cannot be seen in the table). Further, 24 couples had children before the end of four months after the wedding ceremony. Finally, 9 couples were in the same situation in the next four months. Therefore there were all together 65 couples out of 100 who, it became obvious, had lived together as married people before they were so regarded before God and people. In one of the years 1848–1853 I found this interesting item: during a year 32 couples were married, and among these there were only two exceptions to the rule that they had children either before the wedding or an improperly short time thereafter. These two exceptions were the following: one couple in which both the bride and groom were over 50 years of age, and one couple who were still childless after a few years of marriage and would likely be so indefinitely. This improper situation seems also to be very common in these communities.

Here are more situations to note. One which is not seen in table 6.3 I became aware of when I made these excerpts from the church records; I was surprised to find a few instances in which the bride gave birth to her child only a few days, at times less than a week, before or after the wedding. I also know of examples where the wedding ale had been brewed and the cakes baked and the guests invited and their gifts of food ready to be delivered, and so the whole show had to be canceled because

Table 6.3. The wedding day and the birthday of the firstborn in Lom and Vaage[a]

Parish	Year	Married Couples	Couples Having Children: Before the Wedding	Within 4 Months after the Wedding	From 4 to 8 Months after the Wedding	Total Births
Lom	1824–1829	170	28	38	15	81
	1848–1853 (5/15)	171	54	41	16	111
Vaage	1821–1825	224	42	53	48	143
	1848–1853 (6/30)	209	86	36	22	144
			The Condition Calculated per 100			
Lom	1824–1829	100	16	22	9	47
	1848–1853 (5/15)	100	32	24	9	65
Vaage	1821–1825	100	19	24	21	64
	1848–1853 (6/30)	100	41	17	11	69

[a] The table contains an excerpt from the church records, and this excerpt is made as follows: First I have taken the alphabetized list of the couples who have been married one year, and next I have compared names of the married couples, of the parents, and of the children who were born not only in the same year but in the three nearest previous years as well as the following years. By observing the wedding day and the birthday, I could get the result which the table shows.

the bride had given birth. Now when the wedding celebration is set, the expenses arranged, and everything is ready, one does not want to know of such hindrances. Moreover, it can be that the bride, in her very difficult condition shortly before or in her weakened condition after the serious experience, must get on a horse and ride to church and stand at the altar, and after returning home sit some hours at the dining table and then dance with the master of ceremonies and thereafter the best man and the groomsmen and finally with all the guests, and not only for one day but for several nights and days. Is it not then likely that many brides have suffered harm which took a long time to get over, or that a bride has made her child so weak as to be unable to survive? In truth, the whole thing is indefensible! A similar bad practice is often seen—taking much-too-young infants to church and in very severe weather. Strøm tells in his description of Søndmør (1767) that in the parish of Volden during the hard winter of 1755, of 30 newborn infants not one survived, simply because they were taken to church in the bitter cold immediately after birth. This was 100 years ago. But in the church records I still find occasionally recorded for infants: "Died because taken too early to church."

In order to point out another circumstance, I must ask the reader to look again at table 6.3. Of the married couples who had had children at an improper time, the fewest were those who had been married four to eight months after the event; more frequent are those in which this situation is evident before marriage (first category) or shortly after (second category). We could say that the first and the second categories present the most deplorable condition (particularly the first); and what is the explanation for the fact that most of the married couples mentioned here would allow themselves to be found in these two categories? A young couple actually live together; the girl is appalled to discover that she is to become a mother, and she reports it to him; but he is a scoundrel and leaves her immediately so that she remains sitting in shame and wretchedness: this couple is not even mentioned in this table but is recorded only in the lists of the parents of illegitimate children. Another couple lives together irresponsibly and she tells him the serious news, but he becomes distressed, since he had not really decided that he wanted her as a wife; he did not feel that he could abandon her either, but at the same time he could not bring himself to marry her. There must probably be a great deal of persuasion to move him to live up to his obligation, and thereby the matter drags along; and if the marriage takes place at all, it is likely only after the girl has become a mother, so that we might say a forced marriage is counted in the first category. A third couple lives together as lovers, and in the meantime the consequences become known to both of them; she is fond of him and he wants to marry her but they had not thought of the wedding ceremony so soon, and there are many preparations to make. It is not enough to arrange for the pastor's announcement and the wedding; circumstances are probably such that they do not have a house and home; indeed, the young people probably have not yet obtained the permission of the parents, and if they are the children of farm owners they could not ignore it; and it may be that in this connection they had to contend with a struggle, insofar as her parents had possibly chosen another son-in-law. If all efforts were rejected to overcome the obstacles and hasten the wedding ceremony, there are other important matters to be arranged before the birth of the child; and at best this will occur a short time after the wedding ceremony, so that this couple will come to be classified in the first or the second category.

I remember a couple. They were servants. The girl had to quit as a servant, and a little while later she gave birth to their child. The boy did not deny being the father; he did not seem to be completely indifferent to the girl and the child either. He went to the pastor himself and requested the baptism, invited the godparents, was himself at the church, had a celebration for the godparents, a few relatives and friends, provided his part of the food and drink for the feast, and became somewhat tipsy; but while tipsy, he said in the hearing of several that he had put on a feast for the child, and he would not have a wedding celebration with her. And he did not either.

I remember another couple. They were both also servants. Then they found out the serious plight the girl was in. He did not abandon her, but both quit being servants at the end of the year, and they lived together as tenant laborers with a cotter family. The boy was not quick to request a wedding in that he had nothing with which to provide a celebration and less to get married on, as is said. The girl became a mother, and he hung around the community as a day laborer. He could afford little with his earnings; everything appeared to be deplorable, and little by little he came to the conclusion that it was best for them to part. The girl heard this and wept, and he became more and more despondent and had a desire to leave the community. She raised objections, and he became impatient and stubborn; there were daily quarrels. Then the cotter and his wife intervened and suggested that since it had come this far, they should seriously consider remaining together. Eventually he was fortunately persuaded, and in the meantime they were married.

I have read about a third couple. They were children of farm owners. The girl became pregnant and her parents noticed it, but the father, who had never liked the boy, since it seemed to him that the boy did not have enough assets to support a family, opposed the union. The girl died during delivery, and the father requested the pastor to conduct the funeral. The pastor found the matter unpleasant and at first refused, but the father justified his situation as follows: the girl was the eldest of several daughters, and should she be able to defy her father's will in this manner, it would be more difficult for him to discipline his daughters to respect him. The boy became grief-stricken and died a year later. This happened in Nordmør in 1767.

I remember a fourth couple. The boy and girl belonged to highly respected farm-owner families, but he was not liked by her father. The girl became pregnant, but the girl's father pretended not to notice, and no one dared to talk to him on behalf of the young people. The girl spent her time in grief and gave birth to the child in despair; her father did not criticize or reproach her, but he did not give her a glimmer of hope either. Sometime later, a well-regarded farmer came to the girl's father as a spokesman for the boy. "You must not be so obstinate," suggested the spokesman. "The boy has not behaved toward me as to make any claim," the father answered. And he gave the impression that however it went for the daughter, no headway could be made if one wanted to force one's way. Then the spokesman gave in, and the marriage was in the meantime arranged.

I remember a fifth couple. They were also children of farm owners. The boy reported to the father of the girl that he was the suitor when her condition could not be denied, and for the sake of the far-advanced pregnancy of the bride, the wedding ceremony was hastened as fast as possible. It took place at the home of the bridegroom, and the father of the girl was present. But then, probably when the beer was having an effect, he blurted out that he felt the bridegroom had behaved like a scoundrel and he thought the daughter's marriage was degrading. The father of the bridegroom replied in the same manner, and the worthy fathers-in-law became so exercised that the master of ceremonies, who told me the story, had to coax them into separate rooms and lock the doors.

I remember a sixth couple. The boy, a servant fellow, was already named by two girls as the father of their children, and then the same happened to a third. Then he was given the choice: either to be punished according to the law or to marry one of the girls, and he chose the latter.

I remember a whole bunch of couples, and I remember how astonished I became to find that there were so many of them. There was a locality of cotters or a cluster of about 50 cotters' places which adjoin in a row, and all belong to 12 or 13 farms in Gudbrandsdal. One couple were children of cotters, who, of course, could still be sweethearts but who had already lived with each other, some with parents, some with strangers and, to judge by the cradles and screaming infants, many already formed as families. I talked with quite a few of them myself and with their relatives and acquaintances, and I came to the conclusion that one found a pattern: the young people were fond of each other and would have each other, but as people who have still not acquired a piece of land and shelter, they were not likely to marry.

So it is for the thousands of different situations and motives, and there are likewise as many degrees of more or less scandalous conditions. But with the examples presented (which are not all just from Lom or Vaage), one will realize what I mean to be able to point to as common practice: many young people live together in love who have not learned to observe the rules and boundaries to enter into marriage, according to the edicts established by the church and civil authorities; such people experience the most awful complications and often balance between separation and marriage; and to the extent the latter takes place, it is likely so late that the married couple is classified in the first rather than the second category.

Otherwise one often hears another explanation, which will make the whole matter seem more attractive. In the old days—so goes the explanation—the people were accustomed in good faith to regard the betrothal as the accepted beginning of the marriage, and when the betrothal by the decree of the king was abolished (in the year 1799), the wedding announcement was regarded in the same way. But customarily, there is a duration of only a few weeks between the announcement and the wedding ceremony, and to the extent that the improperly born children were conceived during this period, so for the most part they must have been born not before the wedding, and not during the first four months or later, but between four and eight months later. But table 6.3 shows that it does involve most of the married folk included.

Still, I must point out a very significant phenomenon which table 6.3 brings to light; it is that, according to the figures, the conditions complained about got worse from one period to the other which the table covers. "Oh yes, the fear of God is disappearing in the land, and thereby the regard for good religious decrees and humane customs relaxes, and coarseness and all kinds of misfortune take over," as probably many will say. This is easy to say, and such a judgment I made myself on my first visit to Vaage in Lom (in 1852), where I felt that I saw a coarseness and immorality greater than I could grasp. But people were friendly and trusting toward me so that I felt sympathetic toward these communities and was no longer so hasty to emphasize the worst; [and I learned], on the one hand and then on the other hand, that such regression in morality was not easily made sense of simply by the facts, which in other studies I felt I had found, of improvement in education and well-being in these same communities. Therefore I repeated my visit and stayed there a long time (in 1854) and started over again, better prepared to rework the whole chapter on marriage and illegitimate births. And here I will present some of the benefit from the investigation, which strengthened my assumption that the condition maybe really had not changed for the worse as seemed at first glance.

By extracting the church records, which I later compared with the lists of pastors kept by the record office in Christiania, I obtained first an overview of the frequency of illegitimate births for the half-century from 1801 to 1850. During this period, in Lom the number of marriages was 1,433 and the number of illegitimate births was 690. In Vaage the number of marriages was 1,603 and the number of illegitimate births was 1,060. Table 6.4 shows what the conditions were during each of the different years. They clearly worsened, as can be seen during 1821–1830 and still more during 1831–1840, but during 1841–1850 there was a change for the better. This is evident in each of the two parishes.

Table 6.4. Illegitimate births per 100 marriages in Lom and Vaage

Year	Lom	Vaage
1801–1810	38	50
1811–1820	34	49
1821–1830	50	62
1831–1840	66	88
1841–1850	53	79

From 1816 on, the church records are set up to record the ages of the married couples, and in addition to what extent they were unmarried men or widowers, unmarried girls or widows. I went through these designations. During the 35 years from 1816 to 1850, the number of unmarried men who married either unmarried girls or widows was in Lom, 1,959; and in Vaage, 1,136, except for a few whose ages were not recorded.

In table 6.5 I give their age distribution as far as possible for the same periods as for table 6.4. It can be seen in table 6.5 that from the first to the last of the four periods, little by little and quite steadily, a change has taken place in that fewer and fewer unmarried men were married at the young age of under 25. And this is quite remarkable, since during the 10-year period 1841–1850 there must have been a relatively large number of people of the same age, since according to the population tables of people (men and women combined) in the ages from 20 to 30 years there were:

	in Lom	*in Vaage*
in 1825	717	833
in 1835	633	650
in 1845	923	980

The cause of this decreased number of bridegrooms of young age in the last period must be sought in the conditions which made the young people delay marrying. (What these circumstances might reasonably be I have pointed out for Gudbrandsdal in *On Marriage in Norway* [*Selected Works* 2:290].)

Table 6.5. Young men who married young girls or widows

Parish	Period	Under 25 Years	Between 25 and 30 Years	Over 30 Years	Total
		(*percent*)	(*percent*)	(*percent*)	(*percent*)
Lom	1816–1820	36.1	33.3	30.6	100
	1821–1830	34.5	40.7	24.8	100
	1831–1840	34.6	38.4	27.0	100
	1841–1850	31.3	40.9	27.8	100
Vaage	1816–1820	43.8	36.2	20.0	100
	1821–1830	40.9	37.6	21.5	100
	1831–1840	35.8	34.1	30.1	100
	1841–1850	34.9	39.6	25.5	100

But when young people delay marrying, an increase in immoral behavior and illegitimate births can be feared. And anyway, table 6.4 shows us that the decade 1841–1850 was otherwise, in that the illegitimate births were less frequent than in the previous decade.

But we must make use of the observations in table 6.3, which certainly showed us the number of married couples who had children before the marriage ceremony was increasing from around 1825 to around 1850. I believe we dare to draw this conclusion: the disorderly manner of living together outside of marriage was diminishing during the last period (table 6.4); therefore with greater frequency people who had already been living together in a loose manner, sought to correct this impropriety by getting married (table 6.3). To make this matter completely clear and irrefutable, we should have some more clarification (in particular, table 6.3 ought to have covered all the years from 1816, or still earlier), but it seems entirely reasonable to me that in the later time, particularly from 1841 on, comparatively fewer illegitimate children were born and comparatively more of their parents were married subsequently. (Remember that the greater the number of parent couples who had children before marriage [first category in table 6.3], the greater the number of children born illegitimate who after the marriage of the parents became legitimate.) The birth of illegitimate children is always an evil; that the children born illegitimate later became legitimate and also were brought up as legitimate children is a good thing; now it seems the evil has diminished and the good has become somewhat greater, both in Lom and in Vaage. I know that the numbers and the calculations are correct, even if I have not made correct conclusions; the beginning of improvement in morality, which I had expected, was real, and its beginning continued at an even and fast pace.

On this occasion, I wish to give an account of the result of an investigation regarding the condition of marriage in the same communities. By mixing with the general population and by reviewing church records, I have become aware of one thing which has disturbed me greatly: that young boys get married to extremely old women, or that old, gray-haired men get quite young girls for wives. Some examples of this sort aroused my attention even more, since this community in Upper Gudbrandsdal stands lower in my regard because meanness and baseness and all kinds of corruption are found there. So I took to investigating the matter for all marriages reported in the church books year by year from 1816 to 1853, and for the sake of comparison I later had to do the same for the Vaage parish. My approach was as follows: I counted how many unmarried men or widowers had married under the age of 20, between 20 and 25, 25 and 30, 30 and 35, 35 and 40, 40 and 50, and over 50; and next I investigated for these age groups how many of their brides were in different age groups. (Table 6.6 is a test I abstracted from the church records.) One example: bridegrooms between 25 and 30 years and brides between 25 and 30 years I call the same age; if the brides of these bridegrooms are between 20 and 25 years of age, I call them one age-group younger; if they are over 30 years, I call them older. I take the position that it is the most alike parties, when the brides are the same age as the bridegrooms or up to five years younger, who are the most fortunate, and the least fortunate are those who are older than the bridegrooms. What conditions were found for the young men who married girls or widows, plus those for the girls who married young men or widowers, can be seen in table 6.7, in which the years from 1816 to 1853 are divided in two almost similar periods.

Table 6.6. Young men married to young girls or widows, 1816–1835[a]

Age of Bridegrooms	Age of Brides: Under 20 Years	20–25	25–30	30–35	35–40	40–50	Over 50 Years	Total
Under 20	7	5	3	1	1	1	...	18
20–25	31	81	37	14	8	5	1	177
25–30	37	86	47	16	9	5	1	201
30–35	10	48	20	12	1	4	...	95
35–40	3	8	7	6	7	2	2	35
40–50	2	1	3	1	2	2	...	11
Over 50	...	...	2	1	1	...	2	6
Total	90	229	119	51	29	19	6	543

[a] In case a similar count were to be made for other communities and therefore compared, I should point out that when a person was entered in the church records as age 25, I did not enter him in the age group 25–30 years but—perhaps less correctly—in the age group 20–25 years.

Table 6.7. Age difference between bride and bridegroom

Parish	Time Period	Of 100 Brides, the Following Were: Same Age or One Age Level Younger than the Bridegroom	More than One Age Level Younger than the Bridegroom	Older than the Bridegroom
		Bachelors married to girls or widows		
Lom	1816–1835	55.8	22.8	21.4
	1836–1853	63.3	19.0	17.7
Vaage	1816–1835	63.4	17.4	19.2
	1836–1853	63.3	19.1	17.6
		Bachelors or widowers married to girls		
Lom	1816–1835	57.4	25.6	17.0
	1836–1853	62.8	21.5	15.7
Vaage	1816–1835	62.8	19.1	18.1
	1836–1853	63.2	20.8	16.0

If there is agreement with this suggested viewpoint—that the best conditions are found in the first of the three columns of the table and, in contrast, the worst conditions are present in the last column—one will find a change toward the better from the years 1816–1835 to 1836–1853, particularly in the parish of Lom. It is of particular interest to see how the figures from the parish of Lom for the last period have changed so that they are almost exactly like those for Vaage, and it can therefore be concluded that Lom really differed from the neighboring communities in its less orderly and established situation in regard to this point (the several unlike partners or marriages with so great an age difference between partners, where it is difficult to have mutual affection); this must have been so in the early days and not today. Here it can also be noted that mortality (which in large part rises and falls with the cultural level of the people) was—at least as experienced by children under five—much less advantageous in Lom compared with Vaage during 1821–1830, less during 1831–1840, and still less during 1841–1850. Also from this aspect it would seem that the lower cultural level which probably was true of Lom compared with the neighboring parish of Vaage belonged more to the early days.

THE WEDDING DAY AND THE BIRTHDAY OF THE FIRSTBORN IN CHRISTIANIA AND CHRISTIANSAND

Such small-scale investigations which I have undertaken for Lom and Vaage can certainly contribute to informative examples to look at things on a large scale. But it is now time to turn from the individual communities and seek to gain knowledge of conditions in larger areas of the country.

In the first chapter I pointed out the great differences in illegitimacy rates between different parts of the country, and I called attention to this difference as a worthy subject for study. As a contribution to finding the causes for this curious phenomenon, I reported in chapters 3 and 4 some information on how the customs of sleeping in the animal quarters and night courting were related to the frequency of illegitimate births. With the same objective, I shall now report on the dioceses of Christiania and Christiansand in table 6.8, which corresponds to table 6.3 for Lom and Vaage. This table should serve additionally to cast light on the differences shown in chapter 5 between the higher and and lower classes.

The reports to me from parish pastors have gotten me to construct this table, and what is involved is dividing these two parishes into seven groups of deanery-districts. It is then illuminated in addition in appendix D, which in section 5 contains the same material. Here I then need only to point out that each married couple is counted in the owner or the working class (class I or class II) accordingly, as the bridegrooms belonged to one or the other class.

The moral condition of a country is a world full of mysteries, whose relationship and peculiarities are so easily obscured from view. We could hope to obtain limited insight into its vagueness, and table 6.8 gives us such insight.

There is the agreement between the owner and the working class that the married couple who, because of the unseemly conditions counted in the table, are found mostly in the first two columns, which probably show the more deplorable conditions. This agrees with table 6.3 for Lom and Vaage, and with regard to its interpretation, I can refer

Table 6.8. The wedding and the birthday of the firstborn in Christiania and Christiansand

	Children per 100 Consecrated Marriages			
Place	Before Conse-cration	Within 4 Months after Conse-cration	Between 4 and 8 Months after Conse-cration	Total
		Owner Class		
Deanery-Districts				
Group 1	4	16	11	31
Group 2	7	18	11	36
Group 3	6	18	14	38
Group 4	3	12	10	25
Group 5	2	15	12	29
Group 6	1	10	16	27
Group 7	3	8	8	19
Dioceses				
Christiana	5	16	11	32
Christiansand	2	11	12	25
Both	4	14	11	29
		Working Class		
Deanery-Districts				
Group 1	14	22	12	48
Group 2	24	25	10	59
Group 3	15	33	12	60
Group 4	11	21	12	44
Group 5	7	23	15	45
Group 6	2	14	14	30
Group 7	13	25	10	48
Dioceses				
Christiana	16	25	12	53
Christiansand	10	22	13	45
Both	14	24	12	50

to my explanation in the same table. But then there is also the difference between the owner and working classes that in the latter, there are in each of the seven groups more married people who likely experience the most awful conditions, and this agrees with the information contained in chapter 5, which gave evidence of a more extensive heedlessness and irresponsibility within the same class.

In general, when we compare table 6.8 with table 5.2, if we ignore a few minor exceptions, the evidence shows that for both the owner and working classes, in the groups or areas where illegitimate births are frequent, there are also many married couples who had children either before or a short time (up to four months) after the marriage. This can most quickly be seen by comparing group 2, where the conditions in both respects are worst, and group 6 where the conditions are best.

Clearly it is probably so in the areas where (according to table 5.2) the most illegitimate children are born who became legitimate following the marriage of the parents, but this latter is not found to such a degree that the unfortunate excess is thereby evened out.

In brief one can say that two things follow: (1) that people begin their married life without observing the established custom and order of moral people, and (2) that people live an irresponsible life without thought of marriage.

I mean that one can characterize the relationship between most of the bad customs in domestic and family life thus: night courting leads to secret and insecure engagements; in these situations the judgment of other people is not felt, finally not that of the all-wise God either; and the boundary between the permitted and the forbidden breaks down and passion takes over; and for a large part it is a stroke of good luck if the natural attachments which were established under the influence of passion were later hallowed by the marriage ceremony.

Table 4.1 in chapter 4 (about the different distributions of night courting) contains explanations for table 6.8 (about the different degrees whereby the rules for the establishment of marriage are scorned and ignored), and this last table again contains explanations for the puzzles in table 5.2 in chapter 5 (the greater or lesser frequencies of illegitimate births in the different areas).

There are several puzzling things in the world of morality which the cited facts may help us to understand. When one meets with the members of the poor-law commissions in the country or city, one hears quickly about one or another extreme of a man who has deserted his wife and children without the least attempt to care for them, so that they sit in the most extreme grief and misery. How, one asks, how in the world can people become so unnatural? Well, table 6.8 teaches us that very many people get married in such conditions, and it can be assumed that they are forced to do so (to conceal the shame); and then marriage, which should be the open and happy pact of love, becomes forced, easily becoming a hell on earth.

Still, both in the country and the city one must often be taken aback by examples of men who by a long immoral life have acquired the reputation of being fornicators, or of women who by a series of false steps have made themselves almost as despised as whores. How can it be that people to such a high degree can destroy the power of moral conscience and waste the welfare and peace of their lives? After all, table 6.8 teaches us that a great many people begin their love life thoughtlessly and a quite small event can cause some of them to separate. If at first the frail fruit of love is not nurtured, then it is likely that the heart no longer understands the steadiness and dependability without which love cannot bestow a blessing. I take it as evident that these named examples of gross debauchery and moral failure occur more often, for example, in group 2 than in group 6.

And still one hears people try to defend the scandalous conditions which table 6.8 lays bare; yes, curiously enough, in fact from one of the areas in our country, from where in recent times we have often heard of great agitations among the public for the religious and moral concerns, I have a very striking example of such a defense from the common people. It is the deanery-district of Ryfylke that I mean; two pastors have complained, and one of them expresses it as follows: "[There is] an explanation of the fact that with very few exceptions—if exceptions among the farm-owner class are found at all—marriage begins before the consecration by the church (the pastor might well have said "before the marriage is established in the conventional manner," since the situation would reasonably be the same whether the marriage be established by church consecration, by the pastor, or by the civil ceremony of the justice of the peace) while illegitimate births nevertheless are not as frequent in these areas. (They are still more frequent in Ryfylke in group 7 than in group 5 or 6. See tables 1.1 and 5.2.) This fact may indicate that men who otherwise are very sincere in their religion have, when I have expressed disapproval of the aforementioned immoral custom, objected that they do not have God's word that marriage begins with the consecration by the church but feel that when a man and woman begin their lives together with a prayer and invocation, they are also married people if they are not consecrated in church."

A far different justification was presented by a cotter couple to me. They were from Urskoug but now lived in Høland, and I talked with them about differences in morals and customs here and there. About the conditions described in chapter 5, they said that the wickedness had diminished in their community of birth, Urskoug, recently. Eagerly I asked what it might be that had caused such a change, an they thought that it was that the pastor each New Year's Day usually reported to the congregation, first, how many illegitimate children had been born during the year, and next, how many couples had consecrated their marriages and how many of these had half-legitimate children; it was as if the people learned by this method that this was something that should not be (if they knew already of the illegitimate children, it was open), and all who had their thoughts about them desired that there had to be an improvement in this matter in the community.

7

Which of the Two Sexes Is More to Blame?

TO begin with each house is new, and this self-evident circumstance has given both farms and cotter places the opportunity to be called Nystuen [Newhouse] since so many cottages and farmhouses were built on adjoining pieces of land. I am, therefore, free to mention the Nystuen place in Gudbrandsdal where I found a family life which serves as an example of how people can behave. Actually, this Nystuen was not really a place; there was no enclosure with field and meadow, no animal barn or hayloft or granary, not so much as a woodshed by the side of the house; it had only one room, a small one and in the most plain style; the one room had four walls, and the floor was shared by all people, the ground we walk on. And there was no real family life to be found in the house.

The house had been put up by a former servant girl who, with an illegitimate child, wished to withdraw from the world. Here she sat and spun and knitted to feed herself and her child. But the child, a girl, was confirmed and became a servant, and the mother herself, around 50 years of age, left this home of many years and became a permanent servant as a cattle herder. So she turned the house with all furnishings over to a renter, also a former servant girl, and she was the one I met during the visit to the house. She is unmarried but has (or had, but I tell everything as I found it) three children. I will call her *A,* and living with her is sister *B,* who has only one illegitimate child. A third sister is *C,* married in squalor to a cotter on an extremely deplorable place. A fourth sister, *D,* served on a farm and bore children by a farm owner's son and a servant boy there. This servant boy had indeed already had two children with another girl, but *D* took the prize and became his wife. This is still no hopeful marriage; for the time being, she has lived with his parents, and he is still a servant boy, and the future is gloomy in that he is not the eldest son and also cannot expect to acquire a cotter place from his father. Still another sister is *E;* this one had a child with a person who has since had a child with and married another who already had two children; so *E* had another child with a lover, and now these have had a reception (i.e., wedding) and sit as cotters on a piece of land that is so meager that it had been used to grow animal fodder for a long time. The wife should naturally have support money for her first child from the father, but he is poor and the welfare office must help out. A brother of these sisters has recently, in collusion with a girl (an illegitimate child whose mother is also an illegitimate child), become involved in theft and served his time in jail.

All of these family histories were told me by sister *A,* whom I met in Nystuen, and she is the one I am really going to tell about. She is a remarkably capable person. Thirteen or fourteen days before my visit, she had given birth to her third child; three days after the birth of the child, she had gone around to the nearest farms—and eight days later walked with terrible shoes and in deep melting snow over a stretch of ice to a much more remote farm, where she had grown up as a child placed out by welfare—in order to get cream, since nursing children in this community must ultimately have cream porridge of the richest kind, and each mother who is poor has sort of a right to beg for it. When I arrived she had just carried home two loads of wood, and she had to hurry with this task since her oldest child, a boy of six years, was not quite dependable as a babysitter and the sister, who as reported lived in the house, was away. While I was in the house she, the girl *A,* sat at the spinning wheel, and there was no particular opportunity for conversation except when the child needed her attention and the whir of the spinning wheel stopped. She was otherwise a good talker, and she was not bothered that I wrote on the spot what she told. She began in an emphatic tone: "The powerful ones want only to live well themselves and do not care how the poor people have it."

She really lived in mean circumstances. The food she now had at hand consisted of the following items: three merker flour, received yesterday as payment for the spinning (for the time being she spins hemp for six shillings a mark, but she cannot make over one-half mark a day because of the children, who cause her difficulties); also a piece of flatbread, a gift from a cotter's place where she was today to borrow some milk (when she did not get milk, her six-year-old boy was sent to a neighboring farm, and it was a long time before the mother would admit that his errand was to beg); in addition, one-half pint cream in a cup and a dab of cream porridge in another. She owns no other clothing than the rags and bits of shoes she is wearing; her next-to-the-oldest child, a girl of two and one-half years, walks barefoot on the earthen floor, and with some gestures the mother tells how indisposed the little girl was the other day with a cough. Two coverlets are on the bed, plus a fur pelt. The coverlets belong to the boy who is the father of the three children, and he has lent these bedclothes as a sign that he has fatherly feelings; the fur pelt, however, was borrowed from a farm where the girl had served a couple of weeks before childbed. The spinning wheel belongs to the daughter of the girl who owns the house; it is rented for the winter for six shillings. The kitchen utensils belong to the owner of the house; the current occupant still does not pay much rent for a furnished house, only 1 spd. and 12 shillings a year, for which payment she also has the right, connected with the house, to collect some of the bushes which are found here and there on the heath where the house stands. Of this 1 spd. and 12 shillings, I believe that the owner of the house must pay something for land rent, but I do not know exactly the details.

I have already reported that the girl *A* grew up as a placed-out welfare child. Later she became a servant and got acquainted with a boy who also grew up on welfare. Night courting brought them together; he became her lover and she became mother of his child. This happened at an inconvenient time, but then it was fortunate that her mother was alive and took over the child so she could be a servant again. But again they were drawn together, and again she became a mother. From now on she could not really be a servant but had to be by herself in order to care for the children. There were some years of crop failures in the community, and one summer she took both of the children to wander to other communities—actually, she was one of the girls I have seen so often in Gudbrandsdal with a child on her back. During this wandering in a strange community, one of the children became so sick that there had to be a prayer for it from the pulpit, so you see there were great difficulties.

Each time she was to give birth and a long time thereafter, the boy was inclined to avoid her. Their feeling for each other was an alternation of love and quarreling. Finally it went so far that the girl had had no trust or help from him for a long time, and she had to get two well-regarded men to help her get him to come to some agreement about what he should contribute to the children's upbringing. The going rate for a child in this community had been a barrel of grain and a pair of shoes per year, and this the girl claimed, but when he found it severe she took off a little of the grain, for which he had to promise to help her gather wood for the house.

After this agreement, probably particularly following the last little decision about the wood, he "ran" again to her, and look—again she became a mother, a third time. Naturally, they should have married each other, but nothing has come of it to this day, and how it can be from here on is not easy to know.

After the conversation with this child-mother I went directly to the farmer's wife who had brought her up as a welfare child. I wanted to seek all the information which could teach me to understand the mind and character of a person who has behaved so unfortunately. Now the woman I sought was talkative enough, but any direct information which was of value I did not get; on the contrary, I observed that the woman did not really understand my criticism of the girl's behavior; she seemed to give the impression that she had not supported her particularly; she complained about her more for the misfortune that she had taken up with such a strange boy who did not want to marry her. He could well do this because he was an able fellow, handy with whatsoever, a woodsman, carpenter, and shoemaker, so that no one could understand why he did not marry the girl. I understood the woman to say that she found that the girl had been good-natured and for a long time had borne with the boy's strangeness; since he had fooled her for so long [the woman said] she should (as a kind of punishment) not let herself be ruled by him.

DIFFERENCES IN PERCEPTIONS OF THE TWO SEXES

Most of the readers will be surprised by the improper life we found in the cottages, but I direct attention especially to the judgment we heard from the farm owner's wife. She was a respected woman, and when in this case she made a judgment which was so extremely abominable, one can see clearly why the general public regarded the girl's example as ordinary. She is regarded as living in a love relationship and people find it quite natural if she bears her lover's child; if she is left sitting with the child, it is the boy's fault who has deceived her.

A minister in Ryfylke discusses this point of view as follows: "A characteristic view is also that a man should be more severely punished than the woman. That the girl gives in when the man has an opportunity or appeals to her is excused by those who know her. I have even heard mothers excuse their fallen daughters in such matters."

But there are so many ways of looking at things in this world that one contradicts the other. I have heard considered judgments for or against women, and even among people in the country communities, I frequently heard assertions that women are more irresponsible and immoral than men.

Oh yes, there is no lack of examples which are very accepted to support such assertions. Truly, I have not yet found a clear example that women have behaved as whores. But it comes close when one hears, e.g., the foregoing story of the girl in the parish of Lom to whom was brought the midwife or an experienced woman during her serious hour; and first the girl named one person as the child's father, and when that did not help, another one, and when the labor pains continued, a third. The person whose name was mentioned as the child was born served, naturally, as the right one and was recorded in the church records. Another situation is this, that girls with the intention to get married and thereby be supported even engage in night courting with boys, examples of which I have already given: girls who have had a bastard or two and because of one or another misfortune have gotten so bad a reputation that respectable boys no longer seek them, girls who must fear and worry that they will never have the support of marriage.

But the most extreme assertion yet is this, that really often there are examples of women who deliberately have a whole flock of illegitimate children with the abominable thought that they will get their living by subsidy for caretaking, which the authorities and the sheriff will extract from the fathers of the children. I myself have not found any clear example of this lowliness and depravity, but I have often heard it mentioned in support of the assertion that when immorality is extensive in a community, it is mostly the fault of the women. This viewpoint is likely the reason for some of the reflections which the pastors have reported to me and the reason some complain about the laws which guarantee child support from the father. In the discussions in the poor-law commission, expressions like these emerge, that women with illegitimate children need not be supported with a shilling but rather, as a necessary warning to others, should freeze and starve as examples to those who carry most of the fault for the improper events that take place.

It is quite certain that there is a wide difference in the psychological makeup of men and women so that each has distinctive characteristics with regard to the qualities of intellect and feeling. The wide differences in the power of virtue and the dangers of passion's temptation, are unpredictable individually. Therefore it is easy to understand how one strongly influenced by a few strange experiences one believes one has had also can be influenced by an opposite experience. But most of us have still learned to admire the adornment which the father of human beings has given her and which should be an object of the man's love, a protection for the woman's weakness: a natural modesty which often makes even the coarse and sensual man respectful. And still, can the belief persist among a few that women are the seducers?

FREQUENCY OF LOOSE LIVING

How do we find methods to conduct investigations about this problem to clarify the conflicting beliefs and do so properly? I have thought that it would contribute to information if we made note of the repetition of patterns of the offensive behavior which is revealed by the existence of illegitimate births.

The most frequently discussed reports to me from the pastors in the dioceses of Christiania and Christiansand contain problems of these repetitive patterns (appendix D). These reports are unfortunately less complete than the rest, but I must use them as they are and add percentages of fathers and mothers who became such the first time, second time, and so on (table 7.1). In these reports no special attention has been paid to the property and working classes: both classes are counted under one heading.

Table 7.1. Single and repeated illegitimate births

	Fathers *(percent)*	Mothers *(percent)*
First time	82	79
Second time	13	14
Third time	4	5
Fourth time	1	2
Total	100	100

We see immediately that there are instances of repetitions. They might be counted twice if the same couple has had several children together and accordingly lived in more or less actual concubinage or an unwed, unholy relationship, or—more contemptibly—if the man and the woman each lived first with one and then with another. This was not revealed by the figures. However, this matter is of no concern to the present question. On the other hand, the figures do reveal that there is a difference between the two sexes in that there are more repetitions on the part of the women.

And it is obviously precisely this fact that has led to the unfavorable judgment of the female sex, even though such a view had not been confirmed by these figures. But one must not without further thought accept the foregoing conclusion, nor should one forget to take into consideration a very important circumstance, which—notwithstanding the moral condition of the people in the foregoing—is much more influential in exempting the man of blame for backsliding than the woman. I believe it is easier for the man than the woman to enter into a respectable marriage. That this is so can be learned from common experience. This can be observed from the reports in chapter 5 of the many men in the property class who violated women of the working class, while there were few men of that class who married these girls. A parallel is the man who has achieved a legal marriage and is for the most part freed from the temptation of illegal relations. The reverse is the violated, the possibly shamefully reduced woman, who now sits abandoned and rejected, and whom it is reasonable to assume is now more exposed to temptation than before. And it is quite likely that when the temptations are so unequal, no comparison can be made between deed and offense.

There is, of course, a great difference between irresponsible behavior and the law-breaking of thieves. In this connection there can be some interest in knowing the conditions by reporting the 3,773 cases in which men and the 866 cases where women during the years 1845–1849 in this country were convicted for "ordinary thievery." The figures are reported by the Department of Justice annually. The percentage comparisons were as follows:

	Men	Women
1st time	64	70
2nd time	21	18
3rd time	11	10
4th time	4	2
	100	100

Here not only are the numbers of women criminals fewer but the repetitions among them are also less frequent than among the men. So this supports the belief that women are not to the same degree as men disposed to fall into gross transgressions.

But I go further in my explanation of immoral offenses and present in table 7.2 the repeated patterns in different groups of deanery-districts. Table 7.2 teaches us that, with almost no exceptions (for which the fragmentary examples do not have great weight), the repeated patterns are most frequent in the areas where we earlier (table 5.1) found that illegitimate children have on the whole occurred most frequently. This can be seen most clearly by comparing groups 2 and 6. We can express this thus, that where immorality is revealed by a great many illegitimate births, it is also associated with comparatively many more deplorable repetitions; or, where the evil of illegitimate births dominates the most, there it will appear in its worst characteristics. This table thus oddly confirms the belief I told about after firsthand experience, that group 2 is really the one which shows the most scandalous licentiousness.

Table 7.2. Repetitions of illegitimate births

Deanery-Districts	Two or More Illegitimate Births per 100 Fathers and Mothers	
	Fathers	Mothers
Group 1	13	22
Group 2	23	24
Group 3	15	19
Group 4	17	20
Group 5	10	11
Group 6	9	11
Group 7	14	11
Diocese		
Christiania	19	22
Christiansand	11	11
Both	18	21

Before I can continue this investigation further, I wish to point out that there are also repeated patterns of marriages. Although the great majority of marriages are entered into by young men and women who marry for the first time, alongside them there are regularly some widowers and widows who remarry or, as we might say, repeat marriages. Table 7.3 explains (compare appendix D).

When we compare table 7.3 with table 7.2 together with table 5.1, there lies before us a series of different clarifications which we can make use of in such manner as the following examples report.

In group 1, I note 100 married couples, accordingly also 100 bridegrooms. Of these, according to table 7.3, 10 percent, or 10 persons, remarried widowers; those who were married for the first time were accordingly only 90. At the same time that these 100 men were married, there were (according to table 5.1), at the nearest, 37 men who were reported to be fathers of illegitimate children. But of these 37 men there were (according to table 7.2) 13 percent, or around five persons, who

Table 7.3. Remarried widowers and widows

Deanery-Districts	For Each 100 Married	
	Fathers	Mothers
Group 1	10	7
Group 2	9	4
Group 3	11	6
Group 4	10	5
Group 5	12	5
Group 6	12	6
Group 7	14	9
Dioceses		
Christiania	10	6
Christiansand	12	7
Both	10	6

were in this situation a second time or oftener, so of the other 37 who were listed as fathers the first time there were only 32. Now I know that each time there were 90 men married the first time, 32 men were reported as being fathers, and hereafter I can estimate that for each 100 of these, there were at least 36.

If I carry out this comparison for both sexes and for each of the seven groups, I get the result as shown in table 7.4.

Table 7.4. First marriage and illegitimate births

Deanery-Districts	First Time Fathers and Mothers in Each Marriage	
	Fathers	Mothers
Group 1	36.1	31.4
Group 2	55.3	51.7
Group 3	32.0	28.8
Group 4	23.3	21.4
Group 5	14.4	13.2
Group 6	11.8	10.7
Group 7	17.4	17.0
Dioceses		
Christiania	35.8	33.0
Christiansand	14.7	33.9
Both	30.4	28.1

Since there are so extremely few married men and women or widowers or widows who were listed as fathers or mothers, we can thus for the time being leave them out of consideration without much error and sum up the number of births for young men and women; and when we in table 7.4 exclude them for the events dealt with twice or oftener, we can then say that we have an overview of frequencies of illegitimate births which occur in the adult generation which, so to speak, make the first choice between regular marriage and illegal relationships. This is, of course, a new and detailed method to count the frequency of illegitimate births, but it serves to confirm what previously never before could be established: that the frequency is less among the female sex, that immorality is less widespread among women, that there is a fewer number of those who have fallen. (It can also be seen in table 7.4 that when we look at the situation with the first offences among young men and women, the condition is not shown to be so much worse in a few of the seven groups than in the others – for example, group 2 compared with group 6 – when we, according to table 5.1, include repetitive incidents in the calculations.)

But alongside this is also a fact which was presented in table 7.2, that among the once-fallen women there are more whose lives became unfortunate in that the fallen again and again fall oftener than the once-fallen among men.

And perhaps with this dual fact before us one can divide the two sides: The woman does not waste her honor and duty as quickly as the man, but once it is wasted, the woman might then give in to vice more quickly. In other words, it is really the man who first seduces the woman, but the once-corrupted woman can—and precisely because of the first seduction—become dissolute and then probably seduce other men.

In a previous chapter, I have told of a 17-year-old boy who was seduced by a corrupt woman; perhaps the beginning of this misfortune and the blame for both was due to a sensual man who earlier had seduced the same woman. Such an example can still not be applied to the relationships between both sexes, but many fruitful conclusions can be drawn from the relationships to the extent that we know about all women who from one year to another became mothers repeatedly [and that we have] information on how many of them for the very first time fell for men of a higher class and later fell for men of a lower class, plus how many of them at the very first fell at a very young age for old sensualists and later, while older, had relations with young and inexperienced boys.

Clear and dependable insight into the moral condition of both sexes ought not lack practical significance, but for the time being I say this: Men for whom women fell the first time should be watched carefully, since they have likely behaved with deliberate contempt and seduction. And I say this: Women who fell the first time should receive solicitous concern because they probably need the friendly trust of people and other support in order to be saved from new and worse happenings. "Do not talk anymore about the one who betrayed you, do not think of him; do not mourn for yourself, even though you are not really innocent either; but mourn for your child: your whole life must from now on consist of a motherly and Christian concern for your child; your work and your thoughts and prayers you must offer for the well-being of your child; do this faithfully and you will still experience the people's good wishes that God will bestow his consolation"—I have often talked this way to the daughters of cotters whom I found in the cottages in this lamentable state, but oh, when I turned and left, the thought came to me many times that the harsh judgment of the world and poverty and deprivation maybe would submit the shaky will to too great a test and lead the pitiful ones step by step toward complete depravity and misery.

ABOUT ADULTERY

In conclusion, I will still point out a particular condition which might seem not to be connected with the matter which was the actual subject for the investigation in the previous chapter but which in the course of the investigation came out. If we compare tables 7.2 and 7.3, we find it interesting that in the Christiania diocese, where illegitimate births recur most, it is least likely that widowers and widows remarry, but in the diocese of Christiansand, it is the opposite. One could perhaps venture the explanation that a certain greater warmth and liveliness in the folk character in the first-named diocese misleads people to sexual excesses, and in some manner to the opposite direction in the folk character of a greater soberness and thoughtfulness. In the diocese of Christiansand, people are more likely to seek their livelihood with so-called good catches when a young boy marries an elderly but well-off widow, or when a young girl accepts the courting of an old widower because he is rich.

To the extent this is correct, it can be feared that there will occur relatively more frequent acts of adultery in the last diocese than in the first. And to show how extensively this happens in reality, I present (according to appendix D) table 7.5.

If we compare the various groups and dioceses with each other, it seems that as a rule with regard to husbands and wives the condition is better in the diocese of Christiania and most of its four groups (the exception which group 4 forms with its many broken marriages is so striking that it deserves more research); and to the contrary, it is worse in the diocese of Christiansand and most of its three groups. In the former

Table 7.5. Adultery

Deanery-Districts	Fathers or Mothers of Illegitimate Children for Each 100 Persons			
	Husbands	Wives	Widowers	Widows
Group 1	3.3	0.7	7.7	5.9
Group 2	2.4	0.4	5.3	2.5
Group 3	2.4	0.2	8.2	2.4
Group 4	7.7	1.7	6.6	4.7
Group 5	4.5	1.8	8.2	1.8
Group 6	11.1	1.4	5.5	8.3
Group 7	10.0	. . .	5.4	2.3
Dioceses				
Christiania	3.6	0.7	6.6	3.6
Christiansand	8.3	1.0	6.4	3.5
Both	4.1	0.7	6.5	3.6

diocese are found relatively fewer, and in the latter diocese relatively more, husbands and wives reported as fathers and mothers. And this is even more remarkable in that it is not so clearly apparent for widowers and widows.

Adultery is, of course, one of the most despicable kinds of immoral behavior, and what is revealed here seems to conflict with the belief I have expressed before that in the eastern regions where immorality is most widespread (greatest frequency of illegitimate births on the whole), there takes place also most frequently the same despicable occurrences of coarse immorality and depravity. But this conflict is only apparent, and this view can still be correct. Table 7.5 gives only the idea that while married people are much less tempted to immorality than the unmarried, this difference is less in the diocese of Christiansand than in the diocese of Christiania. We could point out the condition as: in the diocese of Christiansand, both the unmarried and married people are characterized by a better condition in this matter, but this characteristic still for one or another reason is less among the married than among the unmarried. This condition can also be seen in table 7.6. Each time 100 persons were married, there were the following number of unmarried and married people who were reported as fathers or mothers. Here the conditions are shown much better for the diocese of Christiansand than for Christiania but with the difference that it is much better for the unmarried and only a little better for the married population.

Still, the investigations which these observations supported are only from the years 1851 and 1852, and the events of the kinds dealt with which could happen in such a short time are too few to uncover fully the elusive matter. But what is reported still permits us to realize that continued research would be useful to assemble information on the remarkable differences, and despite its incompleteness, I have before me the reported information which is of particular interest to me to support a thought which a priori seemed reasonable, namely: that if we could thoroughly see through all situations, it would in many instances show a certain counterweight regarding morals between the population of different areas, so that the area which gratified us by an unusually good condition would perhaps disappoint us by an undesirable situation in

Table 7.6. Immorality in Christiania and Christiansand

	Christiania Diocese	Christiansand Diocese
Unmarried men	38.3	13.2
Unmarried women	39.4	14.3
Married men	1.4	1.3
Married women	0.26	0.14

another area. Or must we not say insofar as it can be confirmed that in the diocese of Christiansand, which stands out with the low frequency of illegitimate births, the bad practice is generated by the so-called good catches, or marriages for the sake of livelihood and not for love—a bad practice which easily leads to broken marriages. (A careful investigation of this must not only include partnerships between young men and women with widows and widowers but must include all of the partnerships with great age differences.) Here might be the place to present the idea that if a comprehensive investigation of the condition of morality were to be of enough significance to judge the culture and morality of the people in various areas, there is needed a parallel description of conditions of other kinds of profligacy (and here can be mentioned major types of lawbreaking, crimes against property and persons, and in addition, particularly drunkenness; it is comprehensible that where there is less inclination to one type of offence, there can be a greater inclination to offences of another kind. Particularly, I have a suspicion that there is probably an association between immorality and drunkenness.

8

Family Life and Morality in Upper and Lower Romerike

"GOOD evening, good evening, so we are going to be together awhile?" Thus I addressed a driver while he gave me the reins. I seated myself in the sleigh and he placed himself on the runners, but I did not hear a sound from him. "It is well over six miles we will be riding together?" I said to him when the sleigh had swung out on the road, but I was taken aback by his "Yah," since it was peculiarly gruff and coarse. "I suppose you are a servant on the farm to which the horse belongs?" I continued in order to start a conversation, and again I got the same hard and grumpy "Yah." I did not look forward to his company. "Tell me, you have probably engaged in hauling dirt today?"—"Yah."—"You are likely tired now?"—"Yah."—"But to change the subject, friend, who do you think is the more tired, you or the horse?"—"Don't know," in the same harsh voice, without a trace of joviality. "Hm! So you have hauled dirt today; I suppose you have hauled dirt, wood, and logs all winter, and eventually you have become tired of all this hauling?"—"Yah."—"But tell me, what can a servant fellow like you amuse yourself with during a week?"—"Not a thing."—"Really, do you say that?" No answer. "Each person usually, of course, has something he takes pleasure in, and I am certain that you also have something which you at times sort of take pleasure in, and what is that?"—"Dancing!" he answered in the same gruff, heavy voice, but not quite as sullen as before. Here I had come upon the subject that he was happy to talk about, and he had happened to give a ride to a traveler who was right willing to have a lengthy report on the same subject; and in this way we struck up a conversation that took six miles of silence that neither he or I remembered.

How often had I in times past talked with servant fellows and such about dancing and other matters associated with what is called the party life, but earlier I never had such a strong impression of how extremely important the thing called the getting-together atmosphere is, or how dominant the judgment and feeling are regarding how people should behave in certain circles when they come together. Here it seemed I could see exactly how this person would jump around the dance floor with his whole weight and forcefully give himself over to the wildest pleasures of the party unless most of the others present could control him and force him to adapt to the customs of better company.

This was in Lower Romerike at the end of the winter of 1856. And on the same road between the same riding points, I had a few days earlier sat in a wide sleigh with one of the well-established farmers of the community. He gave me a lot of information on party life in the higher farm class, where the term *dancing party* was never used, but *balls,* and where Boston and whist are played instead of the servants' bank, knack, and poker [card games].

SOCIAL CUSTOMS

But there was a time when all these party customs were very different from now. In earlier times the party idea was undoubtedly and essentially arranged and determined by the remarkable neighborhood custom which all the way from Lom in Gudbrandsdal to Rødenæs in Smaalenene I have found partly in full flower and partly in various degrees of dying out. The neighborhood party or, as it is also called, the invitation party, is a party circle of nearby farms. At funerals and weddings it was customary that the inviter had to approach first of all the farms in the party circle (for weddings, both the bride's and bridegroom's party circles) and then, in addition, the relatives outside of the boundaries of the party circle. And that is why from olden times the community parties have been divided into such invitation circles, a permanent division so that it is known that the invitation circle of such and such a farm is so and so large, like the schoolmaster knowing which farms belong to his school district. And there is a special characteristic which lies behind this division. Think of a community of 100 farms and imagine that there is an average of 10 farms in each party circle. You would quickly conclude that there should be 10 party circles all together. But there are 100. Each farm is its own individual party circle. The whole will become clear when one considers that the farms in one community follow each other like letters in the alphabet. Farm *E* may have its party circle from *A* to *I,* and then farm *F* its party circle from *B* to *K,* and the party circle for farm *G* includes farms from *E* to *L*. And in this way each family is drawn into a complete and complicated network of associations. When, for instance, a family on farm *I* has a party, it brings together families from *E* to *O,* but when it later is invited to a party at these farms *E* and *O,* it interchangeably comes together with people all the way from *A* on one side and from *S* or *T* on the other side. Yes, these parties and associations which the old folk customs have created overlap the boundaries established for parishes and the smallest judicial districts; and otherwise, strangely enough, in many instances they seem to sort of separate the communities from each other. If we let the letter *Ø* be the outermost farm in a parish and *A* be the nearest adjacent farm in the neighboring parish, *Ø* can then have its party circle, e.g., from *X* in one to *D* in the next alphabet, etc. (A mathematician would probably want to make it look so that the communities are divided into concentric circles, one for each farm, and with this one as the center, together with a certain number of farms inside the periphery. Each circle will always overlap several others.)

These divisions, as mentioned, served essentially for funerals and weddings at home, and it can then be said that these festivities, which party circles call to mind, had a quasi-religious character. Such festivities took place at these ceremonial opportunities before there were church blessings over the dead or over the wedding couple, namely, during pagan times. The custom was transplanted from pagan times to the Christian period, and for the first time during our era it is quite dying out. It was the custom for the guests to bring gifts of food for the banquet. (In 1855 I was in Ullensaker in Romerike at a funeral celebration where the invitation party was observed, and an old farmer explained to me that a "full" gift of food from a "full" farm, according to an old custom, consisted of the following items: 30 loaves of baked bread, one piece of butter of at least six pounds, one ham, in addition one meat dish with one leg of ham, one thigh and piece of breast of beef, one leg of mutton, one side of mutton, one tongue, and one sausage. The same custom was true for several communities in the area.) Thus it was a reasonable custom in the early days for the farm owners and the people of their households to bring foodstuff to offer in the temples to Odin, Thor, and other gods. During pagan times the master of the house blessed the feast (like the director of a feast in the temple) by drinking the first toast to the honor of Odin; in the same manner in the following Christian period, toasts were drunk to the honor of Christ, to the Virgin Mary, and various saints. (Somewhere in Wilse's description of Spydeberg, I have seen that still in the previous centuries it was the custom to drink the Holy

Ghost toast for weddings, either for the pagan period or the early Christian period: Keyser, "The Entertainments of Norwegians in Olden Times," in the *Norwegian Journal of Science and Literature* 2.) Carryovers of this one may point to our master of ceremonies in the previous century who sang psalms and drank toasts to the bishop and the king.

The old-fashioned funeral celebrations and weddings with their many days of festivities and crowds of people have often been criticized. And it is certainly true that they were accompanied by too much drink and ruckus. But still, it is conceivable that the significance that these festivities had must have contributed a seriousness and fittingness to social life as a whole. These gatherings by tradition and custom required invitations to a rather large number of guests, and for the most part in the old days they made up the social life in the countryside. In the parish of Lom, for instance, where the party-circle custom continues in full swing, it is really quite seldom that invitations to festivities are made unless for funerals and weddings, together with baptisms now and then. In the parish of Næs in Romerike, I became aware of another kind of gathering which was a part of the party-circle custom, namely, that each farmer in the circle once during the winter (or, in later times, every other or third year) invites all his neighbors to a party (to which food is not donated); and this kind of a party (it is called a circle party to differentiate it from a party where food is donated) seems more organized compared with what is understood to be informal gatherings for having company, but it is very possible that these parties are continuations of the social gatherings which Olaf the Holy prescribed in his Christian law, and which had a certain ceremonious and religious meaning.

But in all this there have been great changes; in many communities, in any case for the most part, the old-fashioned, one can well say duty-bound and obligatory parties had to give in to new customs, and in place of the old customs, which were common to all classes on the land, a dual custom has been cultivated, one for the farm-owner class and one for the cotter-and-servant class. One of the most influential reasons for this is probably the rapid increase in the cotter people during the last 100 or 200 years, so that a separate class has been formed alongside the farm-owner class. Farthest into the parish of Lom in the area which is called north mountain, it is still the custom that when a farmer gives a party, he invites all the people of the neighborhood, farmers and cotters, big and little, poor and rich, and thus it probably was everywhere in olden days, when the cotters were only few and so new that they still were counted as related to the people on the farms, from which they descended. And on the other hand, the poorest son of a cotter could confidently invite many farm-owner families to his wedding, since he was freed from the costs of supplying food and drinks. But nowadays the farmer limits his invitations to the farm-owner families of the neighborhood, and the only pleasure the servants enjoy is good eating on food-gift days when they bring food baskets to the party farm and later do so in turn. And nowadays it becomes more and more common for poor people to have frugal weddings and funerals, only with the closest relatives, since the farm owners, reasonably enough, are less willing to make these frequent contributions of food and drinks. Even in the farm-owner class, it seems that little by little they have begun to feel it burdensome, particularly for funerals, and unseemly, given the lavish nature of the festivities. In Næs in Romerike a district association was established in 1830, and one of the objectives of the association was to set up a society just to oppose the old custom of food gifts, a society which actually hastened the change in party customs that otherwise, as in other places, would have taken place by itself. In Nannestad, Ullensaker, Gjerdrum, and several communities, gift parties are still being held, but the people themselves regard these as old-fashioned excesses, and within 10 years it is likely there will be no trace left of them here as well.

When the farmers in the parish of Næs stopped the food-gift parties, it was very commendable that they let the custom of parties among the immediate neighbors remain; these gatherings seemed to be a good way to hold on to the feeling of friendship among neighbors which daily petty quarrels can easily disturb. But it seems that nowadays these kinds of gatherings are not enough to satisfy the desire for parties, and therefore one sees now one or another of the same farmers belonging to neighborhood parties having another kind of invitation party alongside these completely open parties, to which are invited relatives and friends outside of the neighborhood, the older to dinner and the younger to a ball in the evening. And such dinner parties and balls have in the recent generation become very common in the communities and the family circles whose well-being and education have brought them in contact with city folk and have given them the desire and ability to adopt city customs. More and more it has become customary in these same circles that a family one fine day travels to visit another, or that a whole circle of friends agree to surprise a mutual friend by a visit, for example, on his birthday, all without invitation, something which is still certainly extremely uncommon in old-fashioned communities like Vaage or Lom. And in Næs, for instance, it is not uncommon that one of the daughters of the house entertains guests with a piano recital, or that several of the assembled youth sing a four-part song, or that the older men entertain themselves by reviewing the content of the daily newspaper, while the farmers in Lom, for instance, where newspapers are few, still as in the days of Halfdan the Black must stick to the subjects of conversation which are provided by the community, primogeniture disputes, and the like.

This was apparent in the new order of things among farm-owner families in Romerike and several of the outer districts in the diocese of Upper Christiania. It is different in the working class, among cotters, servants, and others. I will now report some examples of the character of parties here, although I confine myself to experiences from Upper and Lower Romerike. There is dance and more dance which make up the joy of parties here. The older men naturally have withdrawn from dancing; it is the young people who come together, and the very gathering or party is called a dance. In this meaning of the word, three kinds of dancing can be differentiated: (1) auctioneer, (2) free-dance, and (3) Dutch-treat dance. It sound strange to hear an auction called a dance, and on the whole it is a very bad practice. I have never gotten over how it came about that auctions became gatherings for entertainment, but it is reasonable that the start was made by smart people who held an auction and wanted to attract many people; and for a while now it has been usual that the great majority of the mass of people from all areas are young fellows and girls who do not intend to buy hay or grain. Uninvited also comes a musician with his fiddle, or two or three musicians who will combine, and either in the very auction house or also at a cotter's place nearby, the fun is soon in full swing. If the man who arranges the auction is in such a mean situation that he greatly values earning a shilling or two, he has likewise bought the so-called wine, together with Bavarian beer (earlier, whiskey) which on this occasion is sold at a high price; or there are always some people in the neighborhood who speculate in the same manner, and old women come hauling kettles and cups to boil and serve coffee. The musicians naturally also figure getting money for their services, and during an appropriate intermission they let a trusted person go around with the musicians' bowl, in which the dancers put in as desired 2 or 4 shillings each; yes, in the most recent years when people have so much money, a boy who earlier gave 2 or 4 might now gladly toss 8 or 12 into the bowl, I have been told. In one or another corner also sit some enthusiasts for card playing, with some kibitzers around them. And in one of the communities in Romerike, I heard of farm owners who had gambled away between 1 dollar and 200 dollars in one night. I heard last winter of servant fellows and shoemaker boys who on such occasions could set up stakes for 3, 5, or 7 dollars. And all this auction-celebration could last both one and two nights and days.

The so-called free dance can be described as follows. A cotter or another poor man who needs to earn a shilling by selling coffee, beer, large pastries, etc., and whose house is not too small arranges everything and sets a certain date and lets it be known that there will be a dance at his place. The dance is called free, i.e., anyone who wishes can come and not pay for more than each one consumes. Still, it is a point of honor for the dancers to put something in the fiddler's bowl, since the host of the house has brought the fiddler but has not promised him any other pay than what he can get for his playing. One can imagine how these free dances could lead to coarse and wild behavior at the same time, since whiskey was free, and even now these parties are not free of excesses, where all kinds of girls get together with all kinds of boys. It is to be recalled that there are people who have been brought up in the bad custom of night courting, and while there were older people present at auctions, only the young people themselves run the free dances.

Therefore one can note that young people who conduct themselves a little better do not participate in the free dances but rather in the Dutch-treat parties, and this custom has surely come about in recent times as the immorality of the free dance has been recognized. A few fellows get together to have such a party, contribute 24, 48, or 60 shillings each, and bring with them their sweethearts or other girls whom they wish to impress. One or two of the fellows take on the entire arrangement, make a date with the host about a room, provide the fiddler, and arrange for food and drink. In such a party, of course, only acquaintances get together, and they can assure themselves against roustabouts and too-coarse people in the group. In addition, these Dutch-treat parties also have the advantage in the view of many that one can get a glass of brandy or spiked punch without getting into trouble, since the entire group fetches the goods from a legal outlet and later consumes them together. In very recent times, one has also had a taste of another kind of Dutch-treat party, which I believe is called an invitation party and even a ball; now and then, a master of the house who himself has recently used his dance hall for a ball allows his servants to use it for themselves and their friends whom they will invite to participate. These balls do not cost the participants much since the mistress of the house gladly puts candles in the candle holders and provides coffee cream, and the master has made the condition that no brandy will be drunk. I felt I noticed among a few servant boys who had participated in these more stylish invitation parties that from then on they did not continue to seek to go to either free-dance or Dutch-treat parties in the cotter cottages, and it might be that this situation provoked an older fellow in the parish Næs to complain, "There is really not much fun among young people nowadays as there was earlier, because earlier we were all equally acceptable and like companions, but today there are so many who feel they are too good to join in the fun away in the cotters' homes."

I am more interested in discussing the invitation balls here, which have been strongly supported by the farm-owner class to guide the party going of their servants in a more desirable direction. And that such guidance can be in the right direction will be understood here when I tell what a reliable farm owner told me about a servant girl who had been to 22 dances from the 14th of April to the 14th of October, mostly auction and free dances, about which her fellow servants had asked and were well-informed. This is, of course, only a single example, but it occurs to me that it says much, particularly when a person like me has often heard people around the communities complain about the pleasure seeking and frivolity of the young people.

It can also be pointed out that the working-class youth in the countryside have not experienced proper and well-bred social life and have not by the reading of informative and entertaining works assembled material for self-improvement and conversation outside of the range of ideas which are part of daily community life. "Tell me," thus I approached a seldom-thoughtful cotter up in Lom, "nowadays we city people continually talk about the extraordinary war between Russia and Turkey, but tell me, what do these young fellows talk about when they meet on a road or get together at a party?"—"Oh yes, that I will explain, for now and then someone travels to Håmår (Lillehammer) to bring home a small keg of brandy, and when one meets the other, the question is: do you know if he has come home, you know who? And when he has come home they announce a 'command holiday,' and there they would go even with their last shilling." That there are still more and more young people scattered in the communities, particularly in Romerike, who in recent years have become more thoughtful and readily want to acquire more breeding and proper conduct with others, I am more certain of; there are, after all, many desirable circumstances in our country that must contribute to the promotion of culture even in the so-called lower classes, and I believe that the time is now mature for all such efforts that aim at the removal of the coarseness and bad customs which the higher, more-educated classes have already condemned but which hang on longer in the masses of the working class. I can tell of an example. During Easter this year, on a Sunday afternoon, I sat and smoked a tobacco pipe together with four or five fellows from a remarkably large cotter area near Næs in Romerike; they were people whom one would enjoy talking with, and once I expressed myself as follows: "Now I have a suggestion to make. We all know that the farm owners in these parts subscribe to newspapers and buy books and drive to agricultural conferences and get together to talk about many things that are interesting and informative. You people in the cotter area must also try something so that you also could advance in knowledge and education; otherwise, a really big difference develops between the high and lower classes, as we call it. I see hardly one book in the houses here, except religious books and children's books. What do you think of reading a well-written book? It is, of course, the same as having a conversation with a well-informed and friendly man. Now I know that there are many capable men of goodwill who have written and would gladly write for the benefit and pleasure of the uneducated man—but you pay no attention. Is it the custom? You should establish a book club among you, a book club precisely here in the cotter area for cotters and servant fellows and community shoemakers and day workers, and each one who wants to borrow the books shall contribute a mark per year. No servant fellow is so badly off that he cannot spare the shillings, and a cotter must have a big flock of children who also cannot afford the same."

One said yes to the whole thing but believed, however, that it would be impossible to get the thing started. In answer to these objections, I wrote with a pencil on the spot a few short paragraphs of rules for the club and appointed one of those present, a carpenter, to be the chairman, another, a shoemaker, to be the treasurer, and an absent person, also a shoemaker, to be the librarian. Finally, I wrote up a list of all the cotters and servant fellows and day workers who we thought might be members of the club. "Now see, I would not wonder that the whole thing isn't almost set up. In a couple of days there is an auction at one of the cotter places; you are likely going to be there, and there you will likely meet those whom we now have on the list. Talk to them, explain the matter that they must sign up whether they want to or not." Within a few days, 29 people had signed up, almost exclusively of the working class, and a few weeks later, the treasurer sent me 29 marks with which to buy books. After my acquaintance with the people concerned in the area, I call this a good result, and I would very much doubt that this would have been possible 10 or 20 years earlier when there was hardly a spirit among the people as now. Earlier there had been attempts to establish collections of books in the countryside, but it was mostly for a whole parish, and thereby access to books became too difficult for a great many of the working class who lived far away from the community. Now, after this example, I suggest that young people who are thoughtful act to organize themselves for book collections, for example, in each school district, and I direct this wish particularly to the people of the working class, most of whom need such a method to promote education. If the people of a higher status were to participate and help out, well and good; if not, the working class by its own efforts could get the thing started. And if this might happen and soon,then a great deal of the coarseness and vulgarity that this book describes would be thrown out the door. (I have thought of reading as a means to encourage and restore the spirit and to make people have a higher standard of behavior and, in addition, orderliness to participate in social gatherings, which no person who knows human nature would hinder in order to improve. And here I also think about methods of training that are part of strenuous physical activities—swimming, gymnastics, target shooting, together with the art of singing. It is remarkable how few among the young of the society have interest in such exercises, and therefore so many are clumsy and awkward that they are called country bumpkins. Teachers who could sing, junior officers who can fence and shoot, could do a good deed if they could start such exercises. Let us figure out something new and more useful than the everlasting auction dancing and the free dance, a type of fun which is often vulgar and in time becomes boring.) Several of the pastors who have sent me explanations for the conditions of illegitimate births have—particularly in the eastern part—pointed to the dancing craze and the auction crowds as the reasons why moral standards are so low in many places.

CLOTHES

The dancing craze and the desire for finery—these are the two things that the servant class is criticized for, as I have often heard in the countryside. The latter criticism, I admit, has confused me not a little, for that which is called excessive finery to my eyes looks most often like vulgarity. But the judgment of a single thing must, of course, be related to the concept that the thing has in general, and these concepts differ to a great extent, for instance, in the town and in the country. Thus one learns about the old-fashioned styles of servant clothes in the country. From Lom in Gudbrandsdal to Rakkestad in Smaalenene, from Elverum in Østerdal to Næs in Hallingdal, it is the custom that farm owners provide wages and complete clothing. The wages can vary in amount so that they must be determined and a clear agreement negotiated, but when "complete clothing" is mentioned, both the farm owner and the servant understand, for it is like a rate involving one thing or another, a rate that has an old tradition and that applies to all the farms in the diocese or parish. And this is not enough; except for small and infrequent exceptions, the rate is the same for all communities in a large area, as I just said, the same in the most extreme detail. And for these small exceptions, which are known to have intruded themselves in recent years, people still remember how it really should have been according to the correct old custom.

The servant boy should first and foremost have a set of clothes, i.e., tails or topcoat (in this alternative one can trace the influence of recent styles, for in earlier times there was neither tails nor topcoat but clothing of another style and with the name vest) plus trousers. The farm owner is obliged only to deliver these items of clothing of undyed homespun (lamb's wool, in earlier times entirely white, now possibly gray, a blending of black and white). He shall deliver them ready-made, but actually the servants should accept them without lining and according to an old-fashioned plain-tailoring method. The tailor (without board from the farm owner) for a half-century received, for instance, in the parish of Næs a fee of 12 shillings for the tails and 6 shillings for the trousers; little by little in many and probably in most of the communities, it became customary for the farm owner to add the lining for the waist and occasionally the sleeves, and partly because of this, and partly because of the finer seams now in demand, the fee for the tailor for servant clothes in the same parish of Næs has climbed to 2 spd. for the tails and 12 shillings for the trousers. If now the servant—according to the latest style—still wants the tails lined and to have the chest padded and braces in some of the seams and pockets here and there, it is up to the goodwill of the farm owner to permit the tailor to do so, regardless that it takes more work time and also includes board; but the extent to which the fee to the tailor exceeds the aforementioned sum, plus what kind of cloth is necessary, the servant must pay that himself. Likewise, the servant must himself pay if he wants a finer or better thread for the tailoring than is usual for servant clothes, and more if he wants his homespun dyed and pressed. Finally, he has to provide the buttons for his clothes himself, and this is one of the most certain rules for which it is difficult to find an exception (although the community rules are not destroyed if an individual farm owner here and there shows the servant his goodwill by adding buttons). Further, "full clothing" means two shirts (one of linen and one of burlap, either of hemp or flax, depending on whether one or the other plant is grown in the community), one pair of long stockings and one pair with a knitted foot of old stockings, one pair of mittens (in some communities, one pair of long mittens up to the elbow one year, the other year two pairs of short ones), in a few communities one pair of snow stockings, and in some communities three (but probably in most, two) pairs of shoes. Of these shoes, one pair should be made from the top of the hide (the heavy pair), the other of the thinner part of the leather (the light pair), and the soles should be sewn on with cobbler's thread and be provided with several layers of birch bark in the sole and fortified with a block of birch wood in the heel; yes, and in a few communities there were and in part still are quite a few detailed rules about nails and iron blocks, especially in the heavy pair. But the common rule nowadays is that if the servant wants the light pair to have more decorative welts, he must take from his pay the six shillings, since the charge by the shoemaker for shoes with welts is more expensive than that for shoes with sewn soles (six shillings). In a few communities in recent times, it has come about that farm owners have assumed the full fee to the shoemaker for welted shoes (12 shillings), and in this way it is seen how communities can deviate from the old rate.

This was the complete clothing for servant boys. The clothes for girls are less specified, but a set of rules has been created for them as well, as will be seen by the following, which I have written down as examples of extensive explanations given me by the housewives.

Ringsaker (*Hedemark*)

One year a jacket of homespun and skirt of linsey-woolsey (hemp in the warp and wool in the weft). Another year, a gown of linsey-woolsey (cotton yarn in the warp and wool in the weft), all ready-to-wear (earlier made by men tailors, now by women tailors). Some lining in the gown, namely, in the waist. But the girl must "stretch herself" to get lining in the jacket plus cloth for pockets and hems in the skirts, and likewise hooks.

Rakkestad (*Smaalenene*)

One year a jacket of homespun and a dress of linsey-woolsey, and that a coarse kind of linsey-woolsey. Another year, a gown of linsey-woolsey (with cotton yarn in the warp and wool yarn in the weft), all ready-to-wear (now made by women tailors, earlier by men tailors). The girl pays extra for lining for the jacket and cloth for the hems and pockets plus hooks, if she wants them.

How did this remarkable similarity come about? The schools and welfare and the church—these agencies are established by laws, the specifications of which are the same in all communities, although we find much greater variations in the adaptations and ordinances among individual communities. The natural resources of the communities and attendant methods of making a living and daily way of life and atmosphere and language, etc., reveal so many differences to the traveler on the road from Lom to Rakkestad that, upon the first impression, it seems that all is completely different, and still we find in these rules for clothes a similarity that includes the trivia of buttons and hooks. How has this happened?

There is something called fashion that particularly dominates clothes, which must continually be renewed and can accordingly be easily changed. To the extent that over the country there is contact between relatives among communities, people in one will want to emulate the customs of people in another community, and to that extent one can expect to find similar fashions in clothes; and according to the prevailing fashion, it is reasonable that rules for servant clothing are adapted. It is likely that there are a number of networks of communities or larger areas in the country that separate themselves by different fashions or have the same fashions in clothes, and by looking carefully at this, we should probably find contributions to the not-insignificant knowledge of how the people of many communities have had close or distant relationships with each other or with towns; we could regard this as different cultural streams that in each part of the country have brought with them different customs and ideas and morals, not only in regard to more serious things in life. How useful a full knowledge of these could be one will realize when one recalls that the first chapter of this thesis pointed out a remarkable difference in morality in certain adjoining areas, a difference that one could assume came about because of such various cultural streams, like breezes from the soul of foreign lands.

In Lom I have seen a poverty-stricken old man who, either because he was so old that he was not aware of the new fashion or because he was so poor that he could not afford it, wore a dress coat of a special kind, a vest, as it was called, of white homespun with sides and wide flaps, large pockets, a stiff collar, a lot of embroidery, and finally, white buttons as large as silver dollars. In addition, he had kneepants and buckled shoes. In the same parish on the large farm Graffen, I have also seen in a clothes closet a well-kept set of the same kind of clothes, probably the best collection which can be found on any estate, and thereby, I saw an example of how elegant these clothes could be, the top vest of fine white homespun with dark-colored embroidery, the long undervest in scarlet with sculptured figures, kneepants of suede or plush, garters of dyed yarn, and shoes decorated with large silver buckles. This costume was common in Lom until the beginning of this century. And until the end of the previous century, this same costume, which has been clearly described to me, was worn as far down as Romerike, in Smaalenene, in the diocese of Aken, etc. All the people in Romerike could talk particularly about the "church steeple" in the back, a piece of embroidery that topped out to a point and whose varied colors—blue, green, and red—symbolized the various parishes. But look, this vest-costume, as I call it, was obviously introduced to the people through the townspeople and the government officials, and these in turn got it from foreign countries; it was, you see, a common European style in the previous century. (This costume has been worn in Smaalenene and it seems to be the one Wilse mentions in his *Spydeberg* description of 1779, p. 383). Remnants of the older costume were still known. He writes: "Valdres jacket of gray homespun, edged on the seams and on the shoulders with another fabric, most impressive with black silk or a well-known stitch, is now worn only by a few young people, but earlier even by the aristocracy as daily dress; too bad they are not in fashion." After this glimpse, one can probably assume that this costume was common over the entire diocese, but it was displaced by the vest costume, except in Valdres or Hallingdal, where the new style was likely not introduced, since the old jacket is still worn by the people there.) The fashion was accompanied also by sharp-pointed high-heeled shoes for the women, and such shoes were not lacking in the collections at Graffen; the fashion was accompanied by powder in the hair and pigtail, and old farm-owners' wives in Romerike still talk about amusing incidents from their youth when the French-powder custom joined with the dance around the wooden block and other old Norwegian wedding customs. How many of the foreign sentiments have invaded the breasts of the Norwegian public under the strange clothing? How many foreign ideas have turned the head at the same time that powder has curled the hair?

But at that time, servant boys and cotters also wore white vests and kneepants, and then for the vest, as mentioned, black buttons were worn that were probably expensive but strong as well, so that they could last a man's whole lifetime and go from one piece of clothing to another; thus, one can understand the reason in the old rate for servant clothes that the boy should furnish buttons for the dress coat himself, for the thing was that he must have a set of buttons for everything. (The matter that the mistress of the house does not take care of the hooks in a girl's dress but the girl must provide them herself has been explained to me more simply thus: in former times the servant girl got along with a slip noose at the throat and at the waist. And it is possible that it could have been likewise with the boy's buttonless evening dress, originating from the time that preceded the style of the white vest with the bright buttons, at a time when one probably fastened the jacket together with straps or leather thongs.)

But fashion is after all a changing thing, and the handsome costume that our grandparents wore had to make place for a new one—from I do not know which of the cultural streams. But this change first took place in the towns, then among government officials in the country, thereafter among better-off farmers, and lastly among servant folk and cotters. Some of the servant folk in Romerike at that time are still alive, and they have told me how it went with them when they came to town with a load of lumber and appeared on the streets with their already old-fashioned and conspicuous clothes: red cap, white uniform coat, kneepants, and so forth. The street boys regarded them as people who were outside of the folk customs, and pelted them with snowballs—exactly as I had seen a few years ago in Kongsberg when the coal haulers from Numedal came in with their white uniform coats.

How did the struggle between the old rate for the boy's "complete clothing" and the demands for the new fashions come out? Oh yes, one hears the explanation about it in the parish of Næs: The farm owner still delivered the 16 feet of homespun that the vest and kneepants required, plus the 12 and 6 shillings that the tailor should get for tailoring them, and the boy had to add the extra the tailor should have to make kneepants into long pants, plus one of two: either be satisfied with a short jacket or else two feet of homespun extra in order to get a kind of coat or jacket that could be worn for a few years (with a stand-up collar and not cut off at the waist so that it did not cling to the body). He also had to have the homespun dyed. Still, little by little, the ladies of the house delivered gray homespun, and little by little they took over payment of the somewhat higher fee to the tailor, and little by little the simple topcoat for everyday wear—still following a new demand in taste originating in the towns—was converted into a dress coat with long, tapered tails and finally a topcoat with wide tails, first without any kind of lining, then with lining (of plain burlap) in the back, and thereafter likewise in the sleeves. This is the way it is now and has occurred in most places. But I have a suspicion that in the communities where snow stockings are not part of the rate, the servant has lost thereby, a replacement for the kneepants previously extended by the farm owner.

Now as we have thus dug deeply into details, I believe we can see the evolution of these common things—that when a new fashion spreads over the communities, the servant people themselves must first struggle to keep up, but little by little a larger and larger portion of the increased expenses are borne by the master of the house. And this change takes place annually. Now one and then another good fellow during the negotiations makes the explicit condition that he should get a small addition to the "complete clothing," and in time this addition becomes so common that it almost, in fact does become regarded as a regular part of the payment-in-kind. In this way the many discussions of lining in the topcoat lead to a great deal of haggling, and in recent years more and more servant boys have bargained for a pair of boots a year instead of the one pair of shoes or in addition to the shoes that are part of payment-in-kind. Let a few years pass and a pair of boots for each fellow will become the rule in order to have a "proper wage." In this manner the servant folk indeed become more and more expensive, and a very old woman in Lom told this to a now-living man who passed it on: "These servants today, how expensive they are becoming! In olden days when a fellow had enough (one barrel of grain and 'complete clothes') they took care of themselves and arranged for themselves, but now a great deal must be paid for a worthless one." Accordingly, the complaints that are often heard now are very old.

Still, for my part, I must call the clothes of the working class in the countryside shabby. In this respect the payment-in-kind mentioned for servant clothes is very interesting, for it is an index that has heretofore, and for a large part of the country districts, been regarded as sufficient for a year for an adult in the working class. With several people and in several communities I have examined to the shilling what the "complete clothing" could be worth, and most often I have found the sum to be between seven and nine dalers—possibly a little less for the girl than for the boy. And now there is common knowledge among both the servants and the farm-owner people that the boy, in addition to providing for himself the individual items that are not part of the payment-in-kind (cap, vest, neckerchief), buys besides some homespun or calfskin in order to furnish his work clothes with pieces of cloth, and on the whole he is aware of his clothes and adorns and takes good care [of himself]; he does not get by through the year with just his servant clothes but can even collect a stock of individual items of sets of clothing and of shoes, which is probably more true of the girl. It is also a fact that cotters usually cannot afford to provide for themselves the many new things during the year that they received when they were servants, and therefore I often find when I accompany the wives of cotters to the loft in the granary or to the room where they have their clothes that after a number of years, the man and wife still have as holiday clothing the clothes they received during the last year of their servant period. Yes, most would agree that the frugality is too severe when they see how a large portion of this class of people that we are observing are thus accustomed to the old: two new shirts and one pair of whole and one pair of stockings with replaced lower parts a year, disregarding the inability to collect a supply of this kind of stuff inasmuch as it wears out by the end of the year, and so they probably think at the very least of buying some more of these kinds of clothing. But then one wonders how cleanliness is maintained when there is so little to change! And when there are a great many people who are helped with so little, there are indeed always some, and not so few, who live in worse poverty than usual and get along with less, e.g., with a single pair of stockings. Such stockings are not darned all over but are made shapeless by patches, one on top of the other, and they are so penetrated by dirt that they can stand by themselves.

After all this, it is understandable that it does not take much to seem like luxury and excessive finery. But from the following one can learn that one must be careful in judgment. I visited a wife of a cotter at a place in Romerike. We did not know each other at all; I do not believe she knew my name since I had been in the area for such a short time, though it takes just a short time to become acquainted with our common people. The woman appeared to me to be both sensible and good, and I talked in great detail with her about her domestic life. She had first served on a farm for 10 years, then on another one for four, and on a third for one-half year when she became a bride at the age of 29 years, and this was now five years ago. "So you have direct experience and knowledge about the nature of the life of servant folk. It is said that in this community the girls engage in a lot of finery and frivolity. Might it have been so with you also?" I asked jokingly. One thing followed another and I asked permission to go with her to the little granary loft where she had her things. Up in Gudbrandsdal and Østerdal there are some farms that are well known for their large, well-supplied, and well-ordered storage houses, but none has given me more pleasure than the little one. There was hardly any room for two people at a time among the stacked and hanging items. There were several kinds of flour in a storage chest and two very old chests, but the sifted barley flour was hidden in the lowest drawer. In a can there was a nicely arranged yellow butter, a couple of merker, and from this I heard that the woman usually churns almost all the cream to sell to provide the man with a few shillings. Some linen shears and tows of flax and balls of yarn, even though just that day she was cleaning the fabric she had recently brought down. But I was most taken by a row of clothes that hung under the loft beam.

Since he and she were servants, they had not provided themselves with new sets of clothes, i.e., the proper dress and trousers, jacket and topcoat; they had not needed to, either, inasmuch as they had been supplied since their servant period. When the woman was married, she had ten sets, among which there were four homespuns for women, which came from the wool of her servant sheep. (A grown servant girl in this community has two spdlr. in wages and one spdlr. plus clothes: a ready-made set which can be either a homespun jacket and linsey-woolsey shirt of burlap and wool or a whole dress of cotton-linsey-woolsey [in earlier times, it was 18 feet of good homespun instead of a set, which was regarded more favorably]; still 8 feet of linen, 24 feet of linsey-woolsey, 12 pounds of blended linen [or one spdlr.], three pairs of shoes—plus permission to take care of a sheep of the master and fodder so that its lamb can follow the mother all summer. This right to sheep was still only for the best-paid girls, and the present cotter's wife had it during the last eight years of her time of service. The homespun for women [fall wool in the warp and woof, most desirably Christmas woof, most often woven together with dyed yarn and therefore milled] that an able girl produces from her own sheep for a holiday dress is of the best kind, and the linsey-woolsey she makes is usually better than the "girl linsey-woolsey" that the cotter makes because, reasonably enough, the housewife just as well uses the Christmas woof and the finest wool for the man's and her own clothes, and thus the servant folk get the spring woof. But these and many other small things are brought to one's attention when one has an opportunity to listen to the small mutual complaints between the servant folk and the farm-owner folk. And at bottom the entire farm life consists of a long series of small things.) It was not very much she [the cotter's wife] could earn by spinning for herself on Saturday evenings, considering the amount of free time the servants have in this community, but she paid for both spinning and weaving and bought the dye materials necessary. Of the 10 sets of clothing, she still owned four good ones, namely, two of her own homespun and two servant dresses. I had to give in to the woman and see all of them. Still, she had been able during her servant period to assemble: a couple of chests, a loom chair, a spinning wheel, a cabinet, a cow, a linen sheet (not a pair), three burlap sheets, one patterned tablecloth, and three hand towels. Finally, she had bought a greatcoat (of karlmands homespun, price 3 spdlr.), and all these items were still usable. Further, she had made homespun from her servant sheep that she had promised to her sweetheart for his formal attire as a groom; he did not need it, however, and the homespun was sold to buy kettles. As a bride she still owned four quite new and two to three pairs of wearable shoes that she had received as servant wages, plus 18 pieces of linen and four pairs of stockings; and in answer to an observation of mine that four pairs were too little, she explained that stockings do not have to be washed often, inasmuch as they readily wore out. And now comes the list of the "bought materials" that she as a servant girl had collected, and all lay well protected in the top chest of drawers (in the next drawer there lay a well-dyed piece of well-preserved homespun in a linen cloth of 38 feet, fully milled, dyed, and pressed, nice and beautiful, made from the cotter sheep and destined for clothes for the man):

1 throw, cotton with wool in it	...	spd.	3	ort	12	shillings
1 camel's hair kerchief	...	spd.	4	ort	...	shillings
1 red-checkered wool kerchief, small	...	spd.	1	ort	12	shillings
1 dark wool kerchief	...	spd.	1	ort	8	shillings
1 throw, wool and cotton	1	spd.	...	ort	...	shillings
1 small cotton kerchief	...	spd.	...	ort	22	shillings
1 cape with silk band	...	spd.	1	ort	22	shillings

There were also two aprons whose price could not be recalled. As each piece was taken from the drawer, there were little histories and explanations of the circumstances of the purchase, etc. When the dollar kerchief appeared, I asked jokingly: "Did it not seem to you that the dollar was a lot of money, you, who had two dollars in wages?" In a serious manner she explained that she "had considered that such a piece of clothing could always be useful for when one takes a child to church. One must still have something decent to wrap around it." Thus thinks a servant girl, a girl who is secretly engaged to a night courter (for she was so at the time)! And when such a girl once in a while appears on the way to church with the new kerchief, almost as big and beautiful as the one worn by the farm owner's own daughter, perhaps she can serve as an example of how thoughtless irresponsibility and obsession with finery takes the upper hand in the community!

In this same community I walked on a winter day to and from church in company with some young men from the working class; all walked with boots, a few in addition with overshoes, and most of them in overcoats. At the church I found several of their friends dressed the same, and I noticed that the girls of the working class, with hardly any exceptions, wore cloaks (for greatcoats are old-fashioned now), capes of totencloth [Toten is a district in Norway] or self-made linsey-woolsey, in part also town cloth; plus, most of them wore rather pretty hats, all of which were not part of the "complete clothing," and those who of these young people were servant folk must have added to their wages. But with this evidence I later engaged in a conversation with some well-known men of the working class (among whom were a tailor and a shoemaker) to obtain information on each servant boy in the area, totaling 39; and thereby I learned that the fellows who were best dressed were likely the fellows who were the most orderly in all ways and took on other useful things in addition to clothes. And here the reader must not assume that the people I talked with were probably biased and knew how to conceal or excuse luxury; for I made the same observation here that people of the working class are by no means open in talking about their friends whom they know as drunkards and rascals.

In the last analysis, how should we then judge the frequent complaints about the obsession with luxury in the working class? I have heard these complaints from sensible and thoughtful people so that it is quite certain that there must be a basis for it; it would be foolish to conclude otherwise. The complaints are directed particularly at girls, and it is unfortunately very reasonable to infer that when numerous boys engage irresponsibly in card playing and beer drinking, which I have told about in the foregoing, there are also quite a few girls who are equally irresponsible on their part. And there have been more examples of this scandalous behavior during the last three to four years than before, since the times suddenly have become so unusually good for the working class. But I ask: Why, alongside the frequent complaining, does one seldom hear the master and mistress of the house praise the servant people who show thoughtfulness and prudence, something which clearly there are examples of in each area? And when I summarize the whole matter, I must say: The few who really seem obsessed with luxury must be warned, but the changes in ideas and customs by which people wish to be better dressed than they had to be satisfied with earlier, should not be criticized; yes, one should be happy that the arts and crafts today produce things so cheaply that poor people can appear on the way to church, without scorn, almost as well dressed as frugal rich people. The more respectable folk whose words have some influence in the communities ought to set a good example for those who are born and grow up in impoverished circumstances and are still able to copy the higher born on the outside in clothes; they also at the same time should emulate the more important custom of the more cultured who believe they are too good to participate in the many coarse excesses which seem to be part of the lower classes. You complain, you farm owner, about the luxury in clothes? Rather complain about the luxury of lust and think perhaps there is a rising sense today for more tidiness on the outside that can be the means to arouse the much too slumbering self-regard and overcome the animal crudeness.

MEALS

I now remember a cotter family, still in Upper Romerike. Before I arrived at the house I knew that it was very poor, but I found the man to be a reliable hard worker, and the wife attracted my attention to a high degree: an unusually fine, regular, and beautiful face betrayed feeling and soul, but trouble had overcome her spirit and hid behind her facial expression very clearly when I jokingly tried to divert her to smile and laugh. An awful impression was therefore made on me when, in the course of the conversation, the man told me that a few years ago she was crazy for a few weeks, i.e., mentally ill, so that the man had to stay at home and watch over her, and the woman explained to me that her weakness came upon her when she was pregnant (with the child she now had at her breast) and she came to think of all the difficulties which lay ahead of her. I made jokes, for I had to try to cheer up both myself and the people of the house. When I, for example, tried more or less to take a complete inventory of all items in this house of poverty, items in the house, in the barn, and loft (but not the animals in the barn), I valued all of it, after discussion with the man and wife, at not quite 10 daler. And such things I could consider because it was precisely the objective of my visit here to see how it was with poor people. Oh, how strange it is to sit in a house with a family circle where everything in a way cries out to you: Look around and observe everything well, for here you have an example of how poverty looks, where the greatest effort must be made to survive and not give in to destitution which will lead to charity. (This family stood on the boundary between individual independence and dependence on charity; this woman was "crazy," but only then did the man have to accept help from the welfare agency.) And certainly it was strange for me to sit here, I who had the mission to participate in a Royal Commission's work to prepare a new law about poverty in our country, for here, precisely here, I had to tell myself: "I understand only little of the secrets of poverty."

Something was, of course, easy to understand. First, these were servant people and were married when he was only 24 and she 22 years old; this was now 16 years ago and they had had eight children, of whom seven were alive and six unprovided for at home; during all that time they had besides had a cotter place which was a good deal poorer than usual in this area, and under a master who was of goodwill but had little ability to help his working people advance. In these circumstances lay the cause of the family's poverty, and to that extent the thing was not difficult to understand. But what was and still is for me a mystery is how this poverty, with all its visible destitution, could be rich enough to maintain the patience of the parents' spirit (I heard no sounds of complaint from them) and to bring out the contentment which shone out of the faces of the children—barefoot and half-naked. And it must well have been strange for the man and woman themselves to have a strange man in the house who started to ask and cross-examine about all the things that could cast light on the history of their poverty, a man who, so to speak, made use of the poverty of this house to gather knowledge. "Sister, my good woman," in this way I gave the visit a more cheerful turn, "now the question is if you have a reasonable dinner to give me, for I have walked a long way and have sat here a long time so that I am both hungry and thirsty." I will not easily forget the woman's face when she looked at me questioningly, looked at me to see if I was serious. But then she got into action: she fetched coffee from a container, burned, ground, and cooked this time without a lump in it; she stirred together rye and water and mashed potatoes and fried cakes from a shelf which her resourceful poverty had made out of the bottom of a broken-apart kettle, and only thought herself lucky that just that day she had been able to churn a little dab of butter which really was to have been a small tasty bite for the man on Sunday. There was some coffee cream in a cup, but she set forth the sugar tearfully since there was only a teaspoon of powdered sugar, which was scraped together from the bottom of the tin cup and looked less pleasing. Eventually the food was served and the woman seated herself at the spinning wheel, but all the time she looked to see if I was really eating the food, and when I had almost eaten and drunk everything there was, we were as friendly as if we had known each other for a year. "Now listen, good woman," thus I started the conversation, "your husband has told me what he manages and grows on the place and what he can earn in a year by his work on the farm. Let me hear your explanation! First, how can you with only this clothe your husband and children?"—"Oh, that will be a strange explanation," she answered and laughed, but it was exactly this strange explanation I wanted to hear and got. "And then there is the food!" I continued, "can you explain to me equally well how you get enough for all the mouths you must manage?" But here the woman broke into tears, and I had to harden myself to repeat my question.

But with my introduction of thanking God for food, the explanation was: The woman spins for people, mostly to get a few shillings to buy pieces of clothing. When the man goes to work at 4 o'clock in the morning, she then also rises to make a fire in the fireplace and sit down at the spinning wheel; the children also want to get up, and then there is little peace for her; and the little that she can spin is not enough for food for the children, who want much more food when they are up so early. It is better when the children sleep a little longer for then they help themselves to a meal before the midday dinner, namely, the second breakfast. They then get water porridge (of oatmeal) and often without a drop of milk in it. The children need not be much grown before they understand what the food bell means, which they hear over the woods from the farms, and hardly before the dinner bell rings, they begin to ask. They then get porridge again, remaining from the second breakfast, and leftover potatoes, either newly boiled or warmed in the pan with a little grease in it. The afternoon meal consists of coffee—yes, it is so-called, but it is mostly only whole oats, for 48 to 60 pounds of coffee are bought each year—plus bread. This bread is fried like that I had eaten, but with the difference that it consists mostly of oat flour with only a little barley flour when it is available. The evening meal is like the second breakfast. When the cow—and there is only one cow—gives the most milk, the woman can put together some butter for sale, but otherwise it is often in the houses of the poor that the supply of milk is not big enough to hide from morning to night, and then cream cannot be saved. Also it has not been possible at all on this place to make cheese, and there cannot be cheese at the time of the year when the cow does not give milk. There is also little of meat in the house; the most likely is the suckling calf which must likely be sold the same year for shillings; during the last 16 years these people have kept house, they have only had a pig to butcher three times, and it has always been small. The observant reader will miss flatbread from the foregoing menu, but this is often lacking in the very poor households, and this woman usually makes some only in the fall. The flatbread is so dry when there is no good fish or meat with it. The smallest child, nevertheless, for the most part had a tidbit to enjoy a few times a week. I became aware of it in this way: while on a walk with the man around the grounds and while in conversation with him about his duties and rights as a cotter, I remembered how cotters in many communities had the custom when they ate at the table of the farm owner to fill themselves up with the food placed before them and take home portions, (on meat-days individual portions of meat and pork are set before each person; soup and flatbread, on the other hand, are supplied as desired) e.g., of meat and pork well surrounded by flatbread, and I asked him if he did not do this so that the wife and the children would know how meat tasted. No, he answered, that he did not, because the farm-owner people did not like it; the only thing he could take home with him was a tiny bit of the evening meal bread, and the small ones had become accustomed to knowing which days there was bread for the night meal, and they lay awake in the evening until the father came home. He then had to bring even a little bit, which satisfied them and they did not cry. This bread is really only a very plain ovenbread of barley flour (sometimes only mixed grain flour) with "first-meal" and "last-meal" (top quality and lowest quality) rye in it. But there is enough so that the rye can be tasted.

There is something called sympathizing with people, to get into the thoughts and feelings of a friend, to be happy with the happy, and to grieve with the grieving. And now and then we encounter something which evokes in us the opposite of sympathy. The traveler who travels over the roads of Romerike and from his good carriage looks down at the small, often so shabby, deteriorating hovels along the way may feel ill will toward the people who live in such hovels and peek out of dim windowpanes. Or if one goes in and sees the bedsteads and rags where the hovel people seek their nightly rest, it can be, whether you yourself know it or not, that the great filth brings you to say to yourself: What awful people! And if there is someone who is more used to unexpectedly sitting at the table of a cotter or a poor farm owner and who finds the food so unappetizing that he must close his eyes when he puts the spoon to his mouth and force himself to swallow what the mouth received, it can then be that he is overcome by a certain disgust for the very people who offered him the disgusting food and who appear to eat it with the pleasure of serving food for guests. In such manner there rises an ill will toward one's fellow beings that can make one stone-hearted, for the mind understands quickly how unjust it is against the fellow being, how ungrateful it is toward God. I assert that it will not require little practice and self-control to resist it. And what kind of opposite frame of mind must not be natural for them who notice that they are objects of such unpleasant feelings?

And precisely in the matter of food, I truly have been pained to sympathize with people who are poor. It seems that many times food, and again food, occupies their minds from beginning to end, and it is difficult for me to come to grips with it. In the circles to which I belong, one knows what food means, but for the most part one has or imagines one has so many higher things to think about, to take pleasure in and be concerned with, that one's bread and butter seems to be a less important and noble problem; among poor people, on the other hand, it often appears as if it is really bread and butter that is most important. Yes, there is a great difference in how the mind concerns itself with food; I even believe it is possible to show a distinct and systematic difference in the taste of rich and poor people, which otherwise is regarded as being such a vague thing: rich people think of *good* food that should last until the next meal, and they do not always call good what chemists classify as the most nourishing; poor people think more about if there also will be *enough* for their hunger, and instinctively they are likely to call the best food whatever in reality best satisfies their hunger and nourishes the body. Likewise, in a sense, the artist often calls the wildest landscape lovely, and the farmer says that it is a beautiful land where good grain grows.

And really, inner coarseness clearly reveals a greedy delight in what others call wretched food and drink. The validity of this observation will certainly be acknowledged by one who is accustomed to better and who sees with what relish people enjoy that awful mixture of rotgut and syrup (or whatever it is) that currently is sold under the name of Italian wine.

But is it not strange if both the heart and the tongue are badly trained in people who have grown up in a very poor household, whose food is what I recently tried? Or to the extent that children who leave such a household still show better sense and get along well in the world, do we not then have a double reason to praise the gentleness of the mother, the understanding of the father who brought them up?

After these reflections do I dare conclude that knowledge of the usual food in the country is not unimportant for me who wants the correct understanding of the people's culture and morals? Food has its own history. Gradually, as occupations spread and the standard of living grows and communication becomes easier and industry and commerce compete to serve people, the food situation in the the country will improve, and there is no doubt that this is also one of the means through which Providence will favor the advancement of the people.

Particularly in Romerike, I seem to realize how food is significant for more than the body itself. For while dealing with cotters and farm owners, I was forced to experience how food is a topic for strife that supports an endless little war—a war of the kind one also calls daily fussing and fuming.

The main items in all food are grain for flour and milk, meat, etc. There are communities where most of the food is milk and meat with a little flour, others where there is flour with a little milk and meat. What the combination should be depends mainly on the natural resources of the community and the accustomed methods of tilling the soil; here custom and methods cannot have as great an influence as clothing style, and there is only a small cluster of communities that by mutual copying of custom and use have created a common food style.

Such a cluster of communities is found precisely in Upper and Lower Romerike including Odalen and, as I believe, also Sør. In north

Hedemark the food style is a great deal different, and in Rødenæs, a parish in Smaalenene which lies immediately south of Høland in lower Romerike, I heard people ridicule the "water porridge 21 times a week" of the Hølander, despite the fact that the relatively poor people of Rødenæs by no means fed their population as well as Høland fed theirs. This "water porridge" is the distinguishing characteristic for the food style in the communities mentioned, so that if one wanted to look at different areas according to the food style, [the villages of] Romerike could be called the "porridge communities."

On a large farm it is likely the cook-girl who is first on the job. At 4 o'clock she will put on the porridge kettle to have it cooked by the first breakfast at 5 o'clock. The porridge is cooked with water and mixed grain meal. To be sure, the cotters maintain that on a few farms (sometimes the most, they say) there is only oatmeal; but the thing is that the mix of barley and oats in the so-called mixed grain can vary so that a slight exaggeration on one side or another can call the grain in the same sack either oats or mixed grain, and on that point at any rate, all are agreed that the porridge is mixed grain when it is according to the old custom. Does one want to know more about the preparation? In earlier times it was very common that the cook-girl first stirred the meal in a dish with cold water, then poured the "porridge meal" into the boiling kettle; nowadays the custom is different: she must sprinkle the dry meal into the kettle while cooking and stir it around with a stirring stick. True enough, this last method requires a little more work, and indeed it is difficult to avoid that thereby the porridge becomes somewhat lumpy, but with this method, despite the lumps, the porridge becomes more tasty, as all agree. When the porridge is cooked and the kettle is taken off the fire, the mistress of the house takes over and pours and stirs in some sour milk. This coagulates in the boiling porridge and makes small cheese clumps; it is often mentioned that this is the best of all. Now the porridge is ladled into the bowl, and again the mistress of the house pours in some fresh milk with the foam taken off, which she does not stir around, so that it forms a little lake in the middle of the bowl. And by the size of this lake plus the volume of cheese clumps they recognize the reputation of the house and the kindheartedness of the mistress. Thus we have now first brought this porridge to the first breakfast at 5 o'clock. But during the same cooking, the porridge for the second breakfast at 8 o'clock is also prepared. It remains in the kettle with sour milk in it and is kept warm, but because by the second breakfast it is only lukewarm and accordingly not so "light," a thoughtful mistress needs to add a little fresh milk to the bowl. Finally, newly cooked porridge is served at the evening meal. But since the evening meal's porridge in fact alternates with potatoes, and since for Sunday's second breakfast one or another milk-food is provided, it is then exactly three times a day and not fully 21 times a week that water porridge is served; and thus the scornful expression of the Rødenæs people about the food style of the Romerike people is not true, although it might have been correct some time long ago.

For the first breakfast, and in part for the evening meal, the porridge is served by itself, only with oat flatbread in addition, inasmuch as this is on hand at all mealtimes. But for the porridge at the second breakfast, supplementary food is served. On the farms where there is good food preparation and enough of the various items that are necessary, there is a very definite rule as to what supplementary food belongs to each weekday, although there are certain variations according to the season of the year. And still more definite rules apply to the midday meal, 12 o'clock, and for the afternoon meal, 4 o'clock. On several farms in different communities in Romerike, I have found this rule quite marked even to extreme details. Now today, Thursday, accordingly is meat-day on each farm. On larger farms where the meat kettle must be over the fire several hours, it can be seen already by the second breakfast that the supplementary food consists of a kind of meal-ball cooked in meat soup or fried in the fat. The midday meal then consists of cabbage with meat and pork. The cabbage, i.e., the soup, is evened out with sifted barley flour and there is always hulled grain in it, plus, in the fall, actually cabbage, and in the summer, peas. Potatoes are not ordinarily available and, on the whole, appear to be served economically. Meat and pork alternate, and ordinarily (so believed an artisan who worked constantly in the farmer's buildings and thus was well informed) each person gets a piece of each kind, "about as big as the matchbox there." On many farms this meat-day stops in the summer, and the reason for this was explained by a mistress of the house thus: The midday meal on Friday is warmed-over cabbage with one or another supplement, but in the summer, people do not like this warmed-over cabbage since it turns sour; therefore, on both days something more desirable is served. The custom of cooking the meat so much in soup that there can be enough for the next day should not make one conclude that the soup is very strong. In addition to the real meat-days, smoked ham belongs to Sunday (if there is no fresh meat for this day, for example, a suckling calf). But still more frequently than meat on Thursdays, pork disappears on these days and is changed for a pot of butter.

Still, it would not be correct at this point to present the whole menu with its numerous details. So far I lack, moreover, information on weights and measures of the various grains and other ingredients that make up the courses, information that no farmer or farmer's wife has been able to report to me. But now the reader will still have an idea in large part of what occupies the servant fellow's mind and thought: I have not been able to notice that he worries much over, for example, literary matters, over the various poets' and prose writers' peculiarities, but peculiarities in the various food styles of the mistress of the house he knows very clearly over a wide area, and thereafter he selects the farm that in recent good years appeals to him most.

But I believe it is a fact that the food style—and here I am thinking of the food for the working class—has improved during the last generation, and particularly relative to working hours and food breaks, which little by little have been reduced during a 24-hour day.

I was present at a funeral in Upper Romerike for an old man, and I was told of the deceased that in his youth he had to be in the field with his plow at 2 o'clock in the morning. Today the plowman does not hitch his horses until 4 o'clock. Middle-aged farmers in the parish of Næs described their years as young men: although sons of farm owners they had to get up at the crack of dawn, that is to say, begin in the hayloft at 3 o'clock. "Before breakfast" porridge was delivered to them at 5 o'clock. They rested a while by lying in the hay and—in order to keep themselves warm in the winter cold—beat their feet against the wall. But today, when threshing machines have become common, hired hands and cotters take care of the horses and carry out some fuss work for half an hour until 5 o'clock. Then in a warm house they enjoy their "before breakfast" meal in order to begin the regular work at 6 o'clock. The grain which is now consumed is grain of the superior kind (barley, rye, peas) than earlier when the grain was not always fully mature. Then the fields were largely sowed with oats and mixed grain on land plowed by wooden plows. Also, it is now usual that the crops result in more milk, cheese, and meat, because of the introduction (from the years around 1830) of better fodder than earlier. The situation now is such that a great deal of the best grain is sold in town, but some of the working-class people wish to have me believe that the diet for the working class has become worse in recent times. But in view of the facts presented this assertion can not be believed.

But whatever the situation may be, there is a great deal of dissatisfaction in the working class with the food. In this I am not thinking merely and mostly of the examples I have heard from the mistresses of the house about silly boys who have thrown the spoon on the table or by other boorish methods have made their ill feelings known, but I recall accounts of older people, cotters, who have thoughtfully explained that the food on most of the places was inadequate for those engaged in heavy labor. Against this complaint is heard incessantly from the farm owners' side, and truly not merely unreasonable and strident, that while the workers in recent times have demanded more pay, food, and other things, and actually in large part have had their demands met (now the times are such that even a second-rate fellow can say, "To hell with it, if the master of the place does not want me, I can get just as good or a better job at another place."), there is less eagerness to fulfill their duty and do more in a day, etc.

How should we judge this conflict? Where do we find its origin and what kind of result can we expect?

Older cotters remember and younger people have heard said about a time when the biggest farmers in the communities worked together with their people and ate at the same table and of the same food as they. But then there was introduced at more and more of the larger farms dual dining tables and in part a dual food level—particularly the family of the master, and the workers—and at the same time more and more of the farm owners (to a degree, also their sons) withdrew from participation in heavy labor. To be sure, this did not happen on all farms, but it was enough that it happened on the larger farms and among the more respected, the style-setting families. And even on the other farms, nevertheless, the increasing education of the farm owners and their more visible and significant participation in the public affairs of the community (particularly chairmanships) must have influenced the consciousness of a differentiation; a gap between the two classes, farm owners and workers, spread, and this consciousness wove itself, so to speak, into the outward sign: the dual or separate food and the division of labor between the manager (who could walk in the fields with his tobacco pipe in his mouth) and the manual workers (who "toiled and sweated"). By listening to the stories of older cotters, the younger workers have become very convinced that the farm owner who does not participate in the work himself cannot know how much he can lawfully demand, and that he demands too much rather than too little; and the servant boy who hauls the sack of grain to the mill and sees there how the grain with the best kernel during the sifting is separated for use by the farm-owner people, so only the "top meal and the last meal," or the head of the rye, is kept for these people, believes actually that since the grain was divided, the master and mistress bother only to have it better for themselves and the guests who visit the house; and he believes this so strongly because he heard from the miller that the whole act of sifting the meal has been introduced in this country during the last half-century. In this connection it can be observed, which the housewives cite, that since the farm-owner people have their own meals where coffee is served twice a day, so much good fresh milk remains after the coffee cream that the people now have fresh milk rather than the sour they had before, but on this sensitive point should be mentioned: on the cotters' places (where there is little milk) and on the small farms (where there are few servants and outside workers), coffee has become a daily drink, particularly for early breakfast, where it has replaced water porridge, and for the afternoon meal, but on the larger farms the old custom continues among the people, and coffee is served only once a week, on Sundays. This matter about the coffee is today the most burning question: the workers want coffee and sandwiches for early breakfast instead of the old water porridge, and it is mostly the large farms that are still opposed.

When I put these and several small matters together, I arrive at the following conclusion: The food for the working class has quite certainly improved during the last generation, but this improvement is by no means as great as that for the farm-owner class (which also includes houses, clothing, social functions, etc.) and it has particularly not taken place in such a degree that the workers have replaced the lost satisfaction of sharing with the farm-owner people in days of old, sharing the same table and otherwise living in the same way. On the other hand, I find a lot of reasons for the complaints of farmers about the workers nowadays, that their diligence and competence have not increased as much as could be expected, in truth, with higher and rewarding wages. [I believe this] in part because I have heard complaints from very trustworthy farm owners and partly because I myself have found in a very large part of the working class an atmosphere of great unrest, an atmosphere not usually accompanied by a will to work. (I could also add that I have found precious few signs that the people of the working class think about reading, practice in writing, etc., to master a greater insight and competence in things that truly a farmer and farm fellow could benefit from knowing about.)

Should we turn time around and return to the old condition when the farm owner himself was pulled along on the heavy wooden plow, or hauled out manure on the creaking wagon with wheels on wooden axles, or lived with his servant boys in the wood-cutting valley and hauled lumber to town? No, that no one wants, or in any case most people in the working class recognize that the times and conditions have happily changed to the advantage of the entire society, and the working class as well, and only the foolish or ignorant do not realize this. But I say to the young worker-fellow: make an effort to become competent in everything, clever at using your hands, thoughtful and insightful, and if you cannot find any farm owner in the community who recognizes what you can do, then try your luck in another community and do not walk around here with a festering dissatisfaction year after year! And to the young men of the farm-owner class I say: the running of a farm is not only to understand the application of chemistry on fields and the like but also to have the gift of dealing with the working people and gaining their trust and loyalty, and it will be necessary that the master of the farm quite often—and likely more often than heretofore—himself participates in the work so that he can learn firsthand what a day's work demands of a good fellow, and what food and care a good fellow needs.

And it would seem reasonable in a situation like this that one depends on and expects most from the farm owners and the more educated class. I express my expectation by making the observation that if the farm owners had the ability to win the trust and spread good morale and feeling among their servants, this would not only contribute to educating a cadre of competent people for the improvement of agriculture but also to improving the moral condition in the whole community.

SIMILARITIES AND DIFFERENCES IN UPPER AND LOWER ROMERIKE

Consider how many items in the previous chapter I have brought up: party customs, clothing, food! This is not the place to deal with these items at length, and I might well ask forgiveness for my having dwelt on them so long; it was refreshing to the spirit to look away from the dark side of people's lives, which this book otherwise deals with, and for a moment to fix one's attention on other pictures. But there was another reason for me while I was there in the communities of Romerike and while I had a related objective for my research: the moral condition. This was a reason for me to observe the conditions of domestic life and the routines of daily life and customs in as many directions as possible, and this was then also the reason for me to involve myself in these things in a study like this, as I hope it will become clear with what I am now permitting myself to observe.

Also in chapters 2, 3, and 4, I have reported on the conditions of domestic life and customs, for the most part with regard to Romerike. (Both from my own observations and from the reports to me from pastors, I will separately cite the following for Romerike, with Solør and Odal: The situation regarding night courting must be called similar in

Lower and Upper Romerike, together with the districts in Solør and Odal; in all parishes it customarily or partly prevailed. The situation with the custom to have sleeping quarters in the animal barn was, on the other hand, varied; the custom was not known at all or only exceptionally in the parish in Lower Romerike; in Upper Romerike, on the contrary, there was a place [Næs] where the custom until the most recent times had been very common, and in Solør and Odal it was also true in most of the parishes. But though this custom is found in one of the parishes of Upper Romerike, it cannot be concluded that there is a comparison between the condition of illegitimate births in the deaneries of Upper and Lower Romerike, any more than the condition of illegitimate births is not worse in Solør and Odal, where the custom is more widespread than in upper Romerike.)

When I collate the many reminiscences, of which I have reported a part in the previous chapter, and when I summarize the many and varied observations in one whole, I must say that in domestic and social life and in the whole of the daily milieu a remarkable similarity prevails in the different communities of Romerike, in Upper and Lower Romerike, these tax districts that the old landscape of Romerike has been divided into for a long time. Lower Romerike consists of the parishes of Høland, Urskoug (around the upper portion of the Fredrikshald water course), plus Fet, Enebok, Skedsmo, Nittedal, and Sørum (close to the inland Lake Øieren); Upper Romerike consists of the parishes of Gjerdrum, Nannestad, Ullensaker, Næs, Eidsvoll, and Hurdal (close to Vormen and its small river). But all this can be called a cohesive community; people live together in clusters of farms in Eidsvoll and Næs, in Næs and Ullensaker, in Ullensaker and Sørum, in Sørum and Skedsmo, etc. And as far as the natural environment is concerned, climate and soil, it is quite seldom that two farms are alike, but there is so little difference between parishes that one can easily call agriculture the overwhelmingly important means of making a living for all, so overwhelming that a few different outlying areas, where lumbering and freight hauling are carried on, have no particular significance. And after these considerations one could well say that it is nothing to wonder about but something one would expect beforehand that similarities are to be found in the manner of living and daily customs. But still, in our land many examples are found where the lives of people in quite nearby communities, under the influence of the same natural conditions and means of livelihood, in many instances have developed very differently, and therefore there is something that needs to be observed, that in the communities of Romerike similarities appear strangely in the smallest details where one is not likely to seek them out. It is not enough, as well, that nature has created Upper and Lower Romerike alike; but without doubt (and this is also otherwise known), they were occupied by the one and same kind of people who from the earliest times have been connected with the nearest ancestral tree, and the course of cultural evolution must, in any case for long periods, have been the same overall so that the changes in thought patterns and practices that could have been developed under the most various influences have occurred in the same manner everywhere.

I can also call attention to separate traces of similarities in things, which it is reasonable to assume are dependent on natural conditions and circumstances of time and the dominant thought patterns—similarities that I have determined statistically. But by this comparison I must certainly include Odal and Solør, which until quite recently made up a deanery, together with Upper Romerike.

For each 10,000 people living, I compare the number of marriages that occurred annually, counted as an average of the years (table 8.1). The similarity [in Upper and Lower Romerike] is certainly striking. And even more clearly will the situation appear when we count separately each of the two 10-year periods. Here the great similarities are shown in that in each of the districts, the number of marriages relative to a comparison with the whole country is small for 1831–1840 and medium large for 1841–1850 (see the fuller explanation for this in my study *On Marriage in Norway* [*Selected Works* 2:288, 292]).

Table 8.1. Marriages per year in Upper and Lower Romerike

	1831–1840	1841–1850	During Entire Period 1831–1850
Upper Romerike, Solør, and Odal	60.8	78.4	70.0
Lower Romerike	62.8	77.7	70.5

In the same manner as the frequency of marriages (not the volume) conforms to the means of making a living, the people's concept of what their standard of living should be who wish to start families conforms also to the conditions regarding moving out or moving in for the most part in the same environment; and therefore it is of some interest to note that during the 10 years from 1835 to 1845, a similar outflow took place. In Upper Romerike, Solør, and Odal, the out-migrants made up 2.3 percent of the population, and in Lower Romerike, 2.7 percent.

But alongside all these similarities in the external environment and in the daily morality of domestic life and custom, there is still a marked *difference* between these same communities, and that is the matter of illegitimate births. The part of the Christiania diocese that lies east of the Christiania fjord comes to mind, Mjøsen and the Valdres mountains, and I investigate the condition of illegitimate births deanery by deanery; I find that the matter is unequally worse in each of the four deaneries in the northern part (Gudbrandsdal, Østerdal, Hedemark, plus Upper Romerike with Odal and Solør, together with group 2 in several of the foregoing tables) than in any of the five deaneries in the southern part (Lower Romerike and the four deanery offices in the administrative districts of Borge, together with group 1 in the tables). And the most noteworthy is the steep transition from the better to the worse, and that this steep transition from the lighter area to the darker should fall precisely between Lower and Upper Romerike, which still seem as though they should be the same in all characteristics. I have already mentioned this in connection with table 1 (chapter 1) where we found that for 100 married couples the number of illegitimate children in the first-named district corresponds to that of the place in the kingdom where the conditions are worst, while the condition in the last district is a little better than usual in the kingdom. And this wide difference is doubly noteworthy when we find that it is reflected from time to time so constantly and cannot be explained away as a coincidence. Note the condition in each of the two 10-year periods from 1831 to 1850 (table 8.2).

Table 8.2. Illegitimate births per year in Upper and Lower Romerike

	1831–1840	1841–1850	During Entire Period 1831–1850
Upper Romerike, Solør, and Odal	47.1	55.9	52.3
Lower Romerike	28.1	30.9	29.7

But this situation, where Solør and Odal are calculated together with Upper Romerike, results in figures not quite fitting with the comparison between Upper and Lower Romerike with which this chapter deals. Therefore, I have taken the lists of marriages, etc., which the pastors have sent to the statistics office. From them I have carried out the calculations for the 14 years 1841–1854 for each parish in table 8.3.

Table 8.3 shows clearly that when we take the two first districts, except the small peripheral parishes of Hurdal and Odal, together with Lower Romerike Sørum, one can judge by the table that there is a far worse condition in each of the parishes in the two first districts than in random parishes in Lower Romerike, both during 1841–1847 and 1848–1854, one period after another. The condition is such that when we

Table 8.3. Illegitimate births in Upper and Lower Romerike

District	Parish	Illegitimate Live Births for Each 100 Marriages 1811–1847	1848–1854
Solør and Odal	Hof[a]	78	81
	Grue	48	60
	Vinger	49	52
	Strøm	45	48
	North Odal	30	33
District Total		53	58
Upper Romerike	Hurdal	36	32
	Eidsvoll	62	60
	Næs	55	55
	Nannestad	78	75
	Gjerdrum	54	47
	Ullensaker	68	62
District Total		60	57
Lower Romerike	Sørum	60	60
	Urskoug	30	39
	Høland	20	27
	Fet	26	21
	Enebok	34	26
	Skedsmo	35	35
	Nittedal	23	28
District Total		31	32

[a] Includes Aasnæs and Vaaler

imagine Sørum as part of Upper Romerike, which has a common boundary, there would then be a conspicuously sharp boundary between the southern and somewhat lighter district compared with the northern and dark district. (There is an irregularity in this kind of comparison between different parishes because until 1851, there were, so to speak, different labels used among pastors, so that some recorded as legitimate quite a few of the children whom others recorded as illegitimate. This irregularity becomes reasonably less in investigations for larger districts, where it can be assumed that there are some pastors who use the milder, and others the more severe, labels, so that the difference can be balanced. But more of this in chapter 9.)

For one who has had the patience to follow the entire presentation and put oneself in all the situations, it is reasonable to expect criticism. It is certainly known (see chapter 5) that the matter of the illegitimate births is really clearly worse in the working class than in the owner class, and now one can think thus: "It is possible that the situation regarding illegitimate births, particularly in the working class and in the owner class, is equally bad in Lower Romerike as in the other districts, and the difference that the figures show is only ostensibly because the working class is relatively smaller in number in Lower Romerike." But in reality it is rather the opposite, so that the condition that the figures reveal for both classes is thereby much more marked. Since when I count in the owner class government employees and officials plus farm owners, and in the working class I count cotters and day workers plus servant folk (and the other classes that the population census list are so few that they could be excluded), I find according to the publications of the population census in 1845 the relationships shown in table 8.4.

Table 8.4. Frequency of illegitimate births in different classes, 1845

	Owner Class	Working Class
Solør and Odal	100	190
Upper Romerike	100	180
Lower Romerike	100	213

Here we see that the working class is clearly relatively more numerous in Lower Romerike, and if it were so that the moral condition and therefore the frequency of illegitimate births observed separately for each of the two classes were the same in different districts, then the matter observed separately would look worse in the same Lower Romerike instead of the opposite.

The matter is so extraordinary that I dare to hope the reader will stay with me in the continuation of this investigation.

The figures that have heretofore been presented on the illegitimate births are, as mentioned, found with the help of reports from the pastors to the statistical office, and all pastors have contributed here. Now I shall present some figures from the reports in the foregoing frequently discussed reports from the pastors to me, but unfortunately, these reports are not complete. They have come in only from the following parishes in Solør plus Upper Romerike: Hof, Grue, Vinger, Strøm, Northern Odal, Hurdal, Eidsvoll, and Gjerdrum. For Lower Romerike they have come in from all parishes except Sørum. When in the following I mention figures on the different districts, it should accordingly be recalled that only a portion of them apply. After these two reports, I can initiate investigations separately for each of the two classes of the population, the owner and the working class (classes I and II).

The situation regarding the married couples from each class (each couple is placed in the class to which the bridegroom belonged) during the year 1851–1852 is shown in table 8.5.

Table 8.5. Married couples in different classes, 1851–1852

	Class I	Class II	Total
Upper Romerike, Solør, and Odal	37	63	100
Lower Romerike	32	68	100

In lower Romerike there were relatively more married couples in the working class than in the other district, which agrees with the recently discovered condition between the two classes in the districts (see *On Marriage in Norway* [*Selected Works* 2:300], where the conditions for the married couples are given for the whole of Christiania and Christiansand dioceses).

The frequency of illegitimate births, counted individually for each of the two classes, can be expressed as follows: For each 100 bridegrooms or brides of each class, the numbers of fathers or mothers during 1851–1852 are shown in table 8.6.

Table 8.6. Frequency of illegitimate births in different classes, 1851–1852

	Fathers		Mothers	
	Class I	Class II	Class I	Class II
Upper Romerike, Solør, and Odal	29	83	13	99
Lower Romerike	16	36	9	39

In each of these districts we do find the same thing as in table 5.2, that the condition for each sex is worse in class II than in class I; in addition, the condition for females in class I is better; in class II, on the other hand, it's worse than for males; and this agreement with the previously noted rule can teach us that the current figures, although only supported by reports from a few parishes, are still valid. But therein we see from these same figures that the condition thoughout, both in class I and class II, is worse in Upper Romerike, etc., than in Lower Romerike. It was therefore correct when we already previously arrived at the result that the difference that the figures revealed for both classes were not apparent but real.

Or is it possible that in Upper Romerike with Odal and Solør more illegitimate children were born, that a greater portion of these later became legitimate by the subsequent marriages of the parents, so that the situation is not then in reality as unfortunate as it has appeared hitherto? This will possibly be seen in table 8.7 for the years 1850 and 1851 for married couples; among every 100 of them, the numbers given had children together (1) before marriage, (2) within four months after marriage, or (3) between four and eight months of marriage.

Table 8.7. Married couples with illegitimate children, 1850–1851

	In Class I			In Class II		
	1	2	3	1	2	3
Upper Romerike, Solør, and Odal	7	23	10	25	25	10
Lower Romerike[a]	6	19	8	24	32	12

[a] Here there is a lack of reports for Sørum, also for Skedsmo.

It is certainly true, as we see here, that in Upper Romerike there are a few more married couples who had children together before the ceremony, and these children we must regard as first being recorded as illegitimate and later becoming legitimate. But the difference is so small that it can hardly affect the larger and unfavorable difference in the number of illegitimate children for Upper Romerike. In Upper Romerike it is also the case that a relatively larger number of children are born and brought up out of wedlock (see table 6.7).

Previously we found (table 7.2) that in the areas where, on the whole, there are a relatively large number of illegitimate births, there are also more frequently such outrageous occurrences that one and the same person more often repeats the offence, becoming a father or a mother time after time. Does the pattern apply here? Does it show that these two districts that have the most illegitimate births, namely, Upper Romerike, etc., also have the most repeated occurrences? The answer is contained in the figures that are calculated from reports for both classes for the year 1851–1852 (table 8.8).

Table 8.8. Repetitions of illegitimate births, 1851–1852

	First Time	Twice or Oftener	Total
Fathers			
Upper Romerike, Solør, and Odal	81	19	100
Lower Romerike[a]	87	13	100
Mothers			
Upper Romerike, Solør, and Odal	76	24	100
Lower Romerike[a]	78	22	100

[a] Skedsmo is again excluded.

The condition is more unfavorable for the first district; for both men and women the repeated occurrences are most frequent. That repetitions in both places are more frequent among women than among men is a fact that agrees with what we found before as the usual rule.

What has been presented shows us that the condition of illegitimate births is really worse in Upper Romerike with Odal and Solør than in Lower Romerike, worse in each of the two classes, worse in regard to the volume of illegitimate births on the whole, and in regard to the more outrageous repeated occurrences. It would assist an explanation of the cause for this unfortunate difference in Upper Romerike if we knew that it was more difficult to get ahead and that therefore more of the young people had to delay marriage. In the foregoing we did find a calculation in which the size of the population was taken into account, that there was a conspicuously great similarity in the frequency of marriage in both districts; but the calculation is not so dependable that one might desire to test it with another calculation, and therefore I present a calculation of the ages of the married couples. This calculation relates only to the married young men and women during the years 1851 and 1852 in the various age groups shown in table 8.9.

Table 8.9. Age of marriage in different classes, 1851–1852

	Under 25 Years	Between 25 and 30 Years	Over 30 Years	Total
Class I men				
Upper Romerike, Solør, and Odal	24	42	34	100
Lower Romerike	22	33	45	100
Class I women				
Upper Romerike, Solør, and Odal	53	31	16	100
Lower Romerike	52	32	16	100
Class II men				
Upper Romerike, Solør, and Odal	29	45	26	100
Lower Romerike	30	44	26	100
Class II women				
Upper Romerike, Solør, and Odal	44	38	18	100
Lower Romerike[a]	38	47	15	100

[a] In addition to Sørum, reports from Urskoug are also lacking.

These figures show us that there are in Upper Romerike rather more men and women who marry at a young age, under 25 years of age. People there accordingly do not have an excuse for their fornication because they must delay establishing families because of difficult economic conditions. On the contrary, since there are so many young people among the married couples in Upper Romerike, one should more readily conclude that the two evils are due to casual marriages and fornication.

It was hoped that perhaps one could probably quickly arrive at an understanding of the entire situation by pursuing the investigations a little further—unimportant as it may appear to most people—which I shall now explain (table 8.10).

Table 8.10. Remarried widowers and widows

	Young Men	Widowers	Total
Upper Romerike, Solør, and Odal	90	10	100
Lower Romerike	89	11	100
	Women	Widows	Total
Upper Romerike, Solør, and Odal	96	4	100
Lower Romerike	95	5	100

Here we see that in the district where there were the most illegitimate births and most repeated occurrences of them, there were fewest repeated marriages or fewest remarried widowers and widows, which quite agrees with the previously found pattern for the diocese of Christiania and Christiansand.

In pursuit of these explanations of the reports the pastors gave me, I shall still supply some statistical items that in one way or another contribute to throwing some light on this subject.

I showed some figures in the foregoing from the population census that gave the impression that in comparison with the owner class, the working class population was likely more numerous in Lower than in Upper Romerike. There is a particular circumstance about the same thing that I will show. I group together on one side (as before) farm owners, civil servants, and officials, and these only the heads of families, not the women and children. On the other side, I group the following types of workers: (1) cotters with land, (2) day laborers and cotters without land, and (3) servant men; and I find that for each 100 persons of the owner class, the three types of workers were as shown in table 8.11.

Table 8.11. Numbers and types of workers per 100 of owner class

	Class 1	Class 2	Class 3	Total
Solør and Odal	89	48	53	190
Upper Romerike	81	43	56	180
Lower Romerike	109	39	65	213

It is apparent Lower Romerike has the most numerous worker population when noted on the whole or in a total, which is the reason, as will be doubly clear to most people, that the moral condition is best precisely here. But on the other side, the two districts have relatively the most people of the part of the worker population that must be regarded as having a condition that is critical, namely, day laborers and landless cotters, where on the contrary, Lower Romerike has more cotters with land and permanent servant men. One can then suggest the following observation: in Lower Romerike the moral condition is best because there are relatively more families there in a good and well-regarded position (with many workers under them), families accordingly that can be regarded as occupying a position corresponding to their education and sense of honor. And a relatively larger part of the working class—those at a young age as servant boys and servant girls (for each 100 persons in the working class the number of servant girls were: in Solør and Odal, 86; in Upper Romerike, 85; and in Lower Romerike, 92)—have in a manner been brought up in a better house, as it is called, which encourages order and good morals by better attitudes to acquire the desired level of livelihood of the many cotters with land. (In any case, it has seemed reasonable to me that a division of ownership in the rural areas or a greater tendency to subdivide the land, whereby it became easier for young people to get ahead even though poor and become independent farmers or owners, must—by the encouragement that lay therein for the young—have improved morals. And that there are fewer cotters and servants in Upper Romerike plus Solør and Odal seems to be evidence of a more frequent subdivision of land into smaller farms.)

But before I maintain that this observation should be commonly valid, I must thus point out that the difference in the number of the less fortunate cotters without land plus the day laborers, which the figures presented suggest, seems so small that the great difference in the moral condition can hardly be explained by that alone.

I can still point out another difference between the two districts, according to reports that are found in my study, *About Mortality in Norway.* For each 1,000 living persons and for each 1,000 deaths in Upper Romerike with Solør and Odal, the number in Lower Romerike was as shown in table 8.12.

Table 8.12. Number of persons and number of deaths per 1,000 in Upper Romerike

Year	Living	Years	Deaths
1835	387	1831–1835	424
		1836–1840	432
1845	378	1841–1845	415
		1846–1850	394

Lower Romerike is much smaller than the other district; therefore, the number of people or the number of living and, likewise, the number of deaths is much smaller (387 instead of 1,000, etc.). But now it is apparent that the number of deaths is also not much smaller in Lower

Romerike than the number of living; in Lower Romerike, accordingly, there are more deaths relatively, or mortality is greater than in the other district. The greater number of deaths can probably be attributed to a different physical constitution, and this in turn can probably be attributed to a difference in state of mind, and the difference in state of mind can probably again exercise a different influence on how people manage—these are speculations I still do not dare dwell on longer.

In this connection, it may be of interest to see an explanation of the expenses for poor relief in these districts. And for all of Lower Romerike plus most of the two other districts, I can map out the explanation in table 8.13.

Table 8.13. Expenses for poor relief[a]

	Population 1845	Mean Annual Expenses for Poor Relief, 1850–1853		Annual Expense per Resident
		spd.	*sk.*	*sk.*
Solør and Odal	27,903	10,405	118	45
Upper Romerike	23,812	12,385	53	62
Lower Romerike	23,034	8,652	65	45

[a] According to a position paper regarding the poor relief system that a Royal Commission of that time had prepared. Neither Aasnæs and Vaaler in Solør nor Hurdal in Upper Romerike are included.

Here it can be seen that the expenses are relatively greater in Upper compared with Lower Romerike, and there one can observe a connection with the difference in the moral condition, thus: the greater immorality leads to greater poverty and in turn greater expense for the parishes. But then one should expect greater poverty in Solør and Odal, and this expectation does not follow. We must therefore remember that as certain as it is that immorality contributes to poverty, there are so many other factors that combine to make the public poor-relief expenditures larger or smaller that we should not expect much of this comparison.

It is more likely that knowledge and the level of education must contribute a great deal to the understanding of the moral condition of the people. In the years 1840 and 1843, the Norwegian Department of Education carried out extensive and detailed studies about the educational system nationwide, and these we ought to make use of. I have found that in the aforementioned years, there were so-and-so many (or few) public school teachers (at ambulatory and permanent schools) that each teacher had on average the number of school children shown in table 8.14.

Table 8.14. School children per teacher

	1826	1836	1837	1840
Solør and Odal	89	98	112	113
Upper Romerike		118	113	106
Lower Romerike	91	111	116	107

On average, each teacher had a teaching income and an income as sexton as shown in table 8.15.

Table 8.15. Income per teacher

	1837	1840
Solør and Odal	40 spd.	37 spd.
Upper Romerike	39 spd.	42 spd.
Lower Romerike	35 spd.	37 spd.

According to this information, it does not appear that the more favorable moral condition in Lower Romerike can be attributed to the greater effort of the municipalities to pay the teachers and to pay them better.

But the school system hardly depends entirely on how the school is managed by the school administrators but also on how it is used by the public and sought by the children. About this also the studies contain considerable information, and I will present the following.

Of every 100 children who should be in school, the figures shown in table 8.16 in the years listed reveal quite a bit of neglect.

Table 8.16. Percentage of children not in school

	1837	1840
Solør and Odal	8	7
Upper Romerike	9	12
Lower Romerike	4	8

Of every 100 children, the numbers shown in table 8.17 received instruction in more than the most elementary, namely, (1) writing and (2) arithmetic.

When we ignore Solør and Odal and compare only the two Romerike districts that particularly interest us, these figures reveal to us actually something that is associated with the difference found in regard to morals: in Lower Romerike, there is a more diligent school attendance with both less neglect and more training in the somewhat higher sub-

Table 8.17. Children receiving more than elementary instruction

	1837		1840	
	Writing	Arithmetic	Writing	Arithmetic
	(*percent*)	(*percent*)	(*percent*)	(*percent*)
Solør and Odal	19	7	18	7
Upper Romerike	12	6	14	8
Lower Romerike	15	7	20	10

jects. But I must add that as detailed as these tables are, while constructing them I have found so many traces of errors in the computation of the original lists, particularly pertaining to neglect in school attendance, that not much reliance can be placed on them on the whole. I have produced them to show that I have not spared any effort to get to the bottom of the matter.

When I now summarize the entire content of this chapter, small and great, important and unimportant, I pose the problem thus: What is there about the particular relationships in the moral condition that are revealed in illegitimate births? Is there an unmistakable and quite large difference between Upper and Lower Romerike, outside of what I heretofore have been able to discover, some corresponding great clear difference in the history of the people, in the manner of making a living, in the social conditions, in domestic life, and in the daily customs and practices?

It should be expected that there must be a connection here—that the moral atmosphere and ways of thinking little by little must give domestic life their peculiar character, that within the prevailing concepts of domestic life and customs they must little by little exercise their influence on the emerging generation and give the journey and behavior in life its own direction, etc. And since up to now I have discovered no such relationship, the matter, therefore, is still to me one of the many mysteries of social life.

One will probably say to me: "That which has the major influence on human moral behavior is their religious spirituality, and therefore you should first and foremost have paid attention to what difference there might be between the two observed communities in this regard." But religiosity is the part of the character of a person that is the most difficult for one to make some sense of and that is the least capable of being judged. On the other hand, I have thought that the cause of the revealed differences regarding morality might be the possibility that during a recent or distant past there has been in one community a fortunate group of government officials (and one does not need to think only of the clergy) and other men of great influence who—themselves inspired by a regard for the worth of human beings and duty—have contributed to the maintenance of this spirit in the larger population; and that in the other community, on the other hand, there has been a larger number of prominent men who by word and deed have been destructive rather than constructive. But the actual painful fragmentary reports that well-known men in the communities have given me have not supported the idea that research in this direction would be of any particular yield or any return.

So the whole matter is for me like a mystery; I observe a definite difference between the moral conditions of the two neighboring communities, and I know that this difference must have a cause, but I have not found this cause, not yet. "A poor return," one will probably say, and up to now I might excuse myself by explaining that, in addition to earlier trips and very short visits, my stay in some of the communities in Upper and Lower Romerike has been limited to a few weeks in the fall of 1855 and a few weeks at the end of the winter of 1856, all together 73 days—an explanation that will be accepted when it is known that pastors with regard to their individual parishes say as follows: "I have been here only one year, so I dare not say that I know the condition of the people and their customs clearly yet." But while I naturally must regard my work so far only as a beginning and preparation, the benefit thereof for me is this: I myself have in the past joined in the stories, as travelers often do, saying that in comparison with the peripheral mountain areas, Romerike (as the leading group of communities surrounding the nearby bigger places) is a shameful area with a characterless folk life—and now in the middle of this dullness and colorlessness, there has been presented to me an enigma, a remarkable fact, which is such that it can capture both an idea and has the power to fascinate. Many attempts will probably be made, and there will be a challenge that requires the assistance of several men with the same interest if it is at all possible to succeed in discovering the relationship and to understand the mystery, but the problem arouses interest by the fact that the overwhelming relationship and commonality between the two neighboring communities makes their differences in morality so completely unexpected that—to the extent this mystery *can* be solved—we should undoubtedly have made a long step forward in the understanding of similar conditions in other areas of our country also.

9

Have New Laws Made Moral Conditions Worse?

A highly regarded fellow citizen and scientist, in connection with my conclusion in my study last year, *On Marriage in Norway,* has honored me with an official letter from which I present a few selections.

What has truly prompted these lines is the remarkable increase in illegitimate births during the 10 years 1841–1850 compared with the 10 years 1831–1840, or more specifically, the explanation you made on page 138 [*Selected Works* 2:269—Translator] for the cause of this phenomenon. I have tried to make use of the reasons you proposed; but I have not been satisfied with them. Here it is not a question of "a great number, but not many relatively." (Here the letter writer cites the results of his statistical calculations that I later shall consider.—Sundt) Since I could not arrive at a satisfactory explanation for this steep and distinct increase in illegitimate births during the 10 years, 1841–1850, that you provided, I began to mull over another cause, and I believe I have found one which at least for the time being I have found satisfactory and which I want to report for your consideration and examination. I asked myself if something had been introduced during the 10 years 1841–1850 that could have contributed to this marked rise in the number of illegitimate births, something that possibly had exerted a destructive influence on the moral outlook of the people. And I immediately recalled that the new criminal law with its much-too-mild (I do not wish to say liberal, but rather, irresponsible) views of crimes of adultery and immorality just then went into effect during these 10 years. Already during the five years 1841–1845, the difference is revealed quite clearly, even though the law was in effect for only three years. If one could compare the 10 years immediately prior to its implementation, or 1843–1852 with 1833–1842, it is possible that the difference would have been conspicuous and that my explanation for this sudden and unprecedented increase in illegitimate births could hardly be rejected without good reason. (I am able here to provide the writer with the following information on the number of illegitimate live births: for 1833–1842, 25,386 and for 1843–1852, 35,560, which figures show an increase of not less than 40 percent for the 10 years before the criminal law was put into effect. —SUNDT) Here I must regret in the foregoing that the stillbirths are not reported in your book; these naturally must be included when one wants to use the frequency or the infrequency of illegitimate births as an indicator to judge the moral status of the nation. (This is quite right, but the official lists do not have the information on the stillbirths that were illegitimate before the year 1837. —SUNDT) I am supported so much more in my explanation by recalling a conversation I had with a sheriff in the year 1846. The criminal law had been in effect for 3½ years, and according to the sheriff's experience, had had a destructive impact on the people's morals in his district. He even told me that the dissatisfaction with this new law was so great and general that there was thought of introducing into the Parliament a recommendation for changes in the section that dealt with crimes of adultery and immorality. In particular, he complained about the decision that crimes of adultery are not prosecuted by the authorities unless the offended spouse files a formal complaint. He also reported a recent case that confirmed his opinion about the unfitness of the law in this section. A married man had a wench in his house with whom he lived in an improper relationship. The wench was the dominant one. Even the wife had to obey her. The wife complained to the sheriff, but then she got the message that nothing would be done about the matter if she did not appear before the court as a proper informer and complainant. So the woman declared that she would then rather suffer in silence. Many times I have been sorry that I did not follow up on this line of inquiry in order to gather more information during my short forays that I have made here and there almost every summer in the communities. But I do not need to leave my residence in order to hear about so many examples of increasing irresponsibility by the lowering of the existing barriers that contribute to the idea that adultery is now regarded as a trivial peccadillo. It is not impossible also that the Poor Law of 1845 might have contributed its part. Particularly, I believe that many women in the poorer class have become easier to seduce on the grounds that they now depend more on help from public assistance than before.

That the criminal law has been damaging in other directions as well should not be difficult to demonstrate. With the help of the figures in your book on marriage, page 128 [*Selected Works* 2:262–63—TRANSLATOR], it can be calculated that during the five years that ended two years before the criminal law went into effect, there was one conviction per 855 persons in the country, and during the three-year period beginning after the law was in effect, there was one conviction per 571 persons. Accordingly, since I believe that the criminal law has resulted in more crimes of morality by its mildness and its destructive influence on the attitudes toward such crimes, I likewise believe that the same causes have influenced more crimes on property.

Here the letter writer recalls the law that lay on the public treasury the cost of delinquencies in payments; it is reasonable that this has had an influence on the crimes committed being reported to the authorities, and he continues thus:

> Just as I now on one side am inclined to believe that the greater amount of lawbreaking revealed in the statistical tables for the last 10 to 15 years does not need to be seen without qualifications as undeniable evidence of a greater moral depravity and growing coarseness among the Norwegian people, likewise I am inclined to believe on the other side that if the people's morals have actually become looser in several directions during the last 10 to 15 years, this can be attributed on equal grounds to the unfortunate laws that have come out, like other causes, during that period. Among such laws can be mentioned the criminal law, the poor law, and the laws regarding the distilling of liquor at home and the sale of liquor. The liquor law in particular has brought abut many false oaths or false explanations from witnesses. Might not one well remark that many of our new laws are based more on philosophical speculations than on Christian principles and on knowledge of life and people? That our legal concepts have been based more on judicial theories than the attitudes of the Norwegian people that are the product of the Christian spirit and centuries of human experience? One hears often now that our pastors are more Christian in spirit and more zealous than before, that church attendance is more diligent than before, that the school system is clearly better than before, that drunkenness is decreasing more and more, that the standard of living is improving and spreading in all directions. This is quite true and is very fortunate. But alongside this, still crime and illegitimacy increase. How shall one make sense of this? Truly there must be "something rotten" [This English expression is in the original.—TRANSLATOR] somewhere, and this "something rotten" I assume must be sought in our new laws and their applications. Is this idea valid, and if its validity can be demonstrated with the help of our statistical tables, then . . .

Here the letter writer directs an honorable appeal to me to carry out this work; he means, namely, that a study on this must contain important information for the higher classes. He continues:

> By the higher classes, I mean the bourgeoisie, to which our local government administrators, our parliamentary men, belong. For to

these classes the most convincing arguments are those supported by statistical tables. If the more influential sector of the nation is to be convinced of the need for changes in several of our newer laws, then this must take place to demonstrate their destructive impact. . . . I can well imagine that a change in some of our newer laws (e.g., the criminal law) would be decried by the lawyers as a reversal, a backward step, reactionary. But so be it! History shows us perpetually forward and backward movements, ebbtide and high tide, revolution and reaction in politics, in morality, in attitudes. The Criminal Law of 1842 was a revolution in our legislation, a sudden and violent change in it. It went too far to loosen accustomed bonds on the desires of the flesh. There are now 12 years of experience to cite for its going too far. A little tightening of the bonds, therefore, seems to be necessary. If this need is recognized, well, then tighten the bond again! The most difficult task of a lawmaker is surely to rectify his own misconceptions. It is bad to be wrong in concept, but still worse to let it remain unrectified. But even if one should not want to rectify the legislative misconception of 1842 and 1845 by direct changes in the law complained about, still, a clear presentation of the destructive influence of these misconceptions could be the most convincing argument for the necessity to do more, much more, for the education of society both in city and country than has been done heretofore. What could there not have been accomplished for this cause if the annual expenditures resulting from the criminal law and the law regarding delinquency were directed to the public school system! An annual expenditure of $100,000 must have gone a long way.

When I note in the concluding remark in your book *On Marriage in Norway* that you intend to publish a special study about illegitimate births in Norway, and since I have not been able to find any trace of that in the aforementioned writing, I have taken the liberty in the foregoing to develop the destructive influence of the criminal law in this chapter. Thus, I regarded it as my duty to make you aware of this idea. If you find it acceptable, I ask you to make use of it. In any case, will you subject it to a deeper analysis? And I would be pleased if you would be convinced to try again, since I am fully aware of the difficulties and doubts that the new law can rectify such things.

In this way I have taken the liberty to quote the letter writer in full, because I find in it a clear expression for a thought that I believe is nurtured by quite a few men in this country. Among common people I have found a characteristic inclination for strict laws against immoral behavior, frivolous marriages, drunkenness: profligacies that the coarseness of the lower classes makes them fall into and which should be outlawed. What is particularly concerning about immorality is the common observation that it has gotten worse now for a time, and it is clear that the cause is the change in the legislation which has come about recently. In the frequently mentioned reports from the pastors, I also find many expressions in this direction. A pastor in the Stavanger area deals with this in detail in that he also describes the common people's understanding of the problem. First, he reports for his parish some statistics for the five years 1843–1847 and 1848–1852, which showed that the illegitimate births have increasingly changed to the better during the last five-year period; thereupon he continues as follows: "This is in the meantime certainly only fortuitous, and antoher unfavorable period appears again. Since there are otherwise many causes why the conditions in the later period have worsened, this is completely probable. Above all, it seems here that the milder legislation has had a very destructive influence. Punishment, particularly for the lower classes, has, in effect, diminished, and just because the pastor has now little to do herewith (here we point to the situation that since the reporting of adultery according to the new law was not obligatory but dependent on the complaint of the aggrieved party, thus it is not a matter for the minister to report this kind of crime, which became known to the authorities), it is seen as a result of the indifference on his part that he lets fornication go unpunished. Therefore it is seen almost as permissible, and soon it is not shameful. The attitude that hates this relaxed legislation has been of some support, but this is soon ready to fall. The common people also regard this legislation as initiated by higher-status persons who also want freedom themselves in this behavior—as if it is obvious that the inappropriateness of punishment by bread and water is made up by gluttons who regard happiness as a good meal—and one smiles at the extreme stupidity among those who believe that those who are under the sheriff live as well or better than otherwise."

This view, that it was the stupidity and lust of the upper class that was the origin of the changes in the laws discussed, I have not yet encountered, and there must certainly be extremely few people who are so naive as to think so. But many believe that the newer laws have been unfortunate and have had a destructive influence.

This thought I find expressed at a pastors' meeting in Tromsø in 1852 as reported in the *Journal of Theology* (4: 460): as an associated cause (of the start of the increase in immorality) it is believed that one can suggest that the later milder laws have contributed, even though only indirectly, to the promotion of immorality. "Finally there were complaints that the newer legislation supported the efforts of the church so little, and since this group should not be silent about this, it was agreed that they should express a fervent wish that this legislation in effect must be changed so that it would be more supportive of the efforts that must be regarded as the duty of a Christian nation to recognize."

ACTUAL FIGURES ON ILLEGITIMATE BIRTHS

Recently the number of illegitimate births—the indicator of immorality—has increased to a marked degree, it is certain; in recent times, namely, in 1842, another criminal law also appeared which in a special chapter establishes how crimes of immorality should be handled. And now it is commonly thought that there is a relationship between cause and effect in that this new law with its milder decisions is supposed to be blamed for this evil.

But this view does not hold water, at least not in regard to the condition in the country as a whole.

The following is what Professor Schweigaard says in his explanation of the criminal law with regard to the 18th chapter of the same, which deals with immorality:

> In determining boundaries for the punishability of immorality, the new law is standing in the same footsteps of the previous criminal law in effect. According to the last interpretation, sexual intercourse outside ofmarriage wasn't commonly punishable, and was brought before justice only on the grounds of a particular action by persons or deeds involved. And since in the main, this is the same according to the 18th chapter of the law that has been replaced, the new law continues the law in this part of the criminal law more, therein that the magnitude of the punishment is changed and on the whole diminished in that the grounds of punishability are narrowed or widened.

Accordingly, approximately the same deeds that were punishable before are still so, and the punishments of the same deeds are on the whole milder now than before. But if one undertakes a closer comparison between the magnitude of the punishment before and after the change, the definite impression one gets is that the reduced severity of the law discussed cannot have made much difference one way or another, since it is so trivial that most people were likely not aware of it. By this comparison between before and now, I do not go as far back as the law of the country of 1687, which was hasty in establishing strict punishment; here the comparison can only be made by taking into account the nature of law and justice in the generation that immediately preceded the new law.

On the other hand, the new law has introduced another change that does not concern what deed is punishable, and what punishment can be applied, but is of an entirely different character; the change is that while adultery previously was without further ado an object for the courts, now the courts can act only if the aggrieved spouse places a complaint and calls upon the authorities who can punish. Now it is certainly so that many adulterers thereby escape all punishment in that the aggrieved spouse often and for many reasons will not bring suit and does not want the punishment carried out, and it is certainly not unreasonable to assume that these abominable kinds of offences have become somewhat more frequent now than earlier; it then depends on whether the very indignation among neighbors and acquaintances moved the existing authorities to punish by word. Possibly this had an influence in limiting ungodliness just as effective as that of the previous stricter law, since to an adulterer who does not show serious remorse, the expression "you should not eat with one like that," might be effective. But so be it that these kinds of moral crimes have increased in frequency because of the new law; fortunately, this is the type of immorality that is so seldom practiced in our country that some increase in the number of these cases will not have much moral significance for the complete number of crimes. Most of the illegitimate children (and it is these numbers we should stick to) belong to unmarried parents, and what impact would this matter have on them? Oh yes, it is said that the most abominable violators, adulterers, go unpunished, that they break down the concept of morality in general, and that the young, the unmarried folk, then engage in the improper behavior without any guilt.

But has one also become thoroughly acquainted with the situation? The law went into effect at the beginning of 1843, and from that time the legal system's apparent indifference to adulterers should exercise its unfortunate influence on the weakly established virtues of the unmarried population. Is it conceivable that this had already happened by the end of the same year 1843, such that the moral condition accordingly should in a marked degree be worsened by the beginning of 1844? So? But then we must wait until the year 1845, because as a result there is evidence of some increased numbers of full-term illegitimate children when they were baptized and entered in the church records. But the view that it was the new law that bore the blame for the later marked increase in the number of illegitimate births shows otherwise because the increase occurred and with great suddenness already in the years 1841 and 1842. This is obvious in the simple rows of figures of the number of live-born illegitimate births in the nation, contained in table 9.1.

In trying to determine the circumstances that exercise various influences on the people's morals and status, it is very easy to make a mistake when one does not have an overview of the conditions over a longer time, and therefore I have included the reports for all the years from the beginning of the century. Now glance up and down at the tables

Table 9.1. Live-born illegitimate children in Norway, 1801–1855

Year		Year		Year	
1801	1,470	1820	2,380	1839	2,332
1802	1,323	1821	2,709	1840	2,474
1803	1,509	1822	2,531	1841	2,683
1804	1,556	1823	2,539	1842	3,277
1805	1,594	1824	2,445	1843	3,257
1806	1,749	1825	2,446	1844	3,157
1807	1,732	1826	2,620	1845	3,357
1808	1,697	1827	2,533	1846	3,456
1809	1,373	1828	2,419	1847	3,561
1810	1,521	1829	2,503	1848	3,220
1811	1,761	1830	2,539	1849	3,527
1812	1,771	1831	2,455	1850	3,715
1813	1,557	1832	2,247	1851	4,090
1814	1,374	1833	2,399	1852	4,220
1815	1,845	1834	2,395	1853	4,144
1816	2,585	1835	2,615	1854	4,533
1817	2,455	1836	2,499	1855	4,603
1818	2,384	1837	2,383		
1819	2,332	1838	2,329		

to become acquainted with them so as to have an overview of the many small changes from one year to the next; it is then easy to discover a very striking situation: it is not enough that the number of illegitimate births have increased markedly from the beginning to the end of the 55-year period, but this increase has occurred sort of in fits and starts to certain high levels. In this regard, we can quite clearly differentiate four different periods, namely, the years 1801–1815, 1816–1840, 1841–1850, and 1851–1855. I can make the matter graphic (table 9.2) by putting side by side the figures for the year in each of these periods, which reveals the highest and the lowest figures, a comparison in which I disregard the years 1815 and 1841, which in a way form the bridge from one period to the other. It is obvious that the highest figure in a previous period is lower than the lowest figure in the following period.

The differences between the four periods can also be presented in such manner that we select the annual average of illegitimate births in each period and observe the increase from one period to the other (table 9.2).

Table 9.2. Increases in illegitimate births

Period	Lowest Figure	Highest Figure	Annual Average Annual Income	(%)
1801–1815	1,323	1,771	1,589	
1816–1840	2,247	2,709	2,462	55
1841–1850	3,157	3,715	3,321	35
1851–1855	4,090	4,603	4,318	30

Here I will immediately explain that for the figures for 1851–1855 there is a particular circumstance so that we are unable to use them anymore. In earlier times it was customary for pastors that if a child was born out of wedlock, when baptized it was still entered in the church record as legitimate if the parents by that time were married or desired to get married and their subsequent marriage was regarded as certain. But in 1851, the Department of Internal Affairs, in which statistical agency the pastors belong, issued a directive with the order that all children born out of wedlock should without mercy be recorded as illegitimate; accordingly, a stricter nomenclature resulted, whereby it had to look like there was an increase, although in reality the situation was likely the same as before.

If we stay only with the foregoing overview for the years 1801–1850, we find two circumstances that do not support the view of the law as the cause of the increase in the number of illegitimate births during the later period. First, this increase had already occurred before the law was in effect, i.e., before its presumed influence could become visible, and next, a similar strong and sudden increase had occurred once before, from 1816 on, when there was no such law that could be blamed.

CHANGES IN THE POPULATION

Partly to go to an extreme to show us that the unfavorable view of the influence of the law is not correct, partly to discover what contributes to an understanding of this element in the condition and morals of the people which illegitimate births suggest, we should plan to find out what the true cause can have been for the remarkable condition that has recently been revealed, and the large, sudden, lasting increase in the number of illegitimate births from 1816 and from 1841 on.

In this connection I must make you aware of a remarkable relationship between marriages and illegitimate births that I will first present with the help of table 9.3.

This table is arranged so that by letting the eye follow the line from the left to the right, one finds the number of married couples for one year and the illegitimate births for the next year. The object of this arrangement will be understood when one considers that the greater number of the children who in one year are baptized, or, more correctly, are baptized and entered into the church records and thereafter counted, are not captured in the previous year. Thus with the help of the table it is

Table 9.3. Marriages and illegitimate births in Norway, 1801–1855

Marriages		Illegitimate Births		Number Fewer (−) or Greater (+) Compared with Previous Year	
Year	Number	Number	Year	Marriages	Illegitimate Births
		1,470	1801		
1801	6,089	1,323	1802		−147
1802	6,742	1,509	1803	+ 653	+226
1803	6,790	1,556	1804	+ 48	+ 47
1804	7,069	1,594	1805	+ 279	+ 38
1805	7,227	1,749	1806	+ 158	+155
1806	7,283	1,732	1807	+ 56	− 17*
1807	6,331	1,697	1808	− 952	− 35
1808	5,305	1,373	1809	−1,026	−324
1809	5,370	1,521	1810	+ 65	+148
1810	7,100	1,761	1811	+1,730	+240
1811	7,854	1,771	1812	+ 754	+ 10
1812	7,850	1,557	1813	− 4	−214
1813	6,453	1,374	1814	−1,397	−183
1814	5,801	1,845	1815	− 652	+471*
1815	9,171	2,585	1816	+3,370	+740
1816	9,427	2,455	1817	+ 256	−130*
1817	8,010	2,384	1818	−1,417	− 71
1818	7,713	2,332	1819	− 297	− 52
1819	7,721	2,380	1820	+ 8	+ 48
1820	8,712	2,709	1821	+ 991	+329
1821	8,895	2,531	1822	+ 183	−178*
1822	8,949	2,539	1823	+ 54	+ 8
1823	8,841	2,445	1824	− 108	− 94
1824	8,376	2,446	1825	− 465	+ 1*
1825	9,020	2,620	1826	+ 644	+174
1826	8,806	2,533	1827	− 214	− 87
1827	8,087	2,419	1828	− 719	−114
1828	8,358	2,503	1829	+ 271	+ 84
1829	8,639	2,539	1830	+ 281	+ 36
1830	8,669	2,455	1831	+ 30	− 84*
1831	8,190	2,247	1832	− 479	−208
1832	7,839	2,399	1833	− 351	+152
1833	8,548	2,395	1834	+ 709	− 4*
1834	8,872	2,615	35	+ 324	+220
1835	8,784	2,499	36	− 88	−116
1836	8,424	2,383	37	− 360	−116
1837	8,123	2,329	38	− 301	− 54
1838	7,584	2,332	39	− 539	+ 3*
1839	7,949	2,474	40	+ 365	+142
1840	8,601	2,683	1841	+ 652	+209
1841	9,595	3,277	42	+ 994	+594
1842	9,962	3,257	43	+ 367	− 20*
1843	10,173	3,157	44	+ 211	−100*
1844	10,290	3,357	45	+ 117	+200
1845	10,570	3,456	1846	+ 280	+ 99
1846	11,152	3,561	1847	+ 582	+105
1847	9,890	3,220	1848	−1,262	−341
1848	10,187	3,527	1849	+ 297	+307
1849	10,629	3,715	1850	+ 442	+188
1850	10,648	4,090	1851	+ 19	+375
1851	10,575	4,220	1852	− 73	+130*
1852	10,179	4,144	1853	− 396	− 76
1853	11,257	4,533	1854	+1,078	+389
1854	12,479	4,603	1855	+1,212	+ 90
1855	12,009			− 470	

*[These exceptions are explained in the text.—TRANSLATOR]

easy to be able to compare the number of couples who in each year were married with those who during the same year lived in sin so that they became parents of illegitimate children. And the two last columns in table 9.3 show us how much of the number of the same couples in each year have been smaller or larger than the previous year.

And it is observed that for the most part it so happens that the numbers for each classification fall or rise together. In 1825, for example, the number of marriages rose by 644, and in the corresponding year (1826) the number of illegitimate births rose by 174. In the next year, both numbers fall, and in the following year they fall still more; on the other hand, in the next year both numbers rise. The exceptions to this rule (marked with the sign *) will hardly be found to be so frequent that they refute the rule.

The cause of this relationship can be understood by a single example: the year 1847 reveals a marked decrease in the number of marriages, and in the same year there must be fewer unrecorded births out of wedlock, because the year 1848 shows a distinct decrease in the number of illegitimate births. Such a decrease, although not by any means as marked, was seen also for the legitimate births in 1848. But now we recall that 1847 was a difficult year with high prices, and therein certainly lies the cause of all these changes in the figures: high prices and anxiety and need lowered morale and passion among the young people and inhibited the drive by which many of them followed the normal routines that lead partly to marriage, partly to illegal relationships. It is also possible that the poorer nutrition of the lower classes decreased the fertility of the women. On the other side, it is likely that the very good years led to many marriages in 1853 and 1854, plus many illegitimate births during the years 1854 and 1855. In such manner the tables produce manifold examples for the well-known expression that good or bad conditions increase or decrease the number of marriages during the year, plus the less-known expression: that the same conditions exercise a similar influence on the people's inclination for loose living.

But this by no means explains everything; there is another peculiarity with the increased number of illegitimate births, which quite likely must have another cause than that of annual changing conditions. Regarding this, one can be persuaded by looking at table 9.4.

This table in addition, as was expected, reveals individual exceptions close to those presented in table 9.3 with a simultaneous rise and fall both on the part of marriages and illegitimate births. This is already clearly seen in table 9.1 for the 10 five-year periods during the three longer periods 1801–1815, 1816–1840, and 1841–1850, with fewer marriages and illegitimate births during the first period, more during the

Table 9.4. Marriages and illegitimate live births in Norway

	Actual Numbers[a]		Relationship	
Years	Marriages	Illegitimate Births	Marriages	Illegitimate Births
1801–1805	33,917	7,452	100	21.9
1806–1810	31,389	8,072	100	25.7
1811–1815	37,129	8,308	100	22.4
1816–1820	41,583	12,136	100	29.2
1821–1825	44,081	12,670	100	28.7
1826–1830	42,558	12,614	100	29.6
1831–1835	42,333	12,111	100	28.7
1836–1840	40,681	12,017	100	29.5
1841–1845	50,590	15,731	100	31.1
1846–1850	52,506	17,479	100	33.3

[a] Here, where the numbers are combined for five-year intervals, the differences will not be great if it is desired to use them in the manner presented in the previous table—to compare the number of marriages in one five-year period with illegitimate births in another five-year period that occurred later, e.g., marriages 1801–1805 and illegitimate births 1802–1806. Still, it can be noted that the great increase in the number of marriages 1811–1815 occurs particularly in the one year 1815, in which the number of illegitimate births was not yet rising.

second period, and still more during the third. But what is most remarkable, table 9.4 shows us also in the two last columns that the situation with illegitimate births became worse precisely with a shift from one of these three periods to the other. During the period from 1816 to 1840, five five-year periods in a row, there were never under 28.7 and never over 29.6 illegitimate births per 100 marriages, but during the period 1801 to 1815 the situation was better, and during the period 1841 to 1850 it was worse. The fact is such that when one examines the cause of the obvious worsening from the beginning to the close of the half century, one needs almost only to observe the periods 1816 and 1841, because between these two years the condition is seen to be clearly unchanged from one five-year period to another, while the changes to the worse essentially took place by the time periods mentioned. It is as if by 1816 a new and more numerous generation emerged with other circumstances and morals compared to the previous one, and in wave after wave this generation continued in the same manner until 1840, when again it is as if a new and still more numerous generation starts a new period.

Table 9.3 showed us the changes in the number of marriages and illegitimate births from year to year; table 9.4 shows us more lasting changes from one period to another. These shorter, annual changes could be compared with the smaller waves whereby the overflow of the sea causes ripples from the momentary weaker wind. These more lasting changes are like the undertow, the slower motions in the sea, which the wind of the day before left behind.

In any case, I am unable to conceive how the matter can be explained other than as follows: during the year after 1815 and likewise the year after 1840, there emerged quite suddenly a great increase in people of marriageable age. And this was a result, as I showed in my study *On Marriage in Norway,* of certain enormous changes in earlier times in the entire condition of the people. But the natural outcome is that both during favorable and unfavorable times the number of marriages and illegitimate births had to increase greatly. The too-sudden, large increase among the people of the same age caused distress, so that more young people than previously had to delay marriage, which demands that first one must make a living. This condition, however, does not discourage immorality to the same degree (*On Marriage* [*Selected Works* 2:27 ff.]).

Table 9.4 has shown us that the numbers of people who were married during the years 1841–1845 and 1846–1850 were much greater than before, and at first this might seem unreasonable to discuss, since in the same years 1841–1845 and 1846–1850 there should have been many more people who out of necessity delayed or avoided marriage. But it is true that in these same years when the number of newly married people increased greatly, the number of people of marriageable age increased *still* more, such that the remarkably large number of marriages should have been greater than it was if many of the marriageable people, more than otherwise, had not held back. This must be regarded as completely true and valid since it is found to be used in the census tables (*On Marriage* [*Selected Works* 2:257, 295]). I therefore repeat: the reason the number of illegitimate births from 1841 on increased so extremely clearly, both as such and relative to marriages (thereby naturally also relative to the legitimate births), is quite naturally in the well-known situation that there was a far greater number of people of marriageable age than before, of which many married, more than before; but also, many more than before had to forego marriage, or in any case postpone it, so that the married ones became "many in numbers but also few relatively." Nevertheless, I would still deny the possibility that an increase in immorality can have made the increase in illegitimate births greater than expected, a matter that will be the subject for the research in chapter 10; only it must be asserted that neither the great increase in the number of illegitimate births nor the rather worsened condition between the same and the number of marriages proves the worsening influence of the new law, in that these changes in illegitimate births both occurred before and could be attributed to other factors.

The sentence—that the condition of illegitimate births looks worse (compared with the number of marriages) just at the transition to the period when both the number of illegitimate births and the number of marriages constantly rises to a greater height—seems so remarkable to me that I feel emboldened to use a couple of pages to illustrate with several facts.

The condition that the sentence describes, and which is true for all of Norway, is repeated more or less clearly for each of the five dioceses, particularly for the diocese of Trondheim, which one can be convinced of by the figures in appendix B. It must be remembered that the smaller the areas used for calculations, the more fortuitousness and irregularity are revealed. But it would be of particular interest to initiate research in the diocese of Christiania, the only one of five dioceses for which I have found more or less complete reports (although hardly very dependable) from previous centuries. These reports are held partly in the Royal Archives, partly in the statistical office, and held jointly in the tables in *Statistical Materials from the Danish Government* (in German) for 1784–1786. Of the years that the tables should cover, tables for the years 1731, 1732, 1744, 1749, 1750, 1757, 1760, 1781, 1786, 1787, and 1793

Table 9.5. Illegitimate births in the diocese of Christiania

	Annual Average		Relationship	
Years	Marriages	Illegitimate Births	Marriages	Illegitimate Births
1731–1735	2,145	405	100	18.9
1736–1740	2,114	427	100	20.2
1741–1745	2,084	308	100	14.8
1746–1750	2,252	423	100	18.8
1751–1755	2,482	426	100	17.2
1756–1760	2,242	407	100	18.1
1761–1765	2,462	379	100	15.4
1766–1770	2,471	435	100	17.6
1771–1775	2,413	443	100	18.4
1776–1780	2,756	684	100	24.8
1781–1785	2,475	578	100	23.4
1786–1790	3,009	721	100	23.9
1791–1795	3,151	781	100	24.8
1796–1800	2,877	760	100	26.4
1801–1805	2,838	784	100	27.6
1806–1810	2,654	846	100	31.9
1811–1815	3,402	947	100	27.8
1816–1820	3,660	1,196	100	32.7
1821–1825	3,905	1,258	100	32.2
1826–1830	3,501	1,204	100	34.4
1831–1835	3,442	1,099	100	31.9
1836–1840	3,315	1,118	100	33.7
1841–1845	4,309	1,483	100	34.4
1846–1850	4,592	1,709	100	37.2

were missing. Thus the averages for the five-year period could be abstracted for only three years.

By looking at the numbers revealing the conditions in the last column, we can differentiate between four longer periods, namely (1) 1731–1775, where the condition shows one exception to numbers under 20; (2) 1776–1815, where with one exception the numbers are between 23.4 and 27.8; (3) 1816–1840, where the single exception is not between 31.9 and 33.7; plus (4) 1841–1850, where the lowest is 34.4. If we compare the figures in the first two categories, we find, with almost single exceptions, that the actual number of marriages and illegitimate births rises sharply at the transition from one to the other of these periods (the exception that the five-year period 1811–1815 shows is most evident in the one year 1815, when the number of marriages rose extremely).

COMPARISONS WITH SWEDEN AND DENMARK

I have further endeavored to undertake a comparison with Sweden and Denmark and to present the needed figures in table 9.6.

Table 9.6. Comparisons with Sweden and Denmark

	Actual Numbers		Relationship	
Years	Marriages	Illegitimate Live Births	Marriages	Illegitimate Live Births
Sweden				
1801–1805	94,580	21,828	100	23.1
1806–1810	103,810	23,585	100	22.7
1811–1815	108,248	26,466	100	24.5
1816–1820	107,951	29,478	100	27.3
1821–1825	118,861	33,566	100	28.2
1826–1830	110,107	29,621	100	26.9
1831–1835	110,283	31,289	100	28.4
1836–1840	104,777	32,429	100	31.0
1841–1845	116,694	42,303	100	36.3
1846–1850	123,726	46,570	100	37.6
Denmark				
1801–1805	40,188	10,952	100	27.3
1806–1810	38,720	13,098	100	33.8
1811–1815	46,755	15,094	100	32.3
1816–1820	45,848	14,842	100	32.4
1821–1825	46,996	16,008	100	34.1
1826–1830	48,479	16,338	100	33.7
1831–1835	51,578	18,735	100	36.3
1836–1840	46,218	19,596	100	42.4
1841–1845	52,495	23,124	100	44.0
1846–1850	54,661	24,526	100	44.9

When we first look at Sweden in table 9.6, we find quite a bit of similarity to Norway, particularly during the transition from the period before and after 1841; that the similarity is not greater can be explained as a direct result of Sweden's not having experienced a great increase in population, and this increase did not take place as suddenly as in Norway. In Denmark the similarity to Norway is less and, at its greatest, can be discerned for the period after 1841. If we wished to carry out a similar comparison with England and France and Prussia, we should have less evidence that the conditions have evolved the same there as in Norway. There is something distinctive about our country, and because of certain earlier circumstances in the life of the people, the number of people of marriageable age (and therewith the number of marriages and illegitimate births) grew extremely fast and suddenly during the years 1816 to 1841, and this distinctiveness can be found only somewhat in neighboring Sweden, with which our country has also much in common as regards the so-called population movement. We could explain our circumstances thus, that Norway, with its isolated location, severe climate, and meager agriculture, has been much more harshly affected by the influences which in bad years and war and interruptions of commerce affect the life and well-being of people; among the other countries, Sweden is the one that shares our fate most (*On Marriage* [*Selected Works* 2:248]).

10

To What Extent Have Moral Conditions Deteriorated in Recent Times?

"THE world—she is getting old"—the wife of a cotter said this on the parsonage farm in Lom, as she was approaching 90 years of age and before she died 14 to 15 years ago. "It is so dry now compared with earlier times," she said. "The fields can be maintained by watering, but there is so little in the meadows compared with earlier times. The world, she is getting old," she said. It was the farmer Anders Andvord who told me this, and he had heard the same talk as the old woman's in a conversation with his old father and Hans Tolleifson Bakkum, a cotter up in Bæverdal, who when a young man had stood guard for the king in Copenhagen and who therefore had considerable knowledge of the way of the world.

How often have I not heard the same talk in other places! With only some changes according to the circumstances of the place. In Dalsbygd in uppermost Østerdal I was shown signs of grainfields of previous periods and told of grain storehouses and haymows that had existed until a few years ago, and this is a community where grain is not sown. "They believe, the old ones, that the soil is getting old," in such manner the explanation ended. Even in Hedemark, where one hardly dares complain about the growing of grain and grass, I was still told by a middle-aged farmer about the difference between now and before: when he was a child it was possible every year to find cloudberries in the marshes and fruit on the apple trees in his father's garden, and now both were rare. "One believes that it must be so, as they say, that the world is getting old"; in this way the conversations ended also here.

"And the people in the country, they behave much worse than before"—this is the other pessimistic talk that usually follows.

In northern Gudbrandsdal I had a conversation with a farm owner who was praised by the community for being one of the most enterprising farmers—an old man now. "Yes," he said, "even though I say so myself, I have been one of the most demanding in cultivating the soil; but with all that I have worked to improve them, my fields are not as good now as when I began. It must lie in nature, and it is probably so that the world is getting old." While the conversation continued we touched on the life of the people and social conditions. "Yes," he thought, "it might be well enough with what they call the Constitution, for there was nothing so special with the government of the country before. But I see nothing else than that everything is getting worse now as well."—"Let me hear what it is!" I added. "Why is it that poverty becomes greater year after year?" he asked. "I would like your thoughts for you have lived in the community all your life."—"It is not difficult to understand," he continued, "considering the immorality you talk about. While I was growing up it was not as good either as it should be, but it was nothing like it is now, for now it has become so that it is offensive to talk about it. And so it is in other places as well, because it is precisely at present that people are behaving this way."

In the fall of 1855 I had a conversation in Upper Romerike with an older cotter who farmers pointed out to me as one of the understanding and dependable cotters in the neighborhood, and I became acquainted with him, an upright and trustworthy soul. I can also add that I saw signs in his house of order and well-being beyond the most ordinary among his class. He initiated a conversation for the most part centering on the labor agitation. He took an interest in participating in it. He had himself been one of them who expected that it would improve the lot of the poor people. "For there was talk that they would come forward with a rope against the rich."—"With a rope?" I asked. "Yes," he continued, "you know, as the prophets say, that a rope shall issue forth and divide equally the people."—"Share the earth?" I asked again. "Yes, exactly," he answered. This now became a long conversation, which we stopped before the sharing had taken place.

"In the final analysis, what do you think about the whole matter?" I asked.

"Oh, the poor people have not been hurt," was the answer, and I became aware that these were exactly the same cautious words that several other people of the working class in that area had used for the same question.

"Explain further," I requested.

"Well, it is that working people have it better now than in earlier times, for it is as if the farm owners do not dare—yes, I must say dare—or as if they dare not but better their lot and improve their conditions now, such as wages and food and room; yes, with everything, one might almost say, it has become somewhat better for the common and poor man—that is really true."

I suggested on the contrary a great many other circumstances that must have influenced the improvement in the working class's lot in recent times, but this he would not agree to. "It was still," he believed, "like there was a ferment among the people, in such a way that they were behaving differently from before—exactly like a ferment in talk and thoughts and many things."

I. Ferment? You must explain this more carefully.

He. It was like there was more reflection among people, so they thought about things. Yes, things in some ways were not as they should be, so they came forward with improvements and claims that they wanted to have changes. Because previously they had mostly gone along thoughtlessly and not thought about it, but now they began to think about trying to travel to other communities and places in order to have it better.

I. That people show some thinking is well and good, and I think that is splendid. But tell me: does it seem to you that this ferment and thoughtfulness have also influenced the behavior and style of living of the poor, and has there been an effort thereby so that some good has actually come out of it?

He. Yes, it is only recently that workers and servants have taken to moving from one place to another and holding out for something better and not being so pleased to be subservient, but each sort of wants to be his own man, so to speak. Yes, there is a difference between now and a few years ago—that is right—at least as I understand it.

I. Do you sense that there is more diligence and stability and prudence among the young?

He. Yes, for it is something each one should realize—although it does not occur to everyone—that one must strive and persevere if one wants to get ahead in the world.

I. As for liquor—it has been the misfortune of many a man, and how do you feel about its status now?

He. Oh yes, a lot has appeared in the papers about it, and I must also admit myself that it is something that should not be.

I. Did you mean the Labor paper?

He. Yes, for a few here took the newspaper, and it was often mentioned that liquor drinking should not be.

I. No, I feel exactly it was a big mistake of the Labor newspaper that it said quite little of drunkenness and such immorality.

He. Yes, that is true, and it was mostly the upper classes who were criticized for it; they could engage in it.

I. So it is, the upper class and always the upper class is full of faults. But there was little written about faults among the poor, as if things were in good shape there.

He. Oh no, it is really not so—it is human nature to desire to take to what is bad, both high and low, just the same.

I. Equally, I think, if not just the same. Overbearing and lying, hard-hearted and envious—they are different faults, but equally bad. We were talking about liquor drinking. Tell me, regarding immorality, what has been its status in recent years?

He. Immorality—yes, it is an important matter; I do not know exactly what I can say about it.

I. I know already that this community is one of those that is one of the worst in this regard. But now, since I am talking with an experienced and thoughtful man, I am eager to hear your view of this: has it become worse recently, or how is it?

He. Yes, if I may say so; it is exactly like a vogue.

I. Like a vogue?

He. Yes, so to speak, because it has become much like a custom that must be observed in order to go along [with the crowd].

I. Now, now, I understand the view. But are you saying in all seriousness that the people in this community simply go along in this immorality?

He. Yes, it is correct that many go along exactly as a lark, although they should be ashamed. For one knows it is easy to fall into, but no one should be proud of it. But this is exactly how it has been in this community for a while.

I. It would be even more unfortunate if this would be a product of the [social] movement and the great vogue that you have talked about.

He. Oh no, it is not easy to know if that is so.

I. No, no, it is not possible to know everything. But this much I believe, you and I could know for sure, that when a right and strong [social] movement appears and a change in thinking among people, it should not deteriorate into bad custom and immorality, which truly has caused so many men and women both worldly damage and heartfelt sorrow.

It makes a singular impression on me to have a confidential conversation with an upright man who belongs to another class and is on another level of education. It is as if the surface of the ocean is unruffled and quiet so that one can look into the deep: it is like a different world whose unknown things one sees little of. But now I request the reader to notice the signs in the man's expressions that while he wanted to have both himself and others believe that the moral condition had improved, for example, with regard to drunkenness, he did not consider describing the situation regarding immorality as having worsened.

Given how much I have traveled about in the communities and engaged in conversations with people on all matter of things, it occurs to me that there is nothing that the majority of people, farm owners and cotters, are more agreed on than just this: that immorality has increased in recent times.

Farm owners and cotters do not usually go into the field to make observations and gather facts; they are more likely to be content with the experiences that in their own little circle and in their corner of the parish come to them in the course of daily life, and thereafter they arrive at opinions. Or I might almost say: it is the opinions themselves that are made up inside of them, hardly knowing how. And it is precisely these opinions of such people I have the most respect for; I have the belief that they are very close to the truth, since it is the things themselves that have penetrated the senses of people and led the way to the remarkable depths of the mind. And one can be very moved to hear honest men with all seriousness and worry come forth with the words that "the world, she is getting old," since signs and marks from forest and field that are brought forth to support these sad words are truly often such that one must be somewhat of a naturalist to understand and formulate them any other way. But still worse, spirit and thought can be imprisoned when one hears reliable and experienced men of the community unfortunately give in to this other talk, that "the people in the country actually are behaving worse in many way," since the evidence that is presented as proof is precisely the large number of "love children" or, more correctly, the great number of young people who live in immoral relationships; and by statistics and careful observation or by counting over the entire country year after year, we see that these figures are actually so and their number is unfortunately sadly increased.

This general belief has been adopted by men who have thought so much about the matter that they have found themselves moved to rise up to oppose the disaster. With this objective in mind, a book was published in 1855 with the title *The Bridal Crown, A Story for the People.* In the foreword, the publisher writes about "what appears to be a slumbering moral consciousness in a large portion of the people" and about "an evil, which for a long time has been and is still steadily increasing among us in town and country," an assertion, he says, which he does not want to clarify further.

One has always had the opportunity to observe that men in speech or writing who take a position for or against one or another objectionable practice or misfortune begin by presenting the condition such that it has become worse and worse over time so that everyone should be able to see the threatening danger. And therein surely lies a strong basis for action for many to follow the appeal and to participate in the struggles against the evil and for the good.

But has one really considered what is involved to express such a judgment that moral consciousness is losing out among people and that the moral life is degenerating? The adult generation, who are alive in the country now, have grown up and been brought up during a period when the blessings of heaven in unprecedented measure have poured on the people, blessings mixed with so much opposition and trials that the spirit could be distressed in the middle of the joy—and still the people continue to degenerate? Among the many blessings from heaven there is also that the government administration in the spirit of a free constitution has given the most indolent or demanding the greatest encouragement to work toward a satisfactory and happy position in life, and in addition, the church, by means of its continuously purer and life-fulfilling proclaiming of the Word in the schoolrooms and church services, has addressed the conscience of people—and still selfishness and moral consciousness continue to degenerate? Tell me, if this is so, where is there hope that it can become better? Does the hope lie in the eventuality that the Lord shall send the destruction of war or the fright of plagues over the land, and should we until that time be paralyzed in our struggles by the thought that to work in the service of the good has so little result, such that the evil gets the upper hand anyway?

Since I have felt in my innermost self too much of the paralyzing influence that this thought can exert on the spirit—that the moral condition among people continues to worsen—and my own experience has caused me to assume that if only a strong appeal to the people, which begins with the description of the increase in depravity, can awaken the many to the good, it can also have the opposite effect, so they would think thus: Well now, if the whole thing falls apart, it does not benefit me to oppose; my soul! eat, drink, and be merry while there is time!

STATISTICAL EVIDENCE

Still, truth is the best, whether it sounds so or not. We must seek it, and we must not spare diligence to find it. I said that the consciousness of the people certainly stood close to the truth, but I also believe that it has not grasped the entire truth. To present this shall be the object of the following pages, but the condition is so very complicated that the presentation cannot be very brief.

In chapter 9 I tallied all the live-born illegitimate children in the country for the previous century, first year by year (table 9.1), then for each five-year period (table 9.4). In table 10.1, I give a still more condensed overview for each decade.

Table 10.1. Live-born illegitimate children per decade

Years	Illegitimate Births	Increase or Decrease *(percent)*
1801–1810	15,524	
1811–1820	20,444	+31.7
1821–1830	25,284	+23.7
1831–1840	24,128	− 4.6
1841–1850	33,210	+37.6

If any conclusions can be made about the moral condition, it must be said that it had improved during the years 1831–1840 and later again had gotten much worse during 1841–1850. But most people will immediately understand that this method of observation is much too simplistic.

Let us then, according to the usual method, compare the illegitimate births with the legitimate (table 10.2).

Table 10.2. Legitimate and illegitimate births per decade

Years	Legitimate Births	Illegitimate Births	Illegitimate Births per 100 Legitimate Births	Increase or Decrease *(percent)*
1801–1810	234,401	15,524	6.6	
1811–1820	258,740	20,444	7.9	+20
1821–1830	325,268	25,284	7.8	− 1
1831–1840	328,858	24,128	7.3	− 6
1841–1850	373,078	33,210	8.9	+22

Or we can use the method that I have used elsewhere in this book to compare births with marriages (table 10.3). This method of presenting the comparisons I regard as being more valid than the first (see appendix

Table 10.3. Marriages and illegitimate births per decade

Years	Marriages	Illegitimate Births	Illegitimate Births per 100 Marriages	Increase (*percent*)
1801–1810	65,306	15,524	23.8	
1811–1820	78,712	20,444	25.6	8
1821–1830	86,639	25,284	29.2	14
1831–1840	82,914	24,128	29.2	14
1841–1850	103,096	33,210	32.2	10

A). But in any case, these comparisons show that the condition of illegitimate births in the last period is not as bad as it first appeared when we only looked at the number of illegitimate births themselves.

In the meantime with some reflection, one will discover that some of these comparisons give us very reliable directions for judging the moral condition and its changes. This much we see, that for each 100 legitimate births, there are more illegitimate ones than before, and for each 100 couples who were married, there are now more than before who became parents of illegitimate children, and that a change has taken place is accordingly clear. But it is not clear on which side this change has occurred. Those who are more quickly inclined to look for the worst in the evidence certainly say the changes reveal that the young people are now more inclined to indulge in immoral activities. But it is still possible that the changes are due to people in later times having avoided marriage more. It is like a pair of scales: one pan goes up and the other down, and this change can either be caused by a weight being placed in one pan or by a weight being removed from the other.

Therefore it is very necessary to look around for another method by which to initiate the whole investigation. And this should not require a great deal of thought. Imagine two communities and suppose that from year to year many illegitimate children are born in one and few in the other. Before you undertake some comparisons and draw some conclusions about the moral condition, you ask: Are the communities the same size, with the same number of people, or is there some difference? The same caution must be exercised when we want to compare two different time periods, since the number of people in a country changes from one time period to another in the same way that communities differ one from the other.

The population of Norway is shown in table 10.4. And when I compare the number of illegitimate births for the corresponding ten-year periods, we find that for each 10,000 people in the country, the annual number of illegitimate births averaged the figures shown in table 10.5. But this comparison can still not be depended on. There is the fallacy

Table 10.4. Population of Norway

1801	883,038
1815	885,431
1825	1,051,318
1835	1,194,827
1845	1,328,471

Table 10.5. Illegitimate births per 10,000 people

Decade	Annual Average	Increase or Decrease (*percent*)
1801–1810	18	
1811–1820	23	+28
1821–1830	24	+ 4
1831–1840	22	− 8
1841–1850	25	+14

that the elderly and the children are included in the same count, and a large number of people accordingly whom we had better ignore in the observations when the subject is about offences against morality.

Therefore I will carry out a comparison whereby I pay attention only to the portion of the population that was in the age group from 20 to 40 years (table 10.6). And by the same method as with the previous comparison, I can find that for each 10,000 people of this age group the annual number of births were as shown in table 10.7.

Table 10.6. Population aged 20 to 40

1801	250,735
1815	276,342[a]
1825	320,004
1835	326,457
1845	392,914

[a] How I found this number by an indirect method can be seen in *On Marriage in Norway* [*Selected Works* 2:240].

Table 10.7. Illegitimate births per 10,000 people aged 20 to 40

Decade	Annual Average	Increase or Decrease
1801–1810	62	
1811–1820	74	+19
1821–1830	79	+ 7
1831–1840	74	− 6
1841–1850	85	+15

The letter-writer whom I quoted at the beginning of the previous chapter had initiated his investigations by comparing—as I do now—the illegitimate births with the legitimate by the total population and the population in the age group 20 to 40, and he arrived, as we saw, at the conclusion that the condition of illegitimate births had changed for the worse during the period 1841–1850.

But even the last comparison is not reliable. The situation is that among people in the age group 20 to 40, there are a great many married men and women, and regarding them the illegitimate births are so few in our country that when we here look at the matter in the large, it is best to exclude them and only include the unmarried portion of the population of adults or—in order to correct ourselves according to the population census—for the ages 20 and over.

Table 10.8. Unmarried population over age 20[a]

	Men	Women
1825	105,897	138,297
1835	117,460	148,464
1845	150,935	181,065

[a] Except for extremely few cases the married are over 20 years old; if I extract, accordingly, the figures from the population census of the married from the total population over 20 years of age, I then have left the unmarried portion (bachelors and widowers, girls and widows). But it was at the beginning of 1825 that the population census counted the married, thus this investigation can begin only from that time on.

The annual numbers of illegitimate births for each 10,000 persons are shown in table 10.9. Here the matter immediately looks different from before. Obviously the condition during 1841–1850 looks still worse than during 1831–1840, but it is better on the male side than during 1821–1830, and on the female side in any case just as good.

Table 10.9. Annual illegitimate births per 10,000 over age 20

	Men		Women	
		Increase or Decrease (*percent*)		Increase or Decrease (*percent*)
1821–1830	239		183	
1831–1840	205	−14	163	−11
1841–1850	220	+ 7	...	+12

But is this comparison entirely valid? No, in part there is the same doubt about it as for the above, where we took the total population of the country in the calculation. The doubt rests on the fact that the total number of people—outside of those married over 20-years old—are included, each and all, right up to the highest age, including the most superannuated people, old widowers and widows. Therefore without doubt it would be most valid to undertake calculations so that widowers and widows will be left out and present the case as if illegitimate births were a burden only to those who lived and always had lived outside of wedlock, young men and girls accordingly. Thereby we will certainly exclude some widowers and widows in the younger ages, among whom undeniably some became fathers and mothers of illegitimate children, but this really happens so seldom that the failure to include them obviously cannot be great.

Table 10.10. Unmarried population over age 20[a]

	Bachelors	Spinsters
1835	100,835	105,804
1845	131,867	133,438

[a] In order to be very sure in counting the frequency of illegitimate births, it is necessary to know especially how many of the parents of the illegitimate children were bachelors or widowers, girls or widows, 20–25, 25–30 years of age, etc., plus how many people in the named groups and in the named ages were living in the country. It was first in the population census in 1835 that widowers and widows were counted, thus I have only been able to separate them for 1835 and 1845 and get the number of bachelors and girls.

In table 10.11, we were not able to compare the period 1841–1850 further than with the previous decade, and following these figures there accordingly should be an increase or a worsening in the condition during the last period. But it can still be noted that the worsening does not appear as great as for the foregoing comparisons. Step by step we have accordingly come to the opinion that if the moral condition has worsened during the later period, this condition is still not as bad as it first seemed, and already this shift has its value.

Table 10.11. Illegitimate births per 10,000 unmarried people over age 20

	Bachelors	Increase (*Percent*)	Spinsters	Increase (*Percent*)
1831–1840	239		228	
1841–1850	252	5	249	9

But we cannot stop hereby. The bachelors and girls dealt with were over 20 years of age up to the highest age. But we know that of the married and unmarried together over 20 but under 30, the numbers were as shown in table 10.12.

Table 10.12. Total population between 20 and 30 years of age

	Men	Women
1835	82,809	89,539
1845	116,295	122,971

Thus we can see that among bachelors and girls in table 10.10, a very large portion must have been over 30 years, accordingly beyond the age of temptation and passion. I am certain that the greatest portion of those who became fathers and mothers of illegitimate children are young people of the age when people are most likely to get married, accordingly under 30 years. The two things, marriage and fornication, are associated on the whole with that age group in this country. That it is so in regard to marriage I have indicated in another place (*On Marriage in Norway* [*Selected Works* 2:241]). That it is so regarding fornication we can see in the columns of figures in table 10.13.

Table 10.13. Changes in population between 20 and 30 years of age and numbers of illegitimate births

Population between 20 and 30 Years			Illegitimate Births		
Year	Number	Increase or Decrease	Years	Number	Increase or Decrease
		(percent)			*(percent)*
1801	136,959		1801–1810	15,524	
1815	160,090	+17	1811–1820	20,444	+32
1825	175,482	+10	1821–1830	25,284	+23
1835	172,348	− 2	1831–1840	24,128	− 5
1845	239,266	+39	1841–1850	33,210	+38

Lacking better reports on population counts, I therefore, in order to judge the frequency of illegitimate births most accurately, compare them with the portion of the segment of the population who were living exactly in the age group 20 to 30 years, and I carry out here the comparison both for the births to married couples and the illegitimate births as shown in table 10.14.

Table 10.14. Marriages and illegitimate births per 10,000 people between 20 and 30 years of age

Decade	Marriages	Illegitimate Births
1801–1810	477	113
1811–1820	492	128
1821–1830	494	144
1831–1840	481	140
1841–1850	431	139

There is a decrease in the two last 10-year periods for both marriages and for illegitimate births. In reality, as we have clearly seen before, the very number of marriages and illegitimate births increased precisely during 1841–1850, yes, increased in a significant degree; but relatively there is a decrease, i.e., *there are in the latest period fewer marriages and illegitimate births relative to the number of people who were in the age one could have expected and feared one or the other.*

CORRELATION BETWEEN THE LIFE OF THE PEOPLE AND THE CONDITION OF SOCIETY

The careful reader will note that the calculation is not very certain; the result therefore cannot quite be depended on. But the other calculation, which seemed to show that the change was for the worse, was no more certain either. And when one has torn oneself from the usually accepted opinion about the worsening of this aspect of the life of the people, one will no longer be surprised at the favorable results of these many figures and calculations, but clearly find them reasonable because they agree largely with certain states and conditions in life that we know. We know that the old custom of the servant folk having their sleeping quarters in the animal barn has contributed to offences against morals but that this same custom has far from increased and more likely has decreased in recent times (chapter 3). We know that night courting was one of the old ways that led to immorality, but that also in later times this way was not used as often and constantly as before (chapter 4). It might be common knowledge that the vulgar behavior of youth that manifests itself by drunkenness has now during a succession of years decreased, and it is reasonable to assume that the same has happened to the kind of vulgar behavior we see here. It is still commonly assumed that the school system occupies a definite relationship to the level of morality, such that this level is better or worse according to how it is more or less well administered. It is well known that during the last couple of generations the educational system in our country has constantly improved so that the generation of young people whose situation we have observed during 1841–1850 very surely has received better instruction and upbringing than the generation that came in during the years 1831–1840 or during 1821–1830. It can be asserted as known that the changes in legislation that took place in 1842 have not had so great an influence on the erosion of morality as many have believed (chapter 9).

But it should be emphasized that during the later period there have clearly been various circumstances that must be regarded as having induced temptation to immorality or tested virtue greatly.

First, there was the circumstance that marriages during the later period, despite their magnitude, nevertheless have become fewer relative to the until-then still-greater number of people who were of marriageable age (see in addition the last calculation undertaken in the present chapter and also chapter 9 plus chapters 8 and 9 in the study *On Marriage in Norway*). The cause of this is likely in part the greater difficulty in making a living and in part the greater demand for greater results, accordingly economic reasons. But here it can be assumed that to the degree young people for such reasons must delay regular marriage, they were to the same degree tempted to immoral behavior.

In addition I am reminded of the circumstances that during the later time (I have in my study *About Mortality in Norway* [*Selected Works* 2: 94] noted it for the period from 1835–1845) there have been more instances of people moving from one place to another in the nation, undoubtedly young folk who have sought work and livelihood. As favorable as this may be in many ways—that there is movement and communication in the country—it is also dangerous for the morals of unattached people to have to circulate among strangers, where the fathers and mothers cannot watch over them and where the encouragement or judgment of friends and acquaintances does not exercise its beneficial influence. The significance of this circumstance for our question is seen particularly in that this moving for a great part is done by young people of both sexes who move into the cities from the country districts, where the condition of offences against morality seems constantly to be at its worst.

Is it not so that when we really judge the moral condition among people we should consider two things: the intensity of temptation and the ability or the lack of ability whereby temptation can be withstood? To the extent that the presence of the possibility for profligacy was greater during 1841–1850 than during 1831–1840, we cannot conclude that there was a greater frequency of violations, that the moral capacity had decreased, that self-control had loosened, or that the moral conscience was asleep. If despite the increased temptation and danger the feared profligacy was precisely as numerous as before, we could more likely be driven to the conclusion that virtue was greater and strengthened; if under such circumstances offences had increased only a little bit, we would have to interpret it as a sign that the power of morality had grown extremely great.

And when we seek to arrive at an interpretation of morality by looking at the figures for illegitimate births, we should note that there are certain circumstances that cause errors in the figures, such errors that the matter during the period 1841–1850 looks worse than it really is.

First, I am reminded of what chapter 5 has shown particularly at length, that the conditions of illegitimate births are unequally worse within the working as compared with the owner class. If one counts together all the legitimate births in the country during 1831–1840 plus during 1841–1850, counts them together as they have occurred up to now for both classes, it is illuminating that a comparison between both time periods will only be correct if during both periods there was a similar number of people in the populations of the two classes. On the other hand, if the population in the working class increased faster than that of the owner class, it would then appear as if the illegitimate births had become more frequent for the whole, even if the conditions in reality were just as good or perhaps better within each of the two classes. Now I have from the three last population censuses combined the number of adults, farm owners, cotters, servants, etc., that could be classified in each of the two classes (table 10.15). I made this division according to sex but exactly the same for each of the three census years so I can thereafter carry out such a comparison (a complete explanation can be seen in the study *About Mortality* [*Selected Works* 2:107]).

Table 10.15. Adults in the owner and working classes

Year	Owner Class	Working Class
1825	100	264
1835	100	254
1845	100	278

The numbers are, as can be seen, calculated percentagewise, and the difference is that the number of people in the class in which illegitimate births occur the most was smallest during 1831–1840 but largest during 1841–1850. The only reasonable conclusion is that if the moral condition in reality was just as good during 1841–1850 as before, the sum of illegitimate births must reveal a critical increase. But even if morals in reality had changed for the better within each separate class, it could still be that this change was balanced and more than balanced by the larger number of the working class, so that the improved situation did not appear in the figures or that the figures even show an apparent worsening—an error in the figures and tables that will persist as long as we do not have separate studies for each class.

Another matter I must point out is that the urban population—the part of the people within which, as mentioned, illegitimate births are usually more frequent—has increased in number more than the rural population. The market and coastal towns that existed in 1825 (included here are those that were established later) have the following populations (table 10.16).

Table 10.16. Population in market and coastal towns

Year	Number of People	Percentage of Total Population
1825	115,463	11
1835	128,748	11
1845	158,256	12

The relatively larger increase in the urban population that these figures show for the last year must have, even with unchanged morals and living styles, accompanied a relatively large increase in the number of illegitimate births. And now we will probably say: "The cities grew so rapidly mostly by the moving in of young people from the country, and a larger and larger portion of the nation's youth was exposed to and influenced by the degradation of the cities; it is clearly an assault on the moral condition of the nation." But it is not correct or precise to portray city life as pure depravity and to overlook the favorable influence that it also exercises over its population. I will say that city life more often brings out the stronger difference between vice and virtue: Some or many of the in-migrating young people became subject to vice more certainly than if they had remained in their home communities, but others survived the test and gained stronger characters than if they had continued to live in the stable and accustomed environment at home.

Precisely here in the talk about urban life it is possible that someone may object to my entire concept or point to a circumstance that can be assumed to reveal an error in the figures in an entirely opposite direction, such that the moral condition judged by the figures of illegitimate births may look better than probably it was in reality. It is known that relatively few prostitutes become mothers; prostitution certainly increases with the growth of cities, and thereby immorality becomes more and more invisible for those who look only at numbers in the church records. It is a slippery field I am obliged to deal with, and this field has several other problems that I do not desire to handle but would leave to investigation and description by physicians or police officials. But I need to say something about this problem. Prostitution is surely known to everybody, and no one can think about this knowledge and misfortune without a mixture of anger and sadness. How should we judge it? Here I will first assert that even though I have constantly asked, heretofore I have not found anywhere in the country districts an example of the development of this kind of immorality; or I can be more definite: all over I have been told that there is none. But the fact that immorality is spread over a large part of the country districts or here and there among the major portion of the population is witnessed by this book. Probably the time will come when prostitution also develops in the country districts, if not in the same manner as in the cities, where the police have applied outstanding methods to bring this matter to some kind of order. Probably the time will come in the country districts when a more developed self-regard and modesty will bring the young women to disgust with this indecency, so that only a few will be involved in such an incomprehensibly unfortunate fate. In such a way, the immorality will be changed, but the extent of change will be increased when attention is paid not only to the destroyed individual person but to the entire society. One might believe that this transformation of immorality could take place completely; it would be reasonable to believe that then there would be no more talk about illegitimate births, and instead of counting them—as one must in order to judge if immorality is decreasing or increasing—one would count the women who belong to this cast. Likewise, in the towns where prostitution is found alongside other immorality, surely one must conclude that it is a mixture of factors and must observe both parts. But so far only some of the larger towns, where this problem is significant and where the objection is coming from, can most certainly offset the error in the figures that, according to my previous explanation, was a result of the faster growth in the population of the towns. Thus I have felt much less called upon to proceed more deeply into this matter, for in the main my purpose was to direct attention to the condition of the rural people, who in our country more than in most others make up the largest proportion of the population.

VARIOUS INTERPRETATIONS

If I now finally wish to summarize the overall condition of illegitimacy as it has developed in recent times, I must differentiate between two conclusions as follows:

1. The people who enter into a regular marriage, and the legitimate children God has entrusted to their care and upbringing, I call the fortunate ones. On the other hand, the people who engage in immoral living, and the children who by their irresponsibility they bring into the troubles of the world, I call the more unfortunate. And in recent times, com-

paring the more fortunate and the more unfortunate, the number of the more unfortunate has increased, and this change is to be greatly regretted, not only for the involved parents and children themselves but also for the society to which they belong, for the community in which they live. And to the extent that people complain over the worsened condition in the country, there is no doubt that they are right.

2. But to the extent that the same folk lay blame for the change and destruction of morality to a lessened popular acceptance of virtue and a lessened understanding of the need to strive against and withstand evil, they have not been right. There is not a sufficient basis to assume that the moral impulse among the young has become looser, that indifference to the good, that irresponsibility and wildness, have taken the upper hand. There is a greater basis to believe the opposite. The thing is that when the large number of people of marriageable age increased tremendously during the years around 1845, the number of both marriages and illegitimate births increased tremendously, so it is no wonder that even careful observers could come to believe in an increased irresponsibility among the young. But the thing is also that precisely on account of the large numbers, and possibly also on account of the now much greater difficulties in making a living, there was need for many to believe it most wise and correct to delay establishing a family through regular marriage, but not fully as many possessed a correspondingly heightened moral strength to withstand the corrupt tendency to temptation (on this I have elaborated the explanation I made about the same matter in the study *On Marriage* [*Selected Works* 2:269]).

"*Many in number, but few relatively*"—this sentence is relevant to marriages; it also seems relevant to illegitimate births, only not relevant to the same degree for the latter as for the former. The irresponsibility that led poor people to marriage at a young age must be assumed to have decreased; also immorality seems to have decreased, only not fully as much. Not fully as much—but still some. This "some"—let it be; it is not fully proven, since in matters like this one it is always difficult to provide proof, and we must be satisfied with its probability. This "some" I strongly believe in. And no one assumes that this "some" is so small, so insignificant, since there is an enormous difference between a reversal to the worse and an advance to the better: a little kernel here is like a mountain. With the belief in the start of an advance up to now, the hope rises about a faster advance henceforth, and hope raises the spirit and energy to carry on.

Does the reader remember from the third chapter a miserable man in Gudbrandsdal? He sat in a miserable cottage and fed a small child, while the wife and an older child went begging to the neighboring farm, and the beginning of this family's wretchedness was precisely fornication, a situation which the man himself told about with this quotation: "It is the custom among the people of the poor." It was in the year 1851, and I was not able to answer the man then, or I despaired of finding any answer that could overcome the justification he found in these words; at that time I was myself overwhelmed by the thought that immorality continued to be more and more common, so that it was a momentum in itself and almost everyone had to be part of the stream. But precisely therefore I have again and again thought about the same man, and precisely therefore I have repeatedly considered the problem as a whole; and now I say that no one has permission to justify oneself in this manner, since I do not believe it is still true that all or most practice the old custom. Times have changed; the old custom is being transformed into a new and better one. And what farmer would want to continue to cultivate a field that year after year, despite a great deal of diligence and expense, yielded only more and more weeds? Likewise, the men who govern and administer in the communities could lose patience with their work for schools and all the other things that serve to advance good morals in the country if the sad thought became rooted that it still did not do any good, that people still behaved worse and worse. Therefore, we ourselves must believe that the heart of the people is by no means a barren field that would not be worth the work and care! Truly there are still so many stones to move, so much underbrush to clear, so many improvements to be made, that there shall be hope to begin and persistence to fulfill the task, and one must not let the old complaints kill hope and crush the spirit. (The number of people convicted of crimes has also increased to a marked degree during the later period. In chapter 9, which includes the letter, we have seen how this has also caused thoughtful fellow citizens to worry. But I am certain that an investigation such as was started in this chapter would reveal this problem to be much less serious than at first glance. Moreover, there would be so much else to learn from crime statistics that it is highly desirable that a man with the necessary legal education work up the very comprehensive material that exists.)

11

Education and Good Morals

IN Christiansand I talked with a man of the working class whose thoughtfulness and whose gifts to present his observations I learned to admire. The conversation turned to the condition of liquor consumption, among other topics, and it occurred to me to ask if any difference could be detected on this matter between different classes of the working people. "Yes, it is very clear." Now I asked him to explain this matter to me. "Yes, unfortunately it is self-evident that we must remain in the working class, as we first talked about. For if among merchants and other people of the higher classes there is one or another occasional drunk, it is only an exception. And it is almost the same with genuine craftsmen, those who have had schooling—shoemakers, carpenters and such, masters who belong more to the higher classes and associate much with cultured people, and journeymen who are always thinking of also becoming masters. But then we have a class of working people, which we have many of in Christiansand, and they are building carpenters; with them it is not so good, and I believe this is mostly because it does not take much learning to become a building carpenter. Still, it is not too bad for them yet, for mostly it is only a few people who are building a house, and they work together in a fashion with their own masters, on the same level, and share the earnings equally. Here each one must use one's head and be diligent, and that helps. But then there are ship carpenters. Now the view might be that it is a more difficult matter to build a ship than to put up a house, and that therefore these carpenters should be better educated and therefore be more proper people than others. But then there is the case that in the shipyard there is a master who manages everything, and the working people do not do much more than he tells them to do, and among such people it is true that there must be liquor. Still there is a difference among these, and they are not all equally bad. Some we call caulkers, for you see, from childhood up they are not used to other work than only to caulk (seal the openings between planks with caulk) and they have a boring job: they do not need to think about anything, and there is hardly anything to think about either, while caulking. Oh yes, a drink they think about, which they should get when break comes, because a drink is part of the daily wage in the shipyard, and these people are the worst in the shipyard. Also it is much worse with the beam cutters; they have not been taught anything other than to cut on a line, and so there is the custom, since they work on call, that they can leave the area and walk to and from the workplace whenever they wish. They then have time to talk and money to go to the tavern—because they earned well during the summer. But then there are still some other people, and they are the dock workers. It is deplorable to see how they bum around on the street, and they have done so since they were children—never having had any training or discipline. Their ability consists of nothing but using their arms and backs. It is mostly by fits and starts that they have work, when a ship is to be loaded or when the steamship arrives. Then they also earn well, but they cannot afford to acquire decent clothes for their bodies; what they earn has another destination."

This lifelike and realistic description gives us an example of the few that is surely true in general: step by step the temptation of human beings for vulgar dissipation becomes worse and worse in relation to how education diminishes, or in relation to how childhood discipline, which should have taught the grown-up generation to apply one's brain and use one's hands, has been applied too little. The example concerned drunkenness; the simple generalization concerns certainly all sensual and base excesses, and it particularly also concerns immorality.

Several chapters in this book have shown how offences against morality to an overwhelming degree have occurred in the working class, far more than in the owner class, which were the two classes and estates into which I thought all people were divided. But the working class is still the portion of the people who more than the other class grew up with insufficient education and breeding.

Here one could object that there are people who live in more fortunate circumstances and a more highly regarded situation who have been exposed to other substantial circumstances that could have contributed to their self-regard and feeling for the people and thereby saved them from addiction to these immoralities; thus the great difference need not be attributed to education and upbringing alone. I shall therefore not depend on individual examples to explain common observations but shall direct observations to the more concrete, the relationship between public school and the level of morality.

SCHOOLS AND MORALITY

One of the clearest criteria of a well-run school is that there are many good teachers. It can be remarked that the fewer pupils per teacher, the better he can succeed with each one of them; accordingly, the fewer number to discipline, the better. With this foreword I present the following comparison (but it should immediately be noted that the parenthetical information for the Christiania diocese *a,* the pupils and teachers for Drammen, Jarlsberg, Laurvik, and lower Telemark deaneries, is not included).

In the diocese of Christiansand the schools appear most supplied with teachers, and the illegitimate births are lower than in the other dioceses. The diocese of Bergen is in second place in both respects. The three other dioceses differ widely from them with regard to the number of teachers and the moral condition of the people.

It is surely conceivable that the whole thing could be a coincidence, that in reality the two factors, the school and the moral condition, are not associated, as shown by the figures. There is still also the deficiency with table 11.1 that information on the number of pupils is only for the rural areas and the other information, on the other hand, is for both urban and rural. Therefore we must test the problem further and see if this relationship prevails further than seen heretofore, if it is repeated in the smaller areas of the country within the boundaries of the diocese.

Table 11.1. Pupil-teacher ratio and morality by diocese

	Pupils per Teacher in Public Schools in Rural Areas				Illegitimate Births per 100 Marriages, Town and Country	
Diocese	1826	1836	1837	1840	1831–1840	1841–1850
(Christiania *a*)	(88)	(99)				
Christiania		95	97	92	32.8	35.9
Christiansand	68	66	66	65	10.8	12.6
Bergen	90	75	76	77	19.4	20.5
Trondheim	106	88	89	91	43.9	52.4
Tromsø	105	110	118	111	40.6	39.0
The nation	(88)	85	87	85	29.1	32.2

I shall confine myself to the dioceses of Christiania and Christiansand where the condition of illegitimate births is best and most accurately known and where I have developed for each of the seven groups of deanery-districts a whole lot more extensive information about them (see tables 3.1, 3.2, 5.1, 5.2, etc.). Please refer to chapter 3 or appendix D, where I explain which deaneries I have included in each of the seven groups. I present the following comparison in table 11.2.

Table 11.2. Pupil-teacher ratio and morality by deanery-district

Deanery-Districts	Pupils per Teacher in Public Schools in Rural Areas 1837	1840	Illegitimate Births per 100 Marriages, Urban and Rural 1851–1852[a]
Group 1	95	89	39.4
Group 2	109	103	66.3
Group 3	98	91	36.0
Group 4	79	80	25.7
Group 5	61	59	16.3
Group 6	65	63	11.6
Group 7	77	77	20.2
Diocese			
Christiania	97	92	42.2
Christiansand	66	65	16.5

Here one can first observe that fortunately I have been able to give the condition of the schools for a somewhat earlier period, for the years 1837 and 1840, the years when the people during 1851–1852 were grown up, the people for whom there was information on the moral condition when they were children and attended school. And now observe the numbers in the table! Compared with group 1, there were more children per teacher in group 2 (accordingly fewer teachers) and more moral offenses. It was better in group 3 than in group 2 in both respects. It was still more favorable in group 4, and still more favorable in group 5. As for groups 5 and 6, we can say that they are close. On the other hand, group 7 has more unfortunate figures for both conditions than groups 5 and 6 but more fortunate figures than group 4, to which they are nearest.

Could this strong relationship be coincidental? We can indeed find a deviation from the relationship by comparing group 3 with group 1. But this deviation would probably not exist if the comparison was completely accurate, if the number of illegitimate births could be excluded for the towns of Fredrikshald, Fredriksstad, Sarpsborg, and Moss, which lie in group 1, inasmuch as group 3 has no other town than Kongsberg. And this insignificant deviation from the comparison between groups 5 and 6 is most likely deceptive. In any case, in table 5.2, I have pointed out that when the condition of illegitimate births is observed separately for the owner and working classes, it seems that group 5 has the best condition, and therefore this agrees very accurately in that group 5 according to table 11.2 has the most teachers for its pupils. To make up for the deficiency that the information about the educational system only refers to the rural areas, I will enter this comparison for the cities (table 11.3).

In the towns there were also relatively fewer pupils and therefore

Table 11.3. Pupil-teacher ratio in towns

	Pupils per Teacher in Towns	
	1837	1840
Christiania diocese	129	126
The same, without the city of Christiania	123	121
Christiansand diocese	84	92

more teachers in the diocese of Christiansand than in that of Christiania, and it then appears that the following generally results: more teachers—better moral conditions. Yes, at this time it can also be noted: it is known that the situation with illegitimate births is clearly worse in the towns than in the country, and besides we have seen that the towns have fewer teachers for their children than do the country districts. This last circumstance should not be accepted too readily when it can be balanced off by others.

With regard to the country districts, it might occur to some to say that the reason for the fewer teachers in the schools in the eastern mountain districts (groups 1–4) might well be that that part of the country has a higher density of population, so a teacher can handle more children. And the reason for the greater immorality in the same districts lies in the same circumstance, that people live closer together in dense clusters so that they become more like those in the towns. It is then probably the third and very remote circumstance, the unequal development of built-up areas, that has produced this agreement in the numbers of schools and the moral condition.

But remember that this difference between the towns of the two dioceses does not allow an explanation in this manner. I shall then present something else which rejects this explanation, namely this, that in the districts that are least supplied with teachers, school is attended least diligently, even though the children still have the quickest and easiest way to school. I draw on the conclusion of the studies which are before me, the number of the children under obligatory attendance and the rate of absenteeism (i.e., complete absence from school through the whole year), absenteeism in part as reported due to poverty and in part due to unwillingness. I know well that such studies are often very inaccurate; I also know absenteeism could be more frequent or more infrequent according to the relative prosperity of the country, such that people who are poor have more or less resources to put their children in school. There should, therefore, be studies of a longer series of years and, in addition, studies not only of total absenteeism but also of partial absenteeism. But I still make use of the studies there are and present the calculations contained in table 11.4. If we observe particularly the most

Table 11.4. School abstenteeism

Deanery-Districts	Number of School-Obligated Children Wholly Absent from School during the Year 1837	1840	Average for Both Years
Group 1	3.9	7.2	5.5
Group 2	8.0	10.9	9.5
Group 3	8.9	6.7	7.8
Group 4	6.1	6.5	6.3
Group 5	5.8	5.0	5.4
Group 6	1.0	2.5	1.8
Group 7	3.4	3.8	3.6
Diocese			
Christiania	7.4	8.3	7.7
Christiansand	3.7	3.9	3.8

dependable third column and we compare it with the other columns, we find unmistakably that on the whole there was the least school absenteeism in the districts where the schools were best supplied with teachers, so these three factors are associated: more teachers – more school attendance – better moral condition.

We also see this association in the diocese of Trondheim, for which I present the necessary figures in table 11.5. I have, as is seen, arranged the deaneries beginning where the teacher had the smallest number of pupils (or the schools were supplied with fewest teachers) and continued according to the increase in the number of pupils. And now we show, markedly in the last column, how the moral condition from deanery to deanery by degrees sort of worsens as the number of teachers becomes less adequate, an agreement from which there is only a slight deviation in condition between Nordmør and Fosen.

Table 11.5. Schools in the diocese of Trondheim

Deanery	Pupils per Teacher in Rural Areas 1837	1840	Illegitimate Births per 100 Marriages, Urban and Rural 1841–1850
Namdalen	74	74	32.6
Indherred	83	81	39.0
Romsdalen	89	91	53.3
Darlene	95	92	57.3
Nordmør	101	93	67.3
Fosen	106	105	59.9

With regard to the diocese of Bergen, I shall be brief. On the whole and for the majority of the deanery-districts, the situation with illegitimate births is worse in Christiansand and better than in the Trondheim diocese (see table 1.1). And on the whole paralleling most of the deanery-districts, the teaching personnel in 1837 and 1840 were fewer in the diocese of Christiansand and larger in the diocese of Trondheim (for each teacher there were from 62 to 98 children in 1837, from 65 to 97 in 1840). For that matter there is also agreement. But otherwise one can detect in the diocese of Bergen less agreement with comparisons between its internal deaneries. This last observation is true also of the diocese of Tromsø; and it should be recalled that while the condition of illegitimate births is an unfortunate exception in the deanery-districts of Finmark, the supply of teachers was very meager overall in 1840 (105 to 183 children for each teacher) except in the same two deaneries (in West Finmark, 76 children, and in East Finmark, 53).

In conclusion, I shall explain that in this presentation I have used the very complete statistical tables on the school system published by the Department of Education in 1840 and 1843. I have used only a small part of the many reports. In order to throw light on the matter, I could well have included figures on the wages of the teachers allowed, but these are recorded so variously in money, farm produce, sexton income, and land cultivation that I felt unable to get anything valid from the whole.

After this was first written, by consulting the tables again I thought I could gain some knowledge from the tables for 1840 and observe the reported incomes of teachers. It is actually only the two factors of money income and sexton income that are reported, but the various other incomes (outside of meals on the farms) are for the most part insignificant. It is, of course, natural that a greater desire for schooling is expressed by more generous funds to attract better teachers. But then again, there are many circumstances that make for different ideas about what is a good income for teachers. But in particular, one can imagine that within one and the same diocese, when the whole school system is directly under the Bishop, there arises a common rule for maximum or minimum which probably should make for limiting the comparisons to the different areas within the boundaries of one or another diocese. In table 11.6, I have calculated how much the expenditures for these positions amount to per capita of the population (in 1835). To compare with the moral conditions I have selected the numbers from table 5.2 reported for the class of the population in which the condition of illegitimate births is usually worst, namely, the working class, according to the studies of 1851–1852 from the great majority of the parishes.

It is noted that within each individual diocese there is always a relatively greater number of fathers and mothers in the groups or areas

Table 11.6. Teacher expenditures and illegitimate births in the working class

Deanery-Districts	Expenditures for Teachers' Wages per Capita of the Population	Per 100 Working Class Bridegrooms or Brides: Fathers	Mothers
Christiania diocese			
Group 1	7.4 shillings	45	52
Group 2	7.1 shillings	85	92
Group 3	7.5 shillings	42	46
Group 4	9.2 shillings	32	35
Christiansand diocese			
Group 5	10.2 shillings	17	21
Group 6	7.0 shillings	20	23
Group 7	5.6 shillings	23	28

where the people contribute the fewest shillings to the schools. In the meantime I do not dare place much value on this comparison since there are so many factors that need to be considered, particularly the various permanent schools that are included in the day schools. To calculate the number of pupils, I have used the reported number of school-obligated children as the basis, except for the cities in the dioceses of Christiania and Christiansand, where I only took into account who did not go to the public school, and as far as the teachers are concerned, I have combined the day-school and permanent-school teachers into one class. By dividing the deaneries into the seven groups, I have carefully followed the same order as in the calculation of the illegitimate births (and for those who wish to investigate the accuracy of my calculations, I must point out that what in the published tables is called Christiansand Diocesan Deaneries Country District [i.e., Oddernæs parish] according to me belongs to group 5, in that in recent times it has been turned over to the deanery of Robygdelag). So as not to take up too much space, I include excerpts of tables that I had to make up before I could undertake the calculations whose results I have communicated. I shall only report that which has common interest, that by the end of 1840 it was reported that in the country districts of the nation, there were 179,432 school-obligated children plus 1,888 day-school and 224 permanent-school teachers.

I have now for a long time traveled around the country and talked with many people and searched various kinds of documents and undertaken counting and calculations in order to get at, in any way possible, the probable reason for the great and mysterious differences in the various areas of people's lives that reveal the condition of illegitimate births. At first, during the days when I had finished the book, I again and again reviewed the writing and just then wanted to start the concluding chapter, but it is only now that I have become aware of this certainly extraordinary relationship between school and life. That there must be a certain relationship I knew before, but only in a common-sense manner. And it then occurred to me that a detailed knowledge of the development of the school system over time could serve to cast light on the whole life of the people, but it did not occur to me that there should be such an overwhelming agreement between the more common characteristics of the school and this single factor in the life of the people, or more correctly: elementary research (which the reader will remember I have done in chapter 8) had given me the idea that the studies of the school system which exist today would not be improved much by waiting for more extensive research. But then, at the eleventh hour I gathered my courage and started to go much further into the detailed statistics on the schools, and I admit that I was surprised at the results. Yes, if I remember what I wrote in the first chapter of this book, it is likely that both there and in the following chapters I was coming to comprehend and clarify one or another thing differently than I do now.

RELATIONSHIP TO VARIOUS SOCIAL CONDITIONS

What now? I assume that even the most careful reader grants that in general there has been revealed a clear relationship between the school system and the moral condition. And the exceptions that were found for individual communities are regarded only as reminders that there are still many other factors that could distort or obscure the usual pattern. (It is precisely the newly remembered attempt to explain the difference in morals between Lower Romerike relating to the level of the school system [chapter 8] that gives us an example of how a rule which otherwise can be universal does not always apply to individual instances. Still, it cannot be said by any means that the rule does not also apply there. We learn only to bear in mind that the moral condition is always to be observed as something that has been created by a combination of several simultaneously existing circumstances, of which some are more influential so that the others are not as visible and withdraw from the stage; and the effect of circumstances can change or can have different effects in various places and at different times. Some relationship between the school system and the moral condition can be seen for Upper and Lower Romerike. In these last few pages we have surely learned that in general there is such a relationship, and therefore we also expect this relationship in the named districts; but at the same time we should assume that there must be certain other—so far unknown—circumstances which at the same place have had a more conclusive influence.)

But when we are agreed thereon, what should we make of this relationship? First we could interpret as follows: with the united efforts of some schoolmasters the children will be better taught, and better-taught children will for the most part behave better when they grow up. It follows that if schools in some areas are better supplied with teaching personnel than others, it can be regarded as the cause of the much better moral condition in the same place.

But what is again the cause of the phenomenon that in some areas there are more schoolmasters than in others? It is not to fool around with the reader that I pose this question (since I can surely ask it forever and uselessly) but to approach the problem another way. It is, of course, the same church and the same state which have organized and set up the schools in both the dioceses of Christiansand and Christiania, and we should thus expect a similar development of this public institution in both places. Could the differences be rooted in these places? Can it be shown that bishops, deans, and pastors in early times were more effective in the establishment of the school system in one diocese or community than in another? And that they have been so fortunate in their efforts that the effects on the life of the people should show beneficial results? Hans Holst and Anna Eeg in Kobbervik in the Stavanger area and Dean Winfeld in Hvideseid in Telemark very early established permanent schools with bequests, and these institutions later became teaching schools for future schoolmasters, the first institutions of their kind in the nation. And do we dare believe that from here a greater zeal and competence spread among the schoolteacher group in the diocese of Christiansand to which these schools belonged? We could sufficiently assess the efforts and sacrifices of such individuals for the public good, and in case someone is well acquainted with the histories of the communities, the individuals deserve recognition in a published account of such efforts and undertakings, which could be assumed to have clearly contributed to the promotion of the education and welfare of the people. But still it is not likely that we would be able to explain the entire condition by this method. There would have to be a very unusual group of dedicated persons to advance the school system in one diocese so markedly that one could thereby trace its influence on people's morals, as has been described. And as for the clergy, it is difficult to believe that in one generation (since as a rule it takes a long time to harvest what is sown in this field) a greater fervor could prevail in one diocese ahead of another, since most of the clergy live for a while in one or another diocese.

Just as I was pondering this matter, I came to page through a book that the Norwegian Association Against Liquor has published, which contains an annual report on the Norwegian temperance associations in 1846. In 1836 the first of the 140 associations which were known in 1840 was established, and these at that time had 17,026 members. There is a careful explanation about how many of these belonged to each diocese. In order to make a comparison, I calculate the situation as follows: for each 1,000 people aged 20 or over, the numbers of friends of temperance are shown in table 11.7.

Table 11.7. Friends of temperance per 1,000 people aged 20 or more

Diocese	
Christiania	47
Christiansand	119
Bergen	16
Trondheim	15
Tromsø	26

See, here it is remarkable that in the diocese of Christiansand, where we found that most had been done for the development of the school system, the zeal for temperance is also most widespread (a similar statistic on the mission associations would surely show that both the earliest associations and their relatively most numerous members should be in the diocese of Christiansand). Are there signs ahead of a greater public consciousness among the people, a greater participation in the institutions for education and morals? And here we must remember that arrangements to promote the schools to a great extent certainly do not result from negotiations among the clergy alone, but between the clergy and the public, between pastors and the chairmen of the congregations; thus it is correct to ask about the common sense and the goodwill of the public.

After this signal my mind goes further and asks: Can any circumstance be shown that could be regarded as a reasonable cause of the greater social consciousness and effective participation on the part of the people in social-improvement groups and similar institutions in the dioceses of Christiansand and Christiania, such that the former is ahead? And here we are led to observe the appreciable difference between the two dioceses regarding social conditions. According also to a previously mentioned excerpt from the census tables, I have found that the average for the years 1835 and 1845 showed the proportions of the two large classes of the population (both urban and rural) reported in table 11.8.

Table 11.8. Average proportion of working class to owner class, 1835 and 1845[a]

	Owner Class	Working Class
Diocese		
Christiania	100	281
Christiansand	100	243
Bergen	100	237
Trondheim	100	345
Tromsø	100	292

[a] See the study *About Mortality in Norway* [*Selected Works* 2:107].

This is to conclude that for each 100 farm owners, merchants, etc., there are 281 workers in the diocese of Christiania; in the diocese of Christiansand, on the other hand, there are only 243 cotters, servants, etc.; accordingly, in daily speech, in this diocese [Christiania] there are more masters with fewer underlings, and in that diocese [Christiansand] there are prominent masters with not so many underlings. (A statistic on the labor unions like that on the temperance associations should also have shown relatively more members in Christiania than in the Christiansand diocese.) And this condition is not only found in the diocese as a whole; in each of the seven groups or districts into which I well remember I have divided the dioceses, the studies show how many people of each class were married in 1851 and 1852, and about this I have explained (see *On Marriage in Norway* [*Selected Works* 2:300]). In each of the east mountain districts (groups 1–4) there were about twice as many bridegrooms and brides in the working class as in the owner class; in each of the three west mountain districts (groups 5–7) there was a far lower proportion on the side of the working class, and in group 6 it was indeed the opposite so that the owner class was the most numerous. And if that is not enough, from the same study of the married couples [p. 302] it is seen that in the three west mountain districts where the working class is not as numerous there is rather not so great a differentiation between the classes in social relations. The propertied people and the working people are more on an equal footing with each other there. It is then understandable that cross-marriages between people of the higher and lower classes often occur. "It is reasonable," I said in a talk about this there, "to continue research in this direction and thereby construct comparisons between the different regions of the nation that should result in interesting information and explanations about folk morality and folk conditions."

Now I put the one in association with the other thus: the greater similarity in circumstance among the people in the diocese of Christiansand has served to preserve the natural feeling of community that is so closely related to the true regard for human worth and the rights and duties of people. This feeling of community has been shown to be effective in the age-old efforts to develop good human behavior among the grown-up generations by education (and therefore congregations have established many schoolmasters) and by upbringing (and therefore parents have encouraged children to be diligent in school). The same feeling of community, by applying the named means carefully among the young, has also been shown to be effective in the lives of individuals so that more here than in other places protected themselves from moral crimes and were quicker to join public efforts, such as associations against liquor and for missionary causes. If this hitherto-corrected information seems to place the folk life of the diocese of Christiansand too high and attribute to it such a conscious struggle for the welfare of the public, one can instead express oneself thus—that in the extreme, the atmosphere evoked by the social condition has preserved people's thoughts and morals from some of the bad conduct that easily develops where there is a greater split between the higher and lower states, [where workers are] ignored by the highborn who selfishly misuse their superiority on the one hand, plus [where they feel] low envy on the other. One sign that this misconduct is more prominent in the folk life in the diocese of Christiania could be seen in that the leaders of the congregation, or rather the chairmen of the owner class, haven't provided as much for the school system (most of the children do belong to people of the lower class) so that the working class has especially been spoiled with an excess of immoral behavior. And in this connection it can be recalled that it was especially the working class of the diocese of Christiania whose condition brought the politicians of the nation a few years ago to try by a new law to provide the large cotter class better conditions; plus, it was the working class whose agitation and simultaneous clamor all over the land, and these essentially were the members in that same diocese, won much participation, namely, with the cry for more education. Oh—this cry got lost under other manifold and confused discord, and the zeal for education that flared up on this occasion seems to be lacking in the diocese of Christiania in the final analysis. The parents should provide for schools for their children (table 11.4), but these provisions are often too great for poor people; but it also often seems so to them, since there should already be a certain degree of information and culture in order to realize the good about education that benefits some a great deal.

I have forthrightly given my opinion of the matter. (No one is more willing than I to remember that we still do not have sufficient facts, nor enough compilations of observations to understand the mysteries of folk life, so when we put forth our opinion about one or another matter, it must be done with care and with the thought that another day will probably bring another view. This applies especially to many of the tables in this book, those that support the reports of the pastors for only the two years 1851 and 1852. But I must especially deplore that the school system in this country is not well known. Year after year we should have reports on the number and incomes of teachers, the diligence of school children, etc., district by district. This knowledge is necessary not only for the sake of the schools, whose interests one wants to put in a framework, but also for the sake of the folk life, whose innermost condition and invisible nature one must understand in order by several methods to put the interests of society into a framework. But the studies must be made year after year. An example: How else would it have been possible to formulate a rational opinion about a matter that has caused so much trouble for so many people—namely, the growing number of illegitimate births—if we had not had so many reports of the same for years on end? And in the same way, in the future there can come into existence more and more questions regarding the school system in the nation, which every friend of the fatherland wishes an answer to but which can only be answered by the help of studies for several years.) The conclusion is that depending on the social condition and the public spirit, the chairmen of the congregations and the parents are concerned about the education and nurturing of the children, and so is the public spirit—in such manner are created the ways of thinking and the customs that adults practice in each of their daily lives. In such a way the schools and the moral condition will stand together with each other, mostly because of connections with this third element: the public spirit, the folk character, this invisible activity that we partly learn to know through the most various revelations. A good spirit among the people creates a good school system and much else that aims to promote learning and culture; a good spirit among the people creates good morals and ideas that the multitude will acquire and practice in life.

Will I hereby deny the thought, which at the very first was supported by the observations of the facts I have myself presented in this chapter, this simple thought that a good school system (many teachers, etc.) directly causes the moral condition to become good? For that matter, I will reject the thought that one must still not believe that, for example, an English lord could attempt to improve the moral condition in our communities by turning over some of his wealth to establish and pay some hundred schoolmasters and to feed and clothe the children during their schooling. Human beings cannot be managed by such an external and mechanical method, at least not for the good. But the important thing in this thought I will confirm based on my whole understanding, and with great emphasis I repeat the conclusion that originally resulted from the facts: there is an intense and necessary and unavoidable relationship between the condition of the school system (and the whole educational system) on the one side and the moral condition on the other side. This opinion is based still more clearly on the example I offer: In the eastern part of the diocese of Christiania's hinterland (group 2, or Upper Romerike, Odal and Solør, Østerdal, Hedemark, and Gudbrandsdal), one cannot expect any improvement in the moral condition (which right now is found to be so low) until the spirit comes to the people to want education and to believe in its ennobling influence and willingly and diligently work for its cause—more than heretofore.

NEED FOR DEVELOPMENT OF SCHOOLS

But how? Should this spirit not already be in the people? Must not each person favor education? Is it not precisely this that all people talk about in these times? "Yes, it is true what the political candidate says; here there is really much too much vulgarity among the poor people in the community. But who is to blame? Is it not the ones who have power who have not cared about doing something substantially for education?" In such a way I have heard cotter people express their impatience, but it is a false impatience that hurries to place the blame on others, and such impatience is evidence of a lukewarm desire when it comes to the crunch that poor people should make some provision to send the children to school and let them be absent from their work during schooltime, etc. "Yes, education—that is right: much depends on it, it must come if poverty and poor-relief expenditures are not to dominate. More schools, and more kinds of schools, and good pay for competent teachers! Just give us help from the education budget!" So have I heard farmers express themselves with great impatience, but it is a false impatience that pushes the blame on that source, the education budget, since 50 dalers of this fund is not much more than one shilling or two per capita in the community. "Certainly education is good, but it depends only on what kind of education it is. Look around: do you not also find among highly educated and cultured people ones who still succumbed to wild life of all kinds? No, no, my friend, believe me, it will not become general unless a greater fear of God spreads among the people. That is what will save us." This is also a false impatience. The one who has the gift of prayer may pray in private that the Kingdom of God must also come to us, the Kingdom of God with the enlightenment of the soul and the other gifts of grace, but today he should work to prepare for the coming of God's Kingdom, to prepare by spreading education which is in the power of human beings to deliver—to work with the hope that He who lets the sun shine and the rain fall on the field that human diligence has cultivated, He will also bless the industry that will call forth the growth of thoughtfulness and understanding in the spiritual field of man. Yes, here the word *sun* is important, as mercy falls on both the righteous and the unrighteous: even when the unrighteous, men whose minds are not directed toward the high, decide to provide for the school system ad other educational agencies merely because of human will or because of worldly reasons, for example, to oppose thereby the worst of the vulgarity, or to bring up a generation of more thoughtful and skilled workers. Still the sun's grace will shine on such efforts and result in winning more and more of the grown-up generation to the truth. (Here can be the place to add that in my talk about the entire school system I think of the common school in our country as a school between the grammar school and the university, with the first and most important mission to give the children a sound knowledge of religion which, if possible, is preserved in a pious heart; but at the very least, it becomes the school's objective to develop the whole spiritual person. One example: the boy who under the teacher's encouragement and direction overcomes his childish fickleness to learn how to write and write well at the same time he is practicing the art of self-control. Another example: if the teacher could succeed in lecturing on the history of the fatherland so that the young were cheered and come to love the fatherland, so should this feeling—next to religion the most uplifting—very surely often be an encouragement during the struggles of life, a support against temptation. Nowadays it is remarkable how very little the honor and well-being of the fatherland mean to the youth of the working class; there's a lack of love for the fatherland that can best be compared with the lack of self-regard evident in the many examples of vulgarity.)

In the communities where the social condition at one time evolved so that there is a greater split between the owners and the working people (with few and big masters on one side and on the other side laborers and servants, shabby in appearance and powerless), there the redeeming element will be to seek effective educational agencies to spread education among the people, since education is like light and fire, which do not diminish by being communicated from one to the other. The purpose of education is to be a common good in the main, so that the richest in it can see his poverty in common with the poorest, who can feel that he has part and parcel of it. The higher classes must respond to the call and use the better opportunity they have to go still farther forward on the way to learning, and for each step they go forward, they must behave so that the many who are on a lower level can follow to the extent that their calling and position in life demand, all with the objective that this gap in differences in wealth really does not become greater. Nevertheless, because of the common and mutual acknowledgment of the worth of human beings, this gap must become smaller and smaller. But in order to fill in the wider gap there will be required, as far as concerns the public school, both more teachers, so that the handicaps to the diligent schooling of the children of the poor can more easily be overcome, and more competent and therefore better-paid teachers, who could be expected to have the gift to win the confidence of the lower classes and the respect of the higher classes. But right now in the districts of the two southern dioceses where there was the greatest need, there we found that in reality there were fewer teachers (and that school absenteeism—reasonably enough, as a result—was more frequent) than in the districts where the social and moral condition was better and accordingly did not make so big a demand. And with reference to this I say that no matter how much I join in with the men's talk, which in recent years has resulted in the spread and improvement of the school system in the whole of our country, I must particularly direct the proper authorities' attention to such districts as Upper Romerike, Solør, Hedemark, and Gudbrandsdal, the communities with the extremely deplorable moral conditions shown in this book.

The attention of the proper authorities, I said; but I think mostly of the individual men in the farm-owner class whose voices are usually the decisive factor in the negotiations in congregations or municipalities about such matters, often a very small number of the more thoughtful and zealous men, 10 or 12, whose advice and opinions are accepted by a great many of their peers. This selection of farm owners has been in my mind while writing these observations. If they will take up the work for the cause of public education, take it up such that they do not merely show high-mindedness in appropriating money for schoolteachers, etc., but in such manner that each in his network with a love for the cause spreads the same view in his surroundings, then a transformation will take place in the lives of the folk in the communities in education, in morality: and then, then there will likely be such social conditions as those in the diocese of Christiania, with a mighty and educated owner class and an abundant and skilled working population showing themselves to be fortunate in the development of the standards of living and the promotion of the public welfare.

But if this does not happen, if it comes to be that the men of the communities do not undertake actions for the public school system, which the cause and times demand, then I should wish that a responsible authority could step in and decree what is required. In England, I am pleased to tell, there is a public health commissioner who, when he receives the annual mortality lists for a town or an area that show that mortality has risen a certain degree, can order the municipalities to make certain arrangements to clean the air and eliminate the cause of illness, etc. I would like an authority that in the same manner would keep track of the moral condition and observe, for example, the lists of illegitimate births in each parish, and then—when the number exceeds a certain measure—intervene with its advice or, according to the circumstance, step in with its decisions for arrangements to counteract the moral infections. Yes, I believe that in an orderly society those who administer and govern up to an undetermined degree really could control morality, and I believe that this can and must take place in a *free* society, where freedom has taught individuals to serve the whole voluntarily and gladly.

NEED FOR ADULT EDUCATION

I did not believe that I would dwell so long on the public schools. While I have been very glad for some years to see other men with influence take up the cause of the public schools, I more often have become aware of the great importance of doing everything that can be done to promote increased education and culture among the adult generation, those who recently dropped out of school. I have often had to shake my head when I saw the eagerness of public school officials to use expressions such as "nothing can be done about the adult generation; it is the children we must put our hopes in, those who will become the future generation." In the past the same words were used,but it is sad to see how little the hope of the past was fulfilled for the many persons concerned. It is certainly a familiar saying about children who grew away from school that a large number of them "put the book on the shelf," and it is not unusual to meet people between 20 and 30 years old who have almost forgotten how to read a book. I of course understand it: Teach the children to read better than has heretofore been the case, and then they will be less likely to forget it later. I also understand that not everything is done with book learning and education, but it is always of benefit to master education and preparation, experience and thoughtfulness, the serious mind that life itself can give. In the meantime, when a grown person puts the book on the shelf is still one of the most critical signs, since there are not better things for an 18-year-old boy to usually pass his leisure time with.

And now I permit myself to recall how in chapter 8, in discussions about social opportunities for young people in the country, I suggested establishing community libraries, many in each school district. If the representatives of the municipalities could encourage them by appropriate financial subsidy, it would be fine. There must always be one condition, that such a library must never be dissolved, that if the association dissolves, it must (under the supervision of the municipality) be preserved intact until a new association is established in the same district. There are, as I see from the school statistics which are before me, or there were in 1840 in Norway's country districts, 2,126 day-school and permanent-school districts. Imagine a collection of books in each of them instead of 230 public libraries as there were then! Truly, I do not desire this only for the sake of counteracting coarseness but because I wish the servants and such folk the satisfaction and joy of reading a well-written book. (A book collection begun with 10 dalers the first year and continued with 5 dalers annually—it is a contribution of 24 shillings from 25 members—would after a number of years be considerable, and such book collections in great numbers over the entire country would perforce have a favorable influence on literature: it is more satisfying for authors to write when they know there are people who stand and wait for good books.)

But while this affair certainly must be recommended for private efforts, there is still another current great cause that is dependent directly on political decisions, as you will see in table 11.9.

After this overview it certainly looks like the population increased over the heads of the pastors. And this growth took place during a time

Table 11.9. Numbers of pastors per people

	Number of Pastors[a]		Population per Pastor	
	1815	1855	1815	1855
Diocese				
Christiania	164	168	2,263	3,828
Christiansand	64	74	2,283	3,303
Bergen	68	69	2,348	3,520
Trondheim	62	67	2,260	3,390
Tromsø	47	51	1,627	2,580
Total	405	429	2,190	3,473

[a] Under the word *pastor* I have included everybody called clergy, except curates.

when so many circumstances made the conditions of living more and more complex (think, for example, of how a far greater number of people of all classes left their home communities and settled in unfamiliar places more than before) so that the mission of the church to admonish and comfort could well need a growing corps of spokesmen. But now there are many, many places in our country where it is impossible for even the most zealous pastor to know his congregation, to get to know the individuals.

I know that this matter (increasing the strength of the clergy) to a substantial degree stands and falls with the view that might be taught within the congregations regarding the worth and significance of the spiritual positions and regarding the appropriate organization of the church establishment, and here is not the place to discuss this specifically. But to a very great extent there are extreme difficulties and financial problems that are in the way of sharing among the parishes. And in regard thereto I here want the men who have to negotiate these matters (and here I think once more of the respected and trusted members of the congregation who as chairmen take part in the negotiations) to be aware that regarding the moral condition in certain parts of the country, they have a distinctive mission to help suffering humanity.

FINAL WORDS

After these explanations about the school system and after these comments on the education of the grown-up youth to self-education, plus the increase in the clergy, I venture, since the talk is about education and good morals, still to discuss an educational struggle, which according to my concept should serve to promote good morals in the country; and it is the struggle to cast light on the matter that is actually the moral condition in the country, the struggle to assemble observations and thereby come to understand immorality, its many kinds and expressions, its causes and effects, its relationship to the entire folk life.

And hereby I come, like an epilog to the book, to converse with the reader about my current work.

In the year 1850 one of my reports to the Department of Justice, *Report on the Gypsy or the Vagabond Folk in Norway,* was published and since that time I continue to note in 1856 that many believe I am still occupied solely with the Gypsy folk. During recent years I could do only little for this matter. Nevertheless, my work during recent years, which resulted in this report, is connected to those investigations. By observing the condition of the Gypsies, I gained a great deal of experience regarding the life of the common people that brought me to believe that there were probably hidden things that some persistent and specific scientific study might be able to bring to light, hidden things of suffering and destitution. I have also written in the last chapter about the report mentioned, and at the end of 1850 I humbly requested the authorities to support the work "to start investigations particularly on the lower social classes' condition and morals." From the beginning I had thought that this matter would take several years of work. By a gracious resolution, the sought-for financial support was granted me only for the year 1851. But without any application from me or a recommendation from the government about it, the assembled Parliament appropriated the same budget in 1851 to continue these investigations in 1852 and 1853. By a gracious resolution, there was a grant for still more support for 1854, and after the appropriation for 1854 Parliament extended the support with an increased budget to the end of the budget termination or the middle of 1857. (In addition to up to 200 dalers for travel expenditures, my personal income until the end of 1851 was 500 dalers a year, later 650 dalers.)

In 1851 I traveled over a part of Smaalenene, Hedemark, Gudbrandsdal, and Østerdal, and touched the diocese of Trondheim (Røros). In 1852 I repeated my visit to Gudbrandsdal. In 1853 I traveled over the districts between Christiansand and Bergen. In 1854 I was again in Gudbrandsdal. In 1855 and the current year, 1856, I was in Upper and Lower Romerike for a couple of months. In my count I find that I have used all together 754 days for travel. (A part of my time was devoted to participation in the Royal Resolution of August 5, 1853, a commission established to consider the distribution of poverty, and some of the time for my work was lost with a stay at the Sandefjord Spa in 1854 and 1855.) It is essentially the conditions in the country districts that have occupied me during these years, and—as the citations show—particularly the country districts in the diocese of Christiania.

How many things and many kinds of things during these years I have had to pay attention to, and how many strong opinions and assertions and explanations have I heard from people of all stations! And I, who before that time was so unfamiliar with rural conditions! I arrived at rural communities exactly during the days when worker agitation had enlivened both the hearts and minds. In Sarpsborg the sawyer workers wanted me to believe the strangest accusations against the factory management, and people from other social levels wanted me to believe that in certain worker groups each man drank an average of three half-pints of liquor per day. In Hedemark the cotters took me out to their fields and wanted me to know how bad the soil was and how high the fees for the crops were, and farm owners wanted to explain to me that the cotters at bottom were much too expensive work folk, and I myself found among the cotter class such an excess of immorality that I thought the whole must be regarded as frightful. In Tønsæt the local people wanted me to admit to the rightness of their complaints about certain changes in the rules of the Røros factory management regarding *kulsæt*—a contrivance whose name I had not known before; and at the bottom of the Røros mines, the mine workers on the place with torches in hand informed me how completely backward some of the decisions on pay for digging were, while the managers of the works offered me unrestricted access to the detailed accounting so that there I could see how the mine workers were better off in all ways than they were before. And overall one heard the complaints of the farm owners about the rising expenses for welfare for the poor because of increasing immorality, and the complaints of the poor about the stingy support.

I can say that I have been living a strange life during these years, and most of it has been anxious and insecure. I did not know where I would begin and did not understand how I would arrive at orderly and coherent research on all this. It was as if I stood out in the open to undertake the counting of the stars in the heavens. But under these circumstances I have held out until now with my peculiar investigations and have plucked up my courage to deliver this book also—because I still believe that there can be value in each love of the truth contributing to the knowledge about people, yes, especially about the circumstances and morals of the lower classes.

Most certainly it was my experience that when I lived for 14 days in a community and then went on, I had to tell myself that with all my diligence I still surely had not learned one-tenth as much about the actual circumstances in the same community as the pastor or as each farm owner and cotter knew. And certainly I must consider that when the pastors or other people read this book they will say that much in it they knew before, and further, that it is not entirely valid. But even so, it would be much too strange if not one painstaking comparison of morals and conditions in one area and another, from one time to another, should help us to understand more and more the basis of the life of the people, yes, to give us scientific insight into some of the things on which the people's inner and outer well-being depends.

Or [it would be much too strange if] with deep scientific insight we will not be fortunate to arrive in this matter at exactly the cause of the continuous change that is the reason for the folk life's not having the same characteristics this year as last year, or in any case in one generation as in the other. So let us call it historical research, which also has its value. Have you, reader, experienced the sad night at one of the church cemeteries in the country where there is no grave marker to show concern of the survivors for the memory of the deceased? Such is the life of the people in the past, with its morals and customs, its suffering and longing, in large part forgotten, buried in oblivion. Who does not immediately believe that there should be great interest if we for the same previous century, from 1756 on, had a comprehensive explanation of the people's condition and morals, if only for the reason of the current contribution—love of truth?

And what about transformations in the life of the people? There are, of course, changes in substantive matters—the culture of a nation, welfare, piety—and each thoughtful friend of the people will quite certainly approve a great effort to find out the origin of such changes and direction, since the more this succeeds the more it would be true, as I stated as possible in the foregoing, that the leaders of the people could to a certain degree manage the folk life and control morals.

Because the matter seems so large, I intend to continue the beginning I have made so far—as far as I am able and as long as I believe that in this manner I can best use the abilities I have. But because the task is so complicated, I request that those who possibly approve of my efforts stand by me. In the wish to make this request, I have put not a little effort into publishing this book, since now I can say: "See how much is still lacking in order to give a comprehensive, and in all parts dependable, explanation of the moral life of the people! And see how I cannot in a desirable short time be able to travel over the entire country and with my own eyes and ears get to know everything!"

It is self-evident that I first think of the pastors as especially the ones who can support the study of morality with valuable reports. This book is evidence of their willingness to do so, since a substantial portion of its contents is built on reports which by the goodwill of the pastors have been sent me. Moreover, more than a few pastors took the opportunity to give me their opinion of the statistical reports that I had requested, which were hardly worth the effort and had no significance for the clergy. In newspaper columns and other places, one can often see such expressions of the pastors about the statistics that the government demands that they give. But once in a while in consulting the church registers with care, what else is there than to call on the pastor's memory to organize the entire mass of experiences he had when a new couple was married, a child baptized, etc., experiences regarding significant events in the outer and inner life of the congregation? And if the older pastor does not gain anything new in this way, it becomes easier for a newly placed minister, or for the young man who has just become a pastor, to have important memoranda from his predecessors whereby he more or less quickly can become knowledgeable about the lives of the people. And such memoranda would be annual excerpts in the church register.

"Concern for the soul," says Vinet in his pastoral-theology, "will not be the same in town and country, in a farming area and in factory areas, among people with uncorrupted morals and among folk who are refined and gentle. The pastor must be concerned with everything, as well as the geographical, climatic, economic, dietary, and historical circumstances. He must know his congregation's customs, interests, necessities, prejudices, and desires. He will not limit himself to some individual, permanent views on which he has come to conclusions; he will study them. Since even where the usual circumstances are the same, where there are two congregations both made up of mountain dwellers, or both of farmers, both prosperous, or both poor even there one must differentiate. The pastor above all must know the religious condition of the people who have been delivered to him. This and all the foregoing kowledge are the objective for a continuous and persistent study from the instant he occupies his post; but before his arrival he must be prepared to obtain information about everything that is of some importance, and many small items that seem insignificant are important. If one does not know this, one gets hurt, gives offence, gets badly talked about, and creates prejudices that rise quickly and disappear slowly. One should know the good and the bad, the strong as well as the weak, but one must know what one shall work for, and what one shall work against."

Once before I, as I have so often told, permitted myself to request the clergy for certain special reports from the church register. But that was only to sort of try to see what could be learned from such reports, and the request, therefore, was limited to the clergy in the two southern dioceses. When the current book has been printed, I will permit myself to extend the requests to the clergy in all the dioceses, namely, by sending to the pastors a printed questionnaire to be filled out. (As soon as the current manuscript is delivered to the printer, I will start a longer journey for a continued study of folk life, and it is then a matter of course that I not least will try to collect further information on the subject that has occupied me in these pages. I am accordingly still in the middle of the research work, and it can then be considered remarkable that I already dare to publish the current manuscript. It can be called even more remarkable as the presentation carries much too many traces of being a hasty piece of work, which is surely doubly unfortunate for a study on a subject whose ugly character needs all the appeal that an orderly and polished presentation could offer. But primarily this book gives information about a folk evil that each year brings undetermined misfortune over the country, so there need not be manifested any word or intent to work against it; and for the other, the publication of the current book was almost a necessity for me, for I want, as indicated above, to direct myself to the pastors with a request to contribute to the continuation of the accomplished beginning. I hope that with the assistance of the Department of Education I shall be able to send each of the parish pastors a copy of this book, and that will be my foreword to this request. I perhaps dare to hope that the ministers will let me or several schoolteachers in the district become acquainted with my communications to them.

Regarding several dates here and there in the book, I must add that it was written during May–July 1856.)

But currently I direct myself to the public schools. The greatest part of my knowledge, which a scientist could wish in order to initiate intensive observations of the folk life, is already collected by the schoolmasters, who have a right to go in and act among the people. And among a large portion of the schoolmasters there is the spirit not to limit their work to school hours but to extend their thoughts and efforts to the life for which they are preparing the young, the toilsome and dangerous life. The men of the teaching class who believe that there can be some value in work like mine, and who are not given any special opportunity in journals in one or another way to report their experiences with the condition and morals of the people, I sincerely bid them to send such reports. Community by community, I should wish to see their observations about the moral condition, about the special dangers from immorality, about the improvement in thinking and living style, about the cause of such change. Community by community, I should wish to see their explanations about some of the items that I have touched on in this book, which in some way could seem to relate culture and morality, such as: house equipment and housing (chapters 2 and 3); night courting (chapter 4—if I were a teacher at a day school I should have some kind of opinion on how many families have given up the bad custom and how many have not, separately for farm owners and the cotter class); and further, social customs, clothes, food, rules for working time (chapter 8—I would value highly explanations of the most common food preparation and menus, and for each community, they might dare to give information on the results of the burden of drunkenness, including certainly the many different controls on it around the country); and further, explanations of superstitions and customs (separately for farm owners and the cotter class); plus the total number of families in the districts with schools and the total number of books and newspapers and their titles found in the same families. I cannot, of course, expect that anyone should provide a comprehensive explanation of all these items. But rather one item treated exhaustively than brief and overflowing observations about several! Nevertheless, each contribution, which must be sent to me (in Christiania), will be received with an acknowledgment. And physicians, sheriffs, farmers—perhaps I dare to seek reports from them, reports possibly also about the economic and social conditions of communities. It is, of course, something new to issue such a request, but it is my hope to be able to deliver a continuation of the current writing, a more complete presentation of the people's condition and morals, a description somewhat like those that display the status of agriculture or industry and which are brought about by the contributions of many. Were I able to start to bring in information about the conditions mentioned from all districts in the country, the whole must naturally have a statistical form, with definite terminology, etc. But here, where I can only depend on the goodwill of individuals, the presentation must rightly be turned over to the understanding of each. I dare not expect so many numbers and calculations but rather more descriptions and reflections.

If it should come to pass that I see no visible results of all this kind of work, I still hold to the belief that through the chairmen, through pastors, and through schoolteachers, more basic information on the people's condition and morals will finally lead to an improvement in the condition, to the quickening of the change for the better, which I also believe will take place. But mostly I am encouraged by the idea that when one has come so far that one can control the material and with convincing clarity improve the important elements in the life of the people (elements just as appealing to thought and spirit as those that surprise us in nature), so should writing and studies about it be suitable to awaken the attention among the people themselves, the masses of the youth of the country, who more than any can carry on and attack the bad old customs and stir up the maelstrom of dark conditions, they who therefore are also the main object of the thoughts of this friend of the people. It is remarkable that if one first gets sight of the right and the good, almost anything is possible that one approves of, and there is certainly great truth in the repentant sigh of this unfortunate one: If I had really known this before, how bad it was, I would not have done it! And therefore, I say thus: the effort to search out and cast light on the condition of morality must very certainly be related to the struggle to work against the evil and promote the good.

APPENDIX

A

The Method of Calculating the Frequency of Illegitimate Births

Instead of the common method of calculating the frequency of illegitimate births by comparing them with the legitimate, in this study I have compared the illegitimate births with marriages. In that connection I owe an explanation, and herewith I select an example which includes the figures for Norway in the previous century (see table A.1).

(The figures for 1851–1885 presented an overabundance, and the illegitimate births concerned do not enable any comparison with the foregoing time period because the counting has been carried out by a different method. See the explanation in chapter 9.)

Table A.1. The frequency of illegitimate births

Years	Marriages	Live Births: Legitimate	Live Births: Illegitimate
1801–1805	33,917	118,496	7,452
1806–1810	31,389	115,905	8,072
1811–1815	37,129	116,369	8,308
1816–1820	41,583	142,371	12,136
1821–1825	44,081	157,984	12,670
1826–1830	42,558	167,284	12,614
1831–1835	42,233	169,252	12,111
1836–1840	40,681	159,606	12,017
1841–1845	50,590	179,670	15,731
1846–1850	52,506	193,408	17,479
(1851–1855	56,499	213,004	21,590)

The relationships are as follows:

Years	Marriages	Illegitimate Births	Legitimate Births	Illegitimate Births
1801–1805	100	21.9	100	6.3
1806–1810	100	25.7	100	7.0
1811–1815	100	22.4	100	7.1
1816–1820	100	29.2	100	8.5
1821–1825	100	28.7	100	8.0
1826–1830	100	29.6	100	7.5
1831–1835	100	28.7	100	7.4
1836–1840	100	29.5	100	7.5
1841–1845	100	31.1	100	8.8
1846–1850	100	33.3	100	9.0
(1851–1855	100	38.2	100	10.1)

If one had carried out a comparison between the illegitimate and the legitimate births as in the lower half of table A.1, during 1831–1835 one would have found a clear and steady decrease ever since the five-year period 1816–1820. But this would very likely have been a disappointment. As table A.1 shows, the number of illegitimate births rise and fall in relation to the number of marriages. In actuality both the number of illegitimate children and the number of marriages have essentially responded to the number of people in the marriageable age group, as shown in the comparable study (*On Marriage in Norway* [*Selected Works* 2:241] et al.). The opposite is true for legitimate births. As table A.1 shows, their number rises very fast during 1816–1820 plus in 1821–1825, when the number of marriages increased markedly, but not enough: their number still continues to rise during 1826–1830 and even during 1831–1835, although marriages were not on the rise. The cause for this is obvious in that the number of legitimate births does not respond immediately to the simultaneously established marriages but rather those which were established in the nearest previous five years, and it still includes existing marriages of married people in fertile years. From this it follows that if one compares the legitimate births during the five-year period 1831–1835, it is the same as comparing the group of people who were of marriageable age during the years 1831–1835. A certain percent of them became parents of illegitimate children with the group who during the years 1816 to 1835 or 1821 to 1835 were of the same age, and a certain portion were married year after year and had legitimate children. But this comparison does not work, particularly not in our country, where during the last hundred years there has been an exceedingly large wave of population mobility so that the number of people in different age groups has been very unlike from time to time. Particularly, the age group which includes the largest number of the marriageable people between 20 and 30 years was smaller in 1835 than in 1825, while still the entire population on the whole increased very visibly during the same period (see the related study *On Marriage*). The legitimate births during 1831–1835 stemmed both from the greater number of people in the marriageable age group in 1825 and from the smaller number in 1835; the illegitimate births during 1831–1835 stemmed solely from this smaller number. Accordingly, *if the frequency* of both the legitimate and the illegitimate children in themselves (observed in relation to the class of people to which the parents belonged) were the same during 1831–1835 as earlier, so the *number* of *legitimate* children must be *larger* than before, and the *number* of *illegitimate* children became *smaller* than before. The reciprocal relationship between them must have changed.

By calculating the frequency of illegitimate births relative to the parallel established marriages, I also gain the advantage of undertaking with some ease investigations especially regarding the owner and working classes (see chapter 5). It is really not so difficult to derive from the pastoral records both the married couples and the illegitimate children's parents according to status and position, where on the contrary it would in any case be much more complicated with the same method to count the large number of legitimate children.

It is easy to see that neither one nor the other method of calculation provides a very dependable result. The condition of the illegitimate births according to these calculations can be regarded as more unfavorable during one period than another or in one district than another, and we could see if the illegitimate births are really more frequent, or possibly if the marriages and accordingly the legitimate births are also fewer.

With a more complete population census in 1845, the number of women in the age group 20 and 50 was reported as 269,074. The number of married women under 50 years of age was reported as 144,020. Certainly some of these wives must have been under 20 years of age, but these were at the most very few and can be excluded; so it is conceivable that most of the reported number of women were 20 to 50 years of age, and the remainder or the unmarried portion (girls and widows) number accordingly 125,054.

Since it is quite seldom that married women or women under age 20 years give birth to illegitimate children, the illegitimate births during this time could be attributed to the 125,054 unmarried women in the 20- to 50-year age group.

We therefore stick to this number as the comparison for one generation; for the other generation we take the annual middle number of illegitimate live and dead births for the years 1843–1847, namely 3,570. Here it is found that the illegitimate births which occurred to the women who in 1845 were unmarried and at such age could have given birth to children is at the ration of 285 per 10,000.

If we knew the number not only of illegitimate children but also of this class of women for each of the dioceses or for different periods, we could then make a very accurate comparison. But the population data which were collected in the census of 1835 are not assembled or published. For 1845 the data are also not assembled and published for each of the dioceses but only cited for the whole kingdom (see collection of official population census tables for 1845). Through this means we could accordingly only obtain the single piece of information which has been given as an example. We are not in a position to carry out any comparison between the different time periods or districts in the country. On the other hand, we could with the data presented carry out comparisons with Denmark. Here the situation regarding dead births of illegitimate children can be compared with a completely similar method of counting for the years 1840–1849. The figures were found to be 391 for each 10,000 women in the reported class. The frequency of illegitimate births was accordingly greater in Denmark than in Norway, 37 percent greater since 285:391 equals 100:137. (See *Statistical Tables,* New Series, vol. 1 [Copenhagen, 1850] 69.)

APPENDIX

B

Marriages and Births, Legitimate and Illegitimate, in the Dioceses and in the Country, 1801–1850

As a basis for several of the calculations presented in this publication, I present in table B.1 five-year overviews of the number of marriages and births. This table, which is associated with the tables for the deaths in the appendix for the study *About Mortality in Norway,* contains excerpts from the same official sources as those in the study mentioned [*Selected Works* 2: 152]. In working this up, I made some changes in the official figures where inaccuracies had crept in, namely for 1801 (for the diocese of Trondheim, which had too large a figure), for 1838 (whose annual figure was really for the period of about 13 months from the beginning of the church year 1837–38 to the end of the calendar year 1838), and for 1845 plus 1846–50 (during which the annex parish Flaabygden, which previously had belonged to the diocese of Christiansand, was counted in the diocese of Christiania, whereby the figures compared with the foregoing had become too small for the former diocese and too large for the latter diocese). The detailed explanations of these inaccuracies, plus others which have been corrected by me, are in the study *On Marriage in Norway* [*Selected Works* 2: 184]. (In the last-named publication in the table titled "Births in the diocese of Christiania" [*Selected Works* 2: 207], the figures had not taken into account the situation regarding Flaabygden, an oversight which, however, had no influence.)

There is a deficiency in the calculations of the frequency of the illegitimate births in the present publication in that no attention has been paid to the dead births among illegitimate children. The cause of this, as already noted previously, is that the official tables from the beginning of 1837 only report how many of the stillborn children were illegitimate. Table B.2 shows the number of these for the two last five-year periods.

When these figures are compared with total stillbirths, it can be seen that there are relatively more illegitimate births among those born dead than among those born alive. It can be calculated that the relationship between the stillborn and the live-born illegitimate children has been about the same constantly. One can then estimate the approximate num-

Table B.1. Marriages and births in the dioceses

	Marriages						Legitimate Live Births					
Year	Christiania	Christiansand	Bergen	Trondheim	Tromsø	Country	Christiania	Christiansand	Bergen	Trondheim	Tromsø	Country
1801–1805	14,191	5,223	6,223	5,057	3,223	33,917	50,496	20,482	21,390	16,476	9,652	118,496
1806–1810	13,269	4,742	5,612	4,480	3,286	31,389	50,176	20,419	20,299	15,469	9,542	115,905
1811–1815	17,011	5,863	6,461	4,985	2,809	37,129	53,540	21,298	19,953	14,247	7,331	116,369
1816–1820	18,300	6,259	7,300	6,294	3,430	41,583	63,354	24,304	25,023	18,727	10,963	142,371
1821–1825	19,527	6,742	7,315	6,774	3,723	44,081	73,243	26,352	26,237	19,867	12,285	157,984
1826–1830	17,506	6,634	7,621	6,977	3,820	42,558	74,907	28,928	28,462	21,834	13,153	167,284
1831–1835	17,210	6,897	7,688	6,743	3,695	42,233	71,943	30,400	29,674	23,064	14,171	169,252
1836–1840	16,573	7,065	7,206	6,122	3,715	40,681	67,518	30,392	27,368	21,204	13,124	159,606
1841–1845	21,546	8,213	8,665	7,641	4,525	50,590	75,336	33,894	31,285	24,481	14,674	179,670
1846–1850	22,958	8,253	9,011	7,336	4,948	52,506	85,425	35,098	31,845	24,626	16,414	193,408
Total	178,091	65,891	73,102	62,409	37,174	416,667	665,938	271,567	261,536	199,995	121,309	1,520,345
	Illegitimate Live Births						Stillbirths, Legitimate and Illegitimate					
1801–1805	3,922	495	757	1,609	669	7,452	1,893	633	1,024	514	873(?)	4,937(?)
1806–1810	4,229	565	818	1,685	775	8,072	1,643	638	738	477	303	3,799
1811–1815	4,734	636	831	1,556	551	8,308	1,491	596	606	375	302	3,370
1816–1820	5,979	805	1,211	2,971	1,170	12,136	1,852	756	1,053	650	334	4,645
1821–1825	6,288	829	1,276	2,689	1,588	12,670	2,135	823	1,038	784	365	5,145
1826–1830	6,021	724	1,409	3,049	1,411	12,614	2,399	955	1,126	846	410	5,736
1831–1835	5,495	763	1,421	2,922	1,510	12,111	2,609	1,078	1,263	941	533	6,424
1836–1840	5,588	746	1,468	2,720	1,495	12,017	2,675	1,135	1,324	986	611	6,731
1841–1845	7,415	950	1,796	3,835	1,735	15,731	3,180	1,296	1,610	1,197	663	7,946
1846–1850	8,545	1,123	1,830	4,019	1,962	17,479	3,838	1,365	1,634	1,200	804	8,841
Total	58,216	7,636	12,817	27,055	12,866	118,590	23,715	9,275	11,416	7,970	5,198	57,574

Table B.2. Illegitimate stillbirths

	1841–1845	1846–1850
Christiania	502	529
Christiansand	64	74
Bergen	147	142
Trondheim	239	244
Tromsø	113	149
Country	1,065	1,138

ber of stillborn illegitimate children for the earlier five-year period also.

Otherwise the number of stillborn in the table is uncertain for 1801–1805. For the year 1803, the diocese of Tromsø is reported as having no less than 569 stillborn, while the same diocese during the period otherwise did not usually have more than 70 to 90 a year. Such wide variations do not usually occur, and here there is very surely an error in the figures, but I have found no opportunity to correct them.

APPENDIX

C

Marriages and Births, Legitimate and Illegitimate, in the Deanery-Districts, 1831–1850

In the frequently mentioned studies *About Mortality in Norway,* in chapters 12 and 13, and *On Marriage in Norway,* chapter 10, together with the first chapter of the current study, I have reported some information on the condition of the people in the smaller parts of the kingdom that make up the deaneries. All these reports are based on excerpts from the population census lists for 1835 and 1845, together with those from handwritten lists from the statistical office on marriages, etc., which are drawn up and sent in by the clergy. The figures on the population, together with those on the deaths, I have transferred to the appendix in the earlier publication. In the same place I have given a detailed explanation about my classification of deaneries: this classification had to be entirely similar; each established deanery-district had to contain accurately the same parish and church during each of the years from 1831 to 1850. Where the parish district remained unchanged all the years, there my classification would correspond to that which existed in 1850. On the other hand, where changes had taken place in the boundaries of the parishes during 1831 to 1850, I had to vary from the classification existing in 1850. It is about these variations, as mentioned, that I have given the necessary explanation. Now I will cite the attached tables C.1 and C.2 for the figures on marriages together with legitimate and illegitimate births.

Among the handwritten lists sent in by the clergy (from pastors for parishes, from deans for deaneries, from bishops for diocese), there are now and then writing and calculation failures or lack of clarity. At the statistical office the lists are summarized by diocese for each year in the printed statistical reports. From these I have made the selections for each five years which are contained in table B.1. I summarize the same lists by dioceses in tables C.1 and C.2. There are also different people who each for themselves have made use of the lists, and each in their manner have corrected and deciphered them obligingly. But a result of the various porings over and use of the lists mentioned is that the tables C.1 and C.2

Table C.1. Marriages and Births in the dioceses

No.	Deanery-Districts	Marriages 1831–35	1836–40	1841–45	1846–50	1831–40	1841–50	Illegitimate Live Births 1831–35	1836–40	1841–45	1846–50	1831–40	1841–50
1	Lower Borgesyssel	726	748	776	1,013	1,474	1,789	294	255	302	392	549	694
2	Middle Borgesyssel	738	644	785	893	1,382	1,678	117	109	151	233	226	384
3	West Borgesyssel	633	627	743	847	1,260	1,590	194	194	271	323	388	594
4	Upper Borgesyssel	567	603	681	771	1,170	1,452	159	153	197	241	312	438
5	Lower Romerike	702	655	855	935	1,357	1,790	179	202	278	275	381	553
6	Christiania diocesan deanery	1,051	1,306	1,876	2,105	2,357	3,981	713	759	982	1,252	1,472	2,234
7	Upper Romerike, Odal, and Solør	1,850	1,547	2,308	2,462	3,397	4,770	792	808	1,256	1,412	1,600	2,668
8	Østerdal	633	538	713	702	171	1,415	310	305	390	428	615	818
9	Hedemark	1,028	870	1,225	1,353	1,898	2,578	458	451	581	703	909	1,284
10	Gudbrandsdal	1,239	954	1,549	1,561	2,193	3,110	557	517	758	803	1,074	1,561
11	Toten and Valders	1,440	1,288	1,915	1,853	2,728	3,768	310	359	485	511	669	996
12	Hadeland, Ringerike, and Hallingdal	1,188	1,152	1,526	1,471	2,340	2,997	289	354	417	463	643	880
13	Kongsberg	1,188	1,212	1,504	1,508	2,400	3,012	214	227	302	361	441	663
14	Drammen	842	915	1,108	1,205	1,757	2,313	229	230	281	303	459	584
15	Jarlsberg	1,114	1,112	1,313	1,456	2,226	2,769	252	251	275	318	503	593
16	Laurvik	795	811	947	1,040	1,606	1,987	224	191	234	272	415	506
17	Bamble and Lower Telemark	1,476	1,593	1,722	1,783	3,069	3,505	204	219	255	254	423	509
	Christiania diocese	17,210	16,575	21,546	22,958	33,785	44,504	5,495	5,584	7,415	8,544	11,079	15,959
18	Upper Telemark	832	842	992	954	1,674	1,946	109	108	136	149	217	285
19	East Nedenæs	587	534	614	664	1,121	1,278	46	44	57	54	90	111
20	West Nedenæs	826	793	962	1,050	1,619	2,012	86	103	118	135	189	253
21	Robygdelag	431	459	476	493	890	969	31	35	52	58	66	110
22	Christiansand diocesan deanery	238	321	295	331	559	626	70	80	75	88	150	163
23	Mandal	593	652	691	696	1,245	1,387	34	29	56	54	63	110
24	Lister	881	841	828	766	1,722	1,594	42	41	42	60	83	102
25	Dalerne	563	523	607	613	1,086	1,220	39	45	55	57	84	112
26	Jæder	380	401	473	503	781	976	62	36	57	80	98	137
27	Stavanger	515	613	838	837	1,128	1,675	60	86	121	160	146	281
28	Karmsund	318	384	540	522	702	1,062	42	38	49	57	80	106
29	Ryfylke	733	697	897	823	1,430	1,720	142	101	132	171	243	303
	Christiansand diocese	6,897	7,060	8,213	8,252	13,957	16,465	763	746	950	1,123	1,509	2,073

Table C.1. (Continued)

No.	Deanery-Districts	Marriages 1831–35	1836–40	1841–45	1846–50	1831–40	1841–50	Illegitimate Live Births 1831–35	1836–40	1841–45	1846–50	1831–40	1841–50
30	Hardanger and Voss	793	702	902	885	1,495	1,787	76	83	99	146	159	245
31	Søndhordland	1,108	1,066	1,274	1,513	2,174	2,787	139	160	190	222	299	412
32	Bergen diocesan deanery	812	682	888	930	1,494	1,818	268	258	317	315	526	632
33	Nordhordland	1,276	1,232	1,465	1,637	2,508	3,102	99	101	117	123	200	240
34	Outer Sogn	549	499	596	556	1,048	1,152	192	197	291	230	389	521
35	Inner Sogn	677	660	714	667	1,337	1,381	339	373	364	412	712	776
36	Søndfjord	785	715	837	881	1,500	1,718	90	74	128	102	164	230
37	Nordfjord	644	608	724	740	1,252	1,464	47	63	59	60	110	119
38	Southern Søndmør	495	427	497	539	922	1,036	53	45	70	54	98	124
39	Northern Søndmør	547	614	767	663	1,161	1,430	120	114	160	166	234	326
	Bergen diocese	7,686	7,205	8,664	9,011	14,891	17,675	1,423	1,468	1,795	1,830	2,891	3,625
40	Romsdal	685	582	756	672	1,267	1,428	300	214	360	401	514	761
41	Nordmør	1,019	964	1,166	1,189	1,983	2,355	546	530	778	808	1,076	1,586
42	Fosen	732	712	913	867	1,444	1,780	378	371	526	541	749	1,067
43	Trondheim diocesan deanery	443	414	567	531	857	1,098	312	280	326	314	592	640
44	Dalerne	1,691	1,532	1,798	1,661	3,223	3,459	685	629	935	1,047	1,314	1,982
45	Indherred	1,664	1,467	1,823	1,815	3,131	3,638	523	564	714	706	1,078	1,420
46	Namdal	509	451	618	607	960	1,225	178	142	196	203	320	399
	Trondheim diocese	6,743	6,122	7,641	7,342	12,864	14,983	2,922	2,730	3,835	4,020	5,652	7,855
47	Helgeland	1,029	1,016	1,317	1,263	2,045	2,580	501	441	574	589	942	1,163
48	Salten	727	677	827	846	1,404	1,673	217	214	281	279	431	560
49	Lofoten and Vesteraal	401	464	543	661	865	1,204	203	217	240	287	420	527
50	Senjen	577	492	641	748	1,069	1,389	218	231	247	313	449	560
51	Tromsø	434	498	567	715	932	1,282	225	245	251	285	470	536
52	West Finmark	379	431	449	503	810	952	110	103	95	147	213	242
53	East Finmark	148	137	181	212	285	393	36	44	47	62	80	109
	Tromsø diocese	3,695	3,715	4,525	4,948	7,410	9,473	1,510	1,495	1,735	1,962	3,005	3,697

Table C.2. Marriages and Births in the dioceses

No.	Deanery-Districts	Legitimate and Live Births 1831–35	1836–40	1841–45	1846–50	1831–40	1841–50	Stillborn, Legitimate and Illegitimate 1831–35	1836–40	1841–45	1846–50	1831–40	1841–50
1	Lower Borgesyssel	2,858	2,946	3,072	3,524	5,804	6,596	140	140	134	201	280	335
2	Middle Borgesyssel	3,339	2,896	3,001	3,266	6,235	6,267	92	129	107	127	221	234
3	West Borgesyssel	2,764	2,815	3,165	3,522	5,579	6,687	117	117	134	156	234	290
4	Upper Borgesyssel	2,604	2,359	2,375	2,684	4,963	5,059	82	92	120	126	174	246
5	Lower Romerike	3,165	2,933	3,168	3,610	6,098	6,778	125	125	123	179	250	302
6	Christiania diocesan deanery	3,799	4,004	4,835	6,390	7,803	11,225	247	241	318	408	488	726
7	Upper Romerike, Odal, and Sol	7,900	7,011	7,903	9,126	14,911	17,029	314	293	335	415	607	750
8	Østerdal	2,286	2,227	2,468	2,639	4,513	5,107	94	80	102	129	174	231
9	Hedemark	3,680	3,432	3,864	4,702	7,112	8,566	159	142	178	201	301	379
10	Gudbrandsdal	5,621	4,589	5,244	5,924	10,210	11,168	188	136	207	238	324	445
11	Toten and Valders	5,914	5,619	6,560	7,241	11,533	13,801	118	158	188	225	276	413
12	Hadeland, Ringerike, and Hallingdal	5,109	4,633	5,472	5,874	9,742	11,346	141	117	174	247	258	421
13	Kongsberg	4,987	4,701	5,432	6,016	9,688	11,448	188	170	240	237	358	477
14	Drammen	3,485	3,559	3,863	4,779	7,044	8,342	96	126	178	181	222	359
15	Jarlsberg	4,403	4,324	4,719	5,334	8,727	10,053	184	223	247	264	407	511
16	Laurvik	3,292	2,978	3,441	3,797	6,270	7,238	113	146	131	176	259	307
17	Bable and Lower Telemark	6,737	6,492	6,754	7,297	13,229	14,051	211	238	264	328	449	592
	Christiania diocese	71,943	67,518	75,336	85,425	139,461	160,761	2,609	2,673	3,180	3,838	5,282	7,018
18	Upper Telemark	3,806	3,663	4,038	3,953	7,469	7,991	144	162	158	144	306	302
19	Lower Nedenæs	2,635	2,627	2,739	2,839	5,262	5,578	83	90	119	123	173	242
20	West Nedenæs	3,467	3,586	3,879	4,119	7,053	7,998	92	137	121	134	229	255
21	Robygdelag	2,001	2,063	2,171	2,239	4,064	4,410	70	45	81	80	115	161
22	Christiansand diocesan deanery	1,036	1,090	1,215	1,316	2,126	2,531	54	28	47	60	82	107
23	Mandal	2,903	2,822	2,989	2,966	5,725	5,955	87	71	117	110	158	227
24	Lister	3,488	3,725	3,644	3,700	7,213	7,344	137	143	139	153	280	292
25	Dalerne	2,572	2,470	2,634	2,556	5,042	5,190	121	151	133	127	272	260
26	Jæder	1,706	1,550	1,756	1,883	3,256	3,639	56	55	57	66	111	123
27	Stavanger	2,296	2,462	3,401	3,717	4,758	7,118	79	93	101	127	172	228
28	Karmsund	1,534	1,495	2,049	2,319	3,029	4,368	56	62	81	100	118	181
29	Ryfylke	2,956	2,839	3,379	3,498	5,795	6,877	99	98	142	147	197	289
	Christiansand diocese	30,400	30,392	33,894	35,105	60,792	68,999	1,078	1,135	1,296	1,371	2,213	2,667

Table C.2. (Continued)

		Legitimate and Live Births						Stillborn, Legitimate and Illegitimate					
No.	Deanery-Districts	1831 –35	1836 –40	1841 –45	1846 –50	1831 –40	1841 –50	1831 –35	1836 –40	1841 –45	1846 –50	1831 –40	1841 –50
30	Hardanger and Voss	2,944	2,967	3,112	3,114	5,911	6,226	117	77	114	137	194	251
31	Søndhordland	4,371	4,143	4,869	5,074	8,514	9,943	206	243	290	278	449	568
32	Bergen diocese-deanery	3,203	3,038	3,205	3,353	6,241	6,558	205	175	195	187	380	382
33	Nordhordland	5,114	4,554	5,262	5,509	9,668	10,771	206	267	291	289	473	580
34	Center Sogn	1,916	1,821	2,051	2,036	3,737	4,087	108	114	111	137	222	248
35	Inner Sogn	2,729	2,586	3,036	2,828	5,315	5,864	94	117	126	107	211	233
36	Søndfjord	3,250	2,889	3,402	3,339	6,139	6,741	108	119	154	167	227	321
37	Nordfjord	2,446	2,151	2,457	2,547	4,597	5,004	64	71	82	105	135	187
38	South Søndmør	1,790	1,556	1,738	1,796	3,346	3,534	78	78	101	103	156	204
39	North Søndmør	1,913	1,663	2,152	2,249	3,576	4,401	77	60	127	129	137	256
	Bergen diocese	29,676	27,368	31,284	31,845	57,044	63,129	1,263	1,321	1,591	1,639	2,584	3,230
40	Romsdal	2,354	2,153	2,358	2,430	4,507	4,788	113	99	132	108	212	240
41	Nordmør	3,293	3,047	3,611	3,854	6,340	7,465	189	184	226	252	373	478
42	Fosen	2,745	2,467	2,986	2,897	5,212	5,883	111	103	130	130	214	260
43	Trondheim diocesan deanery	1,590	1,468	1,681	1,649	3,058	3,330	65	85	116	120	150	236
44	Dalerne	5,742	5,387	6,021	5,749	11,129	11,770	199	228	263	247	427	510
45	Indherred	5,629	5,236	6,040	6,104	10,865	12,144	206	229	243	264	435	507
46	Namdal	1,711	1,447	1,784	1,970	3,158	3,754	60	64	87	81	124	168
	Trondheim diocese	23,064	21,205	24,481	24,653	44,269	49,134	943	992	1,197	1,202	1,935	2,399
47	Helgeland	3,588	3,256	3,830	4,015	6,844	7,845	148	157	197	199	305	396
48	Salten	2,951	2,677	2,798	2,982	5,628	5,780	79	120	105	146	199	251
49	Lofoten and Vesteraalen	1,731	1,507	1,677	2,000	3,238	3,677	78	78	90	121	156	211
50	Senjen	2,152	2,146	2,243	2,546	4,298	4,789	84	77	88	107	161	195
51	Tromsø diocesan deanery	2,034	1,854	2,104	2,548	3,888	4,652	71	69	78	92	140	170
52	West Finmark	1,267	1,281	1,429	1,660	2,548	3,089	54	79	71	71	133	142
53	East Finmark	448	403	593	666	851	1,259	18	26	33	43	44	76
	Tromsø diocese	14,171	13,124	14,674	16,417	27,295	31,091	532	606	662	779	1,138	1,441

(or the totals for a diocese for a deanery) are not always as desired comparable to the dioceses in table B.1. More often than not, this lack of comparability is not very noticeable, and it might be said that nowhere is it so great that a significant error will occur in the calculations and conclusions for which the figures are used. The greatest incomparability is in tables C.1 and C.2: illegitimate births in the diocese of Trondheim for 1836–1840, plus 10; legitimate births in the same diocese for 1846–1850, plus 27; stillborn in the diocese of Bergen for 1841–1845, minus 19; and in the Tromsø diocese for 1846–1850, minus 25.

APPENDIX

D

More Specialized Studies of Marriages and Illegitimate Births in the Dioceses of Christiania and Christiansand

As cited, the figures in table B.1 in appendix B are taken from the official statistical tables, and those in tables C.1 and C.2 in appendix C are drawn by me from those sent in by the clergy to the statistical office and kept in handwritten lists. But here I must account for some activities which are the basis for many of my current writings (chapters 3, 4, 5, 6, and 7) together with those in the study *On Marriage in Norway* (chapter 11) and in reports, studies, and data which I have acquired from other sources.

On April 25, 1853, I wrote to all the parish pastors in the dioceses of Christiania and Christiansand (except the diocese-deanery of Christiania, where the large population would make it too difficult to obtain the information), and I requested them to report certain information from the clergy books according to an outline.

The outline has the following parts:

Section 1. Marriages according to social class
Section 2. The relationship between married young men and widowers, etc.
Section 3. Young men and girls married in class I by age
Section 4. Young men and girls married in class II by age
Section 5. About births relative to the time of marriage
Section 6. About illegitimate births
Section 7. About repeat illegitimate births
Section 8. Births, both legitimate and illegitimate, according to the months of the year
Section 9. Illegitimate births according to the months of the year

In addition there was a series of questions regarding the two customs: sleeping accommodations in the animal barns and night courting.

Most of the pastors responded, and almost all of these were complete, thus all the subtopics were included. Some of the responses for one or another of the subtopics were not usable, inasmuch as errors were noted; but these were not frequent. Most of them had handled such matters in their parishes in both urban and rural districts. It is necessary in this summary to show clearly how a large part of the total parishes responded and how fully.

First, the complete number of parishes must be reported, and this can be done together with an explanation which provides some understanding of these reports, namely the statistical classification of the two diocese, which I have done in order to use them according to my objective.

I have combined the deaneries of the diocese into seven groups of adjoining districts, a grouping for a double purpose: that such deanery-districts were similar and that the condition regarding illegitimate births was approximately the same (given that this entire investigation was directed toward illegitimate births), and that the groups into which each diocese was divided came to be approximately equal in size.

The combinations of the parishes are shown in table D.1. Note that without the diocesan deanery (i.e., the city of Christiania and the parish of Aker, population 40,346, for which the reports were not delivered), the inventory for the diocese-deanery of Christiansand is lacking (i.e., the city of Christiansand, population 8,349). The reports which existed in 1853 were used for the classification of the total parishes, with only the deviation that the three deaneries—Gudbrandsdal, Toten, and Valdres—are here handled like the two old deaneries—Gudbrandsdal and Toten with Valdres—when the parishes Gausdal and Faaberg were merged by royal decree, November 30, 1852. I still count, however, the diocese of Toten with Gudbrandsdal. With this deviation from the classification of the dioceses existing in 1853, I have achieved a correspondence with the deanery classifications in tables C.1 and C.2 that I followed for the period 1831–1850. Thus each of the seven groups will have the number of parishes and population which belongs to each group in the total deaneries.

As I said, there is a deviation here which I have not been able to avoid, and that appeared with the annex Flaabyd: in the tables this is seen as belonging to the parish of Hvideseid in the deanery of Upper Telemark in group 5, and in the existing group classification it is counted in the parish of Bo in the deanery of Lower Telemark in group 4. Insofar as complete accuracy was achieved for the rest, the population which Flaabyd had in 1845 (562 persons) had to be taken from the above population which was part of group 5 and added to the population in group 4.

The information in question which the pastors reported I shall now

Table D.1. Groups of deanery-districts in Christiania and Christiansand dioceses

Deanery-Districts		Number of Parishes
Group 1	Lower Borgesyssel	7
	Middle Borgesyssel	6
	West Borgesyssel	6
	Upper Borgesyssel	8
	Lower Romerike	7
	Total	34
Group 2	Upper Romerike, Odal, and Solør	12
	Østerdal	7
	Hedemark	6
	Gudbrandsdal	9
	Total	34
Group 3	Toten and Valders	10
	Hadeland, Ringerike, and Hallingdal	7
	Kongsberg	7
	Total	24
Group 4	Drammen	6
	Northern Jarlsberg	6
	Southern Jarlsberg	6
	Laurvik	7
	Bamble	6
	North Telemark	6
	Total	37
Group 5	Upper Telemark, East Mountan	3
	Upper Telemark, West Mountain	6
	East Nedenæs	5
	West Nedenæs	8
	Robygdelag	5
	Total	27
Group 6	Mandal	6
	Lister	6
	Dalerne	5
	Total	17
Group 7	Jæder	5
	Stavanger	5
	Karmsund	4
	Ryfylke	6
	Total	20

present by groups in tables, and for each group I will enter the figures for the parishes involved. When this number of parishes is compared with the above actually recorded or with the complete number of parishes, which each group has, one will have a conception how great a portion of each group is included. Hereby one can still observe to what extent the reports are missing for quite a few parishes, but still there are

Table D.2. Population in groups of deanery-districts

Deanery-districts	
Group 1	109,017
2	157,235
3	124,475
4	136,085
5	84,176
6	61,708
7	67,118
Diocese	
Christiania (groups 1–4)	567,158
Christiansand (groups 5–7)	221,351

no groups reported in the dioceses which do not have some of the parishes reported.

In order to understand the figures in the tables for the various outlines, the reader still needs some explanation. I will give one for each outline.

SECTION 1

Already in outline section 1 the plan is clear how to find out the differences between the various statuses. In order to avoid too much complexity, the classification of statuses is narrowed to the two large classes which can be regarded as existing in the nation, property owners and the working class (class I and class II). The questionnaires that were circulated were accompanied by an explanation of what kind of people I assumed should be counted in each of the two classes, and the pastors were requested when the section was filled in to follow the same plan for the classification of classes.

The plan was as follows.

> For class I (see the population census tables for 1845, page 26) count government officials and subordinate officials, students, office clerks, farmers (owners and tenants), merchants, mill owners, factory owners, middle-class craft workers or master craftsmen, skippers, and others who, from a middle-class view, are associated with this class.
>
> For class II count cotters with or without land, land-clearing men, craft workers who are not master craftsmen, seamen, ships' pilots, fishermen, mill workers, day workers, servants, and others with whom they are most closely associated.
>
> For each class count the same associated people—widows, wives,

children, and other family members—insofar as they are not regarded as having a definite independent position and must be regarded as belonging to another category than heads of families. Thus, the married ones who at the time of marriage, or when the association ended, were servants, are counted in class II, even if their parents belong in class I.

When anyone occupies several middle-class positions, he should be placed in the class which he appears to belong to and which seems to be the most important economically.

When it appears, for example, that married young men and women are in class I, this means that for this couple the class is the class of the man.

With regard to what is expected of the pastors—that they should be able to carry out this classification of classes in connection with the persons being asked about (married and parents of illegitimate children)—it can be noted that in most cases the clergy books are arranged to contain information about the status of the registered persons or middle-class positions; in the meantime, probably in the fewest places, the clergy books' rubrics are usually filled out accordingly completely. In these cases, plus those where the clergy books do not require the reporting of status, the pastors must be relied on themselves to remember, or with the help of acquaintances they could somewhat easily obtain the status of the persons for the two years which are covered here.

For the present section 1 it is strongly desired that it be filled out for the two years 1851 and 1852.

Section 1 is filled out twice in the tables D.3 and D.4. The reason for this is that in the study *On Marriage* [*Selected Works* 2:300, 302] I have entered two tables, which are calculated from the numbers which are contained in section 1a and which I now take the opportunity to report as evidence for the same calculations. But in the current study I have made use of the reports on the marriages by another method, namely by comparing the number of marriages and illegitimate births (see tables 5.1 and 5.2); for this comparison it was absolutely necessary that it was exactly the same parishes which the two kinds of reports concerned. The reports on the illegitimate births are found in the present table in section 6, but only for 152 parishes. It was therefore necessary to set up outline 1b so that this would also correspond exactly to the same 152 parishes. (Aside from the fact that section 1a involves more parishes than 1b, it involves for individual parishes more years than 1851 and 1852. This is then a reason for a disagreement between a and b.)

Here I take an opportunity to evaluate the completeness of the

Table D.3. Private reports of the pastors

Section 1a Place	Number of Parishes	Grooms and Brides of Class I and Class II Grooms of Class I with Brides of: Class I	Grooms of Class I with Brides of: Class II	Grooms of Class II with Brides of: Class I	Grooms of Class II with Brides of: Class II	Combined Grooms of: Class I	Combined Grooms of: Class II	Combined Brides of: Class I	Combined Brides of: Class II	Total of Both Sexes in Both Classes
Deanery-districts										
Group 1	28	397	109	130	932	506	1,062	527	1,041	1,568
2	25	410	111	114	918	521	1,032	524	1,029	1,553
3	20	467	75	75	868	542	943	542	943	1,485
4	33	563	156	108	1,237	719	1,345	671	1,393	2,064
5	20	250	88	87	422	338	509	337	510	847
6	13	297	97	81	154	394	235	378	251	629
7	17	273	80	86	348	353	434	359	428	787
Diocese										
Christiania	106	1,837	451	427	3,955	2,288	4,382	2,264	4,406	6,670
Christiansand	50	820	265	254	924	1,085	1,178	1,074	1,189	2,263
Both	156	2,657	716	681	4,879	3,373	5,560	3,338	5,595	8,933

Table D.4. The same outline with fewer parishes to compare with section 6

Section 1b Place	Number of Parishes	Grooms and Brides of Class I and Class II Grooms of Class I with Brides of: Class I	Grooms of Class I with Brides of: Class II	Grooms of Class II with Brides of: Class I	Grooms of Class II with Brides of: Class II	Combined Grooms of: Class I	Combined Grooms of: Class II	Combined Brides of: Class I	Combined Brides of: Class II	Total of Both Sexes in Both Classes
Deanery-districts										
Group 1	28	395	107	128	909	502	1,037	523	1,016	1,539
2	25	410	111	114	918	521	1,032	524	1,029	1,553
3	20	467	75	75	868	542	943	542	943	1,485
4	30	484	142	90	1,138	626	1,228	574	1,280	1,854
5	19	230	75	76	400	305	476	306	475	781
6	13	297	97	81	154	394	235	378	251	629
7	17	269	79	84	317	348	401	353	396	749
Diocese										
Christiania	103	1,756	435	407	3,833	2,191	4,240	2,163	4,268	6,431
Christiansand	49	796	251	241	871	1,047	1,112	1,037	1,122	2,159
Both	152	2,552	686	648	4,704	3,238	5,352	3,200	5,390	8,590

reports in section 1 together with section 6, not only to watch out for the number of parishes but to compare with the following figures. From the total reports to the official statistical office for the years 1851 and 1852, the assembled numbers during these years were as shown in table D.5. After these complete reports, the calculations carried out are as given in the first column in table 5.1.

Table D.5. Marriages and live illegitimate births, 1850–1851

Place	Marriages	Live Illegitimate Births
Deanery-districts		
Group 1	1,849	728
2	2,223	1,474
3	1,802	649
4	2,269	583
5	1,226	200
6	829	96
7	1,112	225
Diocese		
Christiania	8,143	3,434
Christiansand	3,167	521
Both	11,310	3,955
(To which are added:		
Christiania deanery	(885)	(609)
Christiansand deanery)	(143)	(36)

SECTION 2

Section 2 applies to the years 1851 and 1852 in the same way as does section 1. It serves as a basis partly for table 7.3 in the present document and partly for the publication *On Marriage* [*Selected Works* 2:304]. [It is] about class levels in section 1.

SECTIONS 3 AND 4

Sections 3 and 4 apply also to the years 1851 and 1852. The number of bachelors and girls should match the corresponding columns in section 2; the number of bachelors and girls in sections 3 and 4 should also agree internally. None of this, though, is always the case. The reason for this is that there are inaccuracies in the incoming reports, inaccuracies which might be due to bachelors who were counted as having married widows or to girls who had married widowers. Since these inaccuracies affected only a few figures, I felt I ought to overlook them. Where the flaw on the other hand became considerable, I chose to leave out the whole report for the parishes concerned. These two sections, in the meantime, are not used in the present study but in the study *On Marriage* [*Selected Works* 2:304 ff.] and in tables D.6, D.7, and D.8.

SECTION 5

Section 5 forms the basis for table 6.7 in in the current study. In order to enable the reader to evaluate adequately the validity of these figures, which certainly have been the most troublesome for pastors to derive from the clergy books, I will show how in my letter I requested that the section be filled out:

> I can well anticipate that this section cannot be filled out with complete accuracy when not all married couples have lived long enough in the same congregation before and after the ceremony so that this matter could be recorded in the clergy books. But it is of interest to learn as accurately as possible about the situation. In a few parishes I have initiated investigations in this direction, but without being able to take into consideration the distinction between the two classes when the status of the people concerned have not been recorded in the clergy books. To this end I had to make an alphabetical list of the marriages in each year, and also a comparable list of the parents of the children born not only for the same year but for several years before (in order to find the number of all the married couples who had had [illegitimate] births together before the wedding) and for the first eight months of the following year (in order to find the number of all the couples who had had children within eight months after the marriage). This was certainly a very onerous task; but in part I assume that it would be easier for pastors who knew the people, and I hope in part that it would interest the pastors to see the final result. For that reason I do not in the meantime have to ask for more than two years for filling out the section, specifically the years 1850 and 1851 (not 1851 and 1852), and when the research must extend over eight months after the end of the last year.

(It should be recalled that this was written in April 1853.)

Table D.6. Bachelors and widowers, girls and widows

Section 2		Married Couples of Class I					Married Couples of Class II				
Place	Number of Parishes	Bachelors with Girls	Widowers with Girls	Bachelors with Widows	Widowers with Widows	Total	Bachelors with Girls	Widowers with Girls	Bachelors with Widows	Widowers with Widows	Total
Deanery-districts											
Group 1	28	410	46	31	14	501	927	78	39	23	1,067
2	25	443	46	20	9	518	934	61	18	22	1,035
3	17	386	53	27	10	476	659	54	23	13	749
4	34	614	72	28	22	736	1,219	93	38	18	1,368
5	20	265	47	14	4	330	432	38	17	6	493
6	12	304	39	15	8	366	188	19	12	3	222
7	17	286	41	13	11	351	348	35	23	21	427
Diocese											
Christiania	104	1,853	217	106	55	2,231	3,739	286	118	76	4,219
Christiansand	49	855	127	42	23	1,047	968	92	52	30	1,142
Both	153	2,708	344	148	78	3,278	4,707	378	170	106	5,361

Table D.7. Married bachelors and girls of class I, by age

Section 3		Bachelors							Girls						
Place	Number of Parishes	Under 20 Years	20–25	25–30	30–40	40–50	Over 50 Years	Total	Under 20 Years	20–25	25–30	30–40	40–50	Over 50 Years	Total
Deanery-districts															
Group 1	27	2	98	139	131	21	7	398	19	162	153	57	4	2	397
2	25	3	89	188	156	22	2	460	27	179	163	79	7	1	456
3	16	...	91	123	96	12	1	323	28	152	91	49	3	...	323
4	33	4	136	256	167	21	7	591	53	250	200	77	6	1	587
5	19	3	63	95	81	15	4	261	31	111	89	26	4	...	261
6	13	1	69	131	120	12	2	335	28	138	120	47	2	...	335
7	17	5	57	116	87	11	1	277	35	138	69	31	4	...	277
Diocese															
Christiania	101	9	414	706	550	76	17	1,772	127	743	607	262	20	4	1,763
Christiansand	49	9	189	342	288	38	7	873	94	387	278	104	10	...	873
Both	150	18	603	1,048	838	114	24	2,645	221	1,130	885	366	30	4	2,636

Table D.8. Married bachelors and girls of class II, by age

Section 4		Bachelors							Girls						
Place	Number of Parishes	Under 20 Years	20–25	25–30	30–40	40–50	Over 50 Years	Total	Under 20 Years	20–25	25–30	30–40	40–50	Over 50 Years	Total
Deanery-districts															
Group 1	27	6	249	404	214	15	4	892	46	314	349	162	12	...	883
2	25	5	303	387	222	27	4	948	26	363	382	166	22	2	961
3	18	7	242	328	140	17	2	736	30	303	294	97	12	...	736
4	33	7	312	587	282	20	1	1,209	33	480	482	203	11	1	1,210
5	19	1	102	214	88	14	3	422	27	184	146	55	9	1	422
6	13	4	54	78	55	4	2	197	9	77	71	34	6	...	197
7	17	2	95	146	76	7	...	326	13	122	133	51	5	2	326
Diocese															
Christiania	103	25	1,106	1,706	858	79	11	3,785	135	1,460	1,507	628	57	3	3,790
Christiansand	49	7	251	438	219	25	5	945	49	383	350	140	20	3	945
Both	152	32	1,357	2,144	1,077	104	16	4,730	184	1,843	1,857	768	77	6	4,735

Table D.9. Marriages and births

Section 5		Married Couples		Couples Of Class I Who Had Children Together				Couples Of Class II Who Had Children Together			
Place	Number of Parishes	Class I	Class II	Before Marriage	Within 4 Months after Marriage	Between 4 and 8 Months after Marriage	Total	Before Marriage	Within 4 Months after Marriage	Between 4 and 8 Months after Marriage	Total
Deanery-districts											
Group 1	25	417	1,028	16	67	45	128	146	231	127	504
2	25	553	1,151	41	100	62	203	274	292	112	678
3	20	555	990	35	101	76	212	146	329	122	597
4	33	708	1,359	22	88	66	176	154	291	161	606
5	20	344	489	8	50	40	98	34	113	74	221
6	13	391	247	4	38	64	106	4	34	35	73
7	17	346	436	13	27	26	66	55	107	42	204
Diocese											
Christiania	103	2,233	4,528	114	356	249	719	720	1,143	522	2,385
Christiansand	50	1,081	1,172	25	115	130	270	93	254	151	498
Both	153	3,314	5,700	139	471	379	989	813	1,397	673	2,883

It is self-evident that it makes no difference here whether or not the births were live or stillborn insofar as the married ones had already had children together within four or eight months after marriage. They need not be counted more than in the first column.

SECTION 6

The need for accuracy applies also to the same parishes for the years 1851 and 1852 as in section 1b. See the additional explanation in the same place.

For the sake of space, a portion of section 6 is included here in table D.10.

Table D.10. Parents of illegitimate children

Place	Married Men	Widowers	Married Women	Widows
Deanery-districts				
Group 1	19	43	4	34
2	24	54	4	25
3	12	41	1	12
4	36	31	8	22
5	5	9	2	2
6	8	4	1	6
7	13	7	...	3
Diocese				
Christiania	91	169	17	93
Christiansand	26	20	3	11
Both	117	189	20	104

The part of the section [reported in table D.11], which applies to the same year and the same parishes as the overall section, can be seen to be drawn up for both classes under one, and the figures are used in table 7.5.

SECTION 7

Section 7 applies to 1851 and 1852, with classes I and II combined. It is used for chapter 7 and for table D.12.

Table D.11. Parents of illegitimate children

Section 6		Fathers of Class I with Mothers of		Fathers of Class II with Mothers of		Together, Fathers of		Together, Mothers of		Total of Both Sexes in Both Classes
Place	Number of Parishes	Class I	Class II	Class I	Class II	Class I	Class II	Class I	Class II	
Deanery-Districts										
Group 1	28	26	80	23	446	106	469	49	526	575
2	25	43	91	20	860	134	880	63	951	1,014
3	20	46	58	19	374	104	393	65	432	497
4	30	18	54	6	392	72	398	24	446	470
5	19	7	23	4	76	30	80	11	99	110
6	13	8	17	6	41	25	47	14	58	72
7	17	11	27	7	85	38	92	18	112	130
Diocese										
Christiania	103	133	283	68	2,072	416	2,140	201	2,355	2,556
Christiansand	49	26	67	17	202	93	219	43	269	312
Both	152	159	350	85	2,274	509	2,359	244	2,624	2,868

Table D.12. Repeated illegitimate births

Section 7		Fathers, First-time or Oftener						Mothers, First-time or Oftener					
Place	Number of Parishes	1st Time	2d Time	3d Time	4th Time and More	Un-known	Total	1st Time	2d Time	3d Time	4th Time and More	Un-known	Total
Deanery-districts													
Group 1	21	343	39	11	2	73	468	346	68	19	9	27	469
2	26	771	175	40	17	71	1,074	790	175	57	21	32	1,075
3	18	343	46	10	6	75	480	364	60	18	9	29	480
4	26	208	25	18	1	148	400	273	43	20	4	51	391
5	16	77	7	2	...	14	100	86	9	2	...	4	101
6	12	53	5	...	...	6	64	56	5	2	...	...	63
7	10	75	10	1	1	11	98	80	5	5	...	8	98
Dioceses													
Christiania	91	1,665	285	79	26	367	2,422	1,773	346	114	43	139	2,415
Christiansand	38	205	22	3	1	31	262	222	19	9	...	12	262
Both	129	1,870	307	82	27	398	2,684	1,995	365	123	43	151	2,677

Sections 8 and 9, which for the 10 years 1841–1850 contain the explanation for the figures of both legitimate and illegitimate births that occurred for each month of the year, are not reported here since I have not used them in the current study. The objective of developing these reports was to follow and show the unusual circumstance which influenced immoral behavior during particular seasons of the year such that the illegitimate births coincided with the corresponding time of the year. But a presentation of the (not great) result which this research has given me can more appropriately be published elsewhere.

Finally, there is the content of the reports from the pastors, as will be recalled, the information about the custom of sleeping quarters in the animal barns, together with night courting; but this information is already reported in table 3.1 and table 4.1.

E I L E R T S U N D T

by Arvid Brodersen

Eilert Sundt (1817–1875) was the pioneer, and in many ways is still the unsurpassed master, of social research in Norway. He left a vast legacy of publications, collected in eleven volumes. The one presented here in an American edition by Odin W. Anderson holds pride of place in the current curriculum of sociology at Oslo University.

The story of how Eilert Sundt embarked upon the career of a social scientist and then proceeded to create an impressive body of research in the field is worth retelling, for it meant breaking new ground in a still-traditional and old-fashioned scholarly world. A son of a relatively well-to-do merchant, he was offered the best available academic education, and with his keen mind and intelligence he made the fullest use of the opportunities granted him. After primary school in his small native town of Farsund, he entered at age thirteen the *Latinskole* in the provincial capital, Stavanger. There he received the prerequisite preparation for the university study of theology and the prestigious career of a minister of the Lutheran State Church, a profession which his parents fondly wished him to pursue.

Eilert dutifully devoted himself to the study of theology at the University of Christiania (today, Oslo University), finishing with a brilliant examination and the diploma entitling him to service as a resident pastor of the church. However, his studies at the university extended far beyond the subject matter of theology. He was keenly interested in church history, including the varieties of doctrines, a marginal topic of divinity. He especially loved literary and linguistic studies and passionately read the classics from Homer to the Icelandic sagas, as well as Dante, Shakespeare, Schiller, and Goethe, all in the original languages. Moreover, he was an enthusiastic member of the academic community, the intellectual elite of the country in and around the university. Its members assembled in the Students' Association and participated in the debating society, not

Professor Arvid Brodersen, a native of Norway, is a former member of the graduate faculty at the New School for Social Research. In a long and distinguished career as linguist and sociologist, he has been visiting professor at universities in Berlin, Zurich, and Mexico. He was head of the Social Science Department of UNESCO in Paris from 1946 to 1949.

only of the student body itself but of the academic professionals in general.

Sundt's student years were a golden age of Norwegian art and letters under the nation's greatest poetic genius, Henrik Wergeland, the inspiring leader and friend of the people. Wergeland was a true humanist who fought for the rights of the poor and humble in Norwegian society and against the exclusion of the Jews.

Sundt became an ardent admirer and friend of the poet, and speaking as chairman of the Students' Association at Wergeland's funeral, he expressed the nation's bereavement and his own grief at the loss of a friend whose personality and work inspired his own efforts—just then starting—in the service of the people.

> He not only beautifully described the age-old nobility of the Norwegian freeholder, but he himself worked for the latter's ennoblement by the cleansing bath of enlightenment. He not only spoke up for the cause of the suppressed and the victims of injustice, but he sacrificed himself for them. He did not merely speak fine words about Abraham's unhappy children, but labored for them during the long days and sleepless nights. For this, our joyful admiration is glorified by our knowing about his unflagging, restless, happy activity during the long public walk through his short life.

In this spirit, Sundt stated his own life's program, which was to follow the lead of his friend by dedicating himself to the enlightenment and ennoblement of the people. His path was open for him to do so as a minister of the church, but he hesitated, doubting whether this was his real calling, and refrained from applying for a post as clergyman. By now he had finished his university studies, after an inordinately long period of eleven years, but with the rare distinction of a *laudabilis,* at his final examination. In 1846, at age twenty-nine—and, as it turned out, exactly in midlife (Dante's *nel mezzo del camin de nostra vita* comes to mind)—to earn a modest living, Sundt sought and got a post as a teacher at a penitentiary in Christiania. Here, as if through a strike of lightning, his life's real calling became clear to him: he was not to be principally a preacher and evangelist but a scientific researcher, a sociologist, long before the word was yet current in his native language. Coined by Auguste Comte some ten years earlier, the word only later became common usage in France and, especially through Herbert Spencer, in England.

Sundt started his social research at the very bottom of society, studying at close quarters the poverty-stricken, downtrodden, and delinquent inmates of the jail. Among them he found many characters who were different from the rest, a class of homeless vagabonds who lived roaming the roads of the countryside, begging, stealing, and occasionally performing small services of repair work for the farmers. On the whole, they were hated and feared by the resident population, considered a nuisance and a criminal element. Sundt paid special attention to this group of inmates, speaking to them individually. He soon discovered that they were not, as commonly believed, a uniform group but consisted of two distinctly different components: in part they were Gypsies of Asiatic origin, in part simply drifters and hoboes of Norwegian parentage who had landed on skid row. Yet in popular usage, they were all referred to by the same term—*fanter* (roughly, derelict vagabonds).

In the course of systematic interviews, Sundt studied each of the two subgroups and particularly the Gypsies, describing their exotic language and customs. During the period from 1847 to 1849, he wrote his first extensive report on his subjects. It was addressed to the authorities, who received it well, as they were seriously concerned with this social problem. The report was printed in 1850 at public expense, and the interest was such that a second edition appeared in 1852. As a reward Sundt was granted a state stipend for studies in church history, but he continued his work as teacher and investigator at the penitentiary, where his experiences as a sociologist had completely captivated him. He pursued his research on the Gypsies and their fellow outcasts, drawing on continuing personal observation as well as the mostly German and French literature on the subject. This resulted in a series of further extensive reports in the years 1859, 1862, 1863, and 1865. With these he succeeded in persuading the authorities to grant considerable subsidies for the *fants* from the modest treasury of the period.

This unusual preoccupation with an otherwise neglected topic earned him the popular nickname "Fante-Sundt." However, during these years he also went much farther afield, devoting his prodigious energies to broader social problems as well. Traveling all over the country, he studied the ways of life and the conditions of the population in general and especially of its lower classes, issuing a series of monographs on various crucial subjects. In the year 1855 he laid the scientific foundations for these by two studies of demographic statistics: one on mortality and life expectancy, the second on marriage in contemporary Norway (Drake 1980). Drawing on the rich data of the national census, supplemented by primary reports he elicited from clergymen on vital records in their various parishes, he gained solid background material, especially for his major study of contemporary sex mores in Norway, here presented in English translation. The first part of this comprehensive report was published in 1856–1857, followed by sequels in 1859, 1864, and 1866, a total of 537 printed pages.

During this period, he managed to complete a number of other monographs as well. In 1858 they included a study on the laborers of the mining town of Røros and one on the slum areas of the capital, Christiania, Piperviken, and Ruseløkbakken. In the following year he published a study of temperance in drinking (more precisely, of alcoholism) in rural and urban Norway. The almost equally painful problem of cleanliness was the subject of two studies in 1869 and 1870.

In addition he published a number of ground-breaking studies in Norwegian culture. One was about the construction and architecture of rural housing (1863–1865). His work on boat and ship building in connection with studies of the fishing industry (in the 1860s) appeared as the first of two volumes entitled *The Natural History of Norwegian Labor.* The second volume, on arts and crafts in rural homes, concluded his purely empirical sociological work.

However, throughout his studies and in countless popular articles and public lectures, his overriding concern was the practical application of his research on the problems of Norwegian society to policy making at the time. And the crucial matter he urged upon his readers and listeners was the enlightenment of the common people through better schooling and public information. He was a leading force in the Society for the People's Enlightenment and was editor of the periodical *Folkevennen* (People's Friend), all in line with his life's main objective: to open the way to freedom through knowledge for the poor and underprivileged classes.

His reports aiming at social reforms and addressed to the official Commission on Poverty, on which he served as a consultant-member, were greatly appreciated by the authorities, guiding them in their legislation and public-support policies regarding the poor classes. In 1864 Eilert Sundt was awarded the highest honor of the country, the Order of St. Olav, but nobody thought of offering him a post at the university, for which he had amply demonstrated competence and which would have granted him and his family material security.

In 1870 he found himself unable to continue his social research on a hand-to-mouth basis, and at age fifty-three, he at last applied for a position in the church. He was given the parsonage at Eidsvoll, a relatively prosperous rural place, historically famous because the select representatives of the nation had assembled there in 1814 and on May 17 had completed and signed Norway's Constitution—valid, with some amendments, to this day. Eidsvoll had also played an important role in the life of Henrik Wergeland. So, all told, this seemed an auspicious new beginning for Eilert Sundt. Yet it turned out to be a rather unhappy experience. The atmosphere at Eidsvoll was rife with religious dissent and disharmony, hard to cope with. Sundt's son Einar subsequently said his father's entry into the church occurred too late in life, and in fact Sundt died after only five years of service. But his unhappiness was more deeply rooted in his basic spiritual orientation all along.

Of course, he was a true Christian in his compassion and charity toward his fellow human beings, "neighbors" all, whom he loved and cared for, particularly those of the poor and downtrodden classes. But in his innermost mind he also harbored a profound commitment to other values than those of the Sermon on the Mount. In his long years at the university, he had steeped himself in the culture of classical humanism as created by the great European poetry, literature, and philosophy. He was devoted to the idea of Enlightenment, which is essentially incompatible with the Christian dogma of the unalterable sinfulness of human nature, utterly dependent on God's grace and love. Sundt believed in the power of rational knowledge, of science, to improve not only humankind's external condition but also the minds and inner natures of the people. It was by virtue of this faith that he became a social scientist.

During a visit to England in 1862, he was deeply impressed by Darwin's recently published and immediately famous *Origin of Species*. The historian H. O. Christophersen in his monumental book on Eilert Sundt's life and work (Oslo, 1962) writes: "He at once saw the extraordinarily fruitful method for research in cultural history here presented. No doubt the evolutionist point of view had a liberating effect on Eilert Sundt's scientific energy." Unlike some others who primarily were impressed by Darwin's emphasis on the struggle for survival as an evolutionary force (equally agreeable to Marxists and capitalists), Sundt found himself above all confirmed in his belief in the natural perfectibility of the human species through the evolutionary process. From Darwin he took fresh courage to strive to improve not only the social condition of his fellow Norwegians but also their mental and moral disposition.

There was nothing amateurish about his approach and method. He aimed above all at a systematically scientific treatment of his subject matters. To this end, he familiarized himself with the most advanced methods of the age. He read much of the relevant literature in French, English, and German, such as Frédéric Le Play's book on the European worker, the long series of the British *Reports of the Poor Law Commission,* Robert Pashley's *Pauperism and Poor Laws,* the German Carl Godeffroy's *Theorie der Armuth,* and numerous other works. He also regularly read the statistical and other periodicals.

In his sociological research, he aimed at an objective statement of the facts, his method being "value-free" in the sense of Max Weber. Yet, in his choice of subjects, and likewise in the ethical intent which motivated his research, he was directed by a commitment to human and social values.

In the present work, for instance, he methodically draws a statistical map of the occurrence of illegitimate births in the country as a whole, showing significant local variations in their frequency. He then proceeds to explore the objective causes of illegitimacy, not being satisfied with the simple explanation taken for granted by most theologians: that the deviant behavior is rooted in the essential sinfulness and immorality of human nature. He discovers its real causes principally in two facts of Norwegian rural life at the time. First, he cited the housing situation of the hired farm laborers; they were mostly offered sleeping quarters, males and females together, in the haylofts and cow barns of the farms. Second, there was the time-honored rural custom of *nattefrieri*—the socially approved visit of a young man on certain Saturday nights to a girl in her bedroom, for chaste courtship and mutual acquaintance in privacy, without intercourse. Obviously, this custom involved temptations, sometimes leading to lapses, pregnancy, and childbirth, but not always to marriage.

Eilert Sundt was deeply concerned with the rather high incidence of illegitimate births. It was indeed a serious problem, causing public expenditure and, above all, human misery, hitting the unwed mother and her child, aggravating their poverty. There were sufficient reasons for the compassionate observer to make the problem a major subject of research.

Some recent critics have maintained that Sundt's overall approach was essentially a conservative pleading for peaceful reform rather than for revolutionary social change by militant class conflict. The answer in Marxist terms is that Norway's society at that time was hardly ripe for an organized class war. It was predominantly rural, with only the faintest rudiments of an industrial proletariat. The landowners were all freeholders of modest properties, with only a handful of somewhat larger estates. Unlike Denmark and Sweden, let alone the continental countries, Norway had and still has, according to its Constitution, no aristocracy lording it over a numerous peasantry. The temper of the nation's intellectuals was and remains egalitarian; they do not form an elite group apart from and above the madding crowd, but in their devotion to the country they embrace the people as a whole. Nationalism is and always was strong in Norway, but it is a popular emotion, not a cold and aloof authoritarianism.

Eilert Sundt embodied this typically Norwegian brand of nationalism and in his life and work became the architects of today's modern welfare state and industrial society. It was a peaceful passage, and it also had the drive and guidance of the organized labor movement from the 1920s onward.

REFERENCES

H. O. Christophersen, *Eilert Sundt: En dikter i kjensgjerninger* (A poet in facts)(Oslo: Gyldendal Norsk Forlag, 1962).

Eilert Sundt, *On Marriage in Norway,* trans. Michael Drake (Cambridge Univ. Press, 1980).

A F T E R W O R D

by Stephen G. Wieting

The year 1848 marks the beginning of a pivotal quarter-century in European intellectual history. The great thinkers of this era provided ideas, installed forms of association, redirected the study of society and culture, and redressed linkages among institutions and countries that define contemporary life more than a century later. Eilert Sundt began his first publicly supported fieldwork in 1848 and published his final book in 1873. These temporal brackets place him squarely in the period in European and British history that was so extraordinarily volatile politically, culturally, and socially.

Consider Sundt's intellectual contemporaries, individuals who have strongly influenced the formation of Western sociology. Among the English were Walter Bagehot (1826–1877), Sir Francis Galton (1822–1911), Charles Darwin (1809–1882), John Stuart Mill (1806–1873), and Herbert Spencer (1882–1903). The French included Frédéric Le Play (1806–1882), Alexis de Tocqueville (1805–1859), August Comte (1798–1857), and Count Joseph Arthur de Gobineau (1816–1882). Continuing the intellectual traditions and participating in the formation of modern Germany were Friedrich Engels (1820–1905) and Karl Marx (1818–1883). The availability of this volume of Sundt's work fortunately increases the chance that he can be located properly within this array.

Sundt's study stands at the center of the long period, lasting through the nineteenth century (from 1814 to 1905), of Norway's struggle for independence. This struggle—most immediately involving Denmark and Sweden—was linked with French, German, and English efforts to increase political, economic, and social freedoms. These intellectual battles and political events were reverberating around Sundt, so that what he said about Norway allows the history of his country to be placed among histories of the others.

How best to locate Sundt and his contemporaries? What is the basis of our commonality with them more than a century later? Our own forms of association and ways of thinking are so determined by the changes Sundt and others of his period were effecting that we must

---

Stephen G. Wieting is associate professor of sociology, at the University of Iowa.

exercise considerable control to see truly what they were participating in and creating in the years 1848 to 1873. Strategies of analysis and interpretation that begin with the metaphors and presuppositions of the late twentieth century will hamper appreciation of this time of change and reformation. Instead, we best represent their efforts and maintain our commonality with them by recovering their acts of cultural creation within their times. These creative acts are like our own in displaying a web of social relations by a series of referential acts. In other words, by his acts of referencing, Sundt is social. By enumerating his referential acts and those of others of his period, we begin to open up the social context of his cultural contribution.

A variety of sources dealing with the study of culture give us some useful suggestions on ways to locate Sundt and his contemporaries; they include subject-object relationships, the conception of self held by the writer or investigator, the macro-entities referenced by speaker or writer, and finally the matter of audience response, evaluation, and retention of the cultural item.

Subject-Object Relationships

Several sociologists and philosophers in the pragmatist tradition of the study of humans and society—such as George Herbert Mead, John Dewey, and Arthur Bentley—have emphasized the role of the acting subject (in this case the investigator-writer) in the selection of topics to study. Michel Foucault in much of his work has called attention to the importance of noting the particular objects (institutions, people, problems) that investigating subjects select.

Sundt's plan of study was enormous: a description of the social relations and norms of the "common people" and an explanation of these social objects using social variables. Within his broad orientation, the breadth takes texture from the specific studies he has produced—again highly varied. A recent effort in Oslo to provide modern versions of his production yielded eleven volumes. Beginning with Sundt's first publication on gypsies, his research and writing sustain major themes of demography and social anthropology (for example, his book on marriage and this on sexual customs), problems of work (studies of temperance, and of the construction and maritime trades), and social epidemiology (his late study of cleanliness).

The Conception of Self

Jean Piaget's studies of the conditions needed for the emergence of the human sciences, Foucault's publications, and suggestive work that has brought pragmatic traditions into semiotics discussion (Finlay-Pelinski 1982) have stressed the importance of where the investigator locates himself or herself in the analysis. The placement of the self relative to the objects being analyzed is thus a matter of contemplation and concern in evaluating Sundt's cultural contribution. Piaget stresses that the capacity to decenter, as he calls it, is a crucial ingredient for all of science and particularly for the human sciences. The decentering includes several steps.

First, each human science has needed to recognize that one's own expression of society is only a partial view of humanity and that its uniqueness and its similarity might profitably be seen through a comparison with that of others. Second, each has had to understand the need to see material conditions relative to the past and future. Third, both of these crucial steps of decentering require some way to assess spatial and temporal observations. This has given rise to a variety of mechanisms of verification, including the incorporation of rational proof, measurement, the assignment of symbols according to rule, the logic of experimentation, and the use of statistics.

In his work Sundt often expresses judgments that may by late twentieth-century standards appear partial and value-laden. In these instances, Sundt only partly realizes Piaget's decentering. However, most of Sundt's analysis and writing contains a clear commitment to a comparative evaluation of his country and his period. Sundt, with consummate patience and caution, resists analyses and conclusions that do not admit comparison across time or across some group (for example, region, cohort, or country). He resolutely grounds his analysis in basic universal standards of rational proof and in the logic of experimentation, measurement, and statistics.

Piaget's emphasis, and the heart of modern social science, concerns placement of the investigating self with respect to an object of interest. This is betrayed by what investigators actually say about their identity. Sundt consistently identifies himself as a scientist, but he qualifies this by claiming his fundamental advocacy of the people. Analytical placement becomes evident in how investigators understand and assess their relation to the object. At several points Sundt evaluates similarities between himself and the perspective of the individuals studied. He acknowledges sources of error that might be associated with his particular perspective on the data.

Accomodation to Formal Expectations and Macroentities

Michel Foucault and Randall Collins (1981) have emphasized the need to consider social discourse at interactional and at the more public levels of rituals and celebrations in the light of the norms and information referenced. Sundt and his contemporaries are of necessity engaging in such macroreferential activity. The problems they attack, the issues they address, the priorities of their work all gain additional significance when we observe the formal standards of research, writing, and institutional orders they invoke. In Sundt's case his writing emphasizes issues of equality and political economy, national identity and independence, the need for scientific ideas in the study of humans, and the use of scientific standards in the formation of social agents (such as schools) for the common good.

Throughout his life Sundt argued the case of largely disenfranchised groups. He worked in an era when Norway struggled for national identity; for creation of colleges, banks, and currency; and ultimately for independence, which was not fully secured until Norway achieved freedom from Sweden in 1905. Sundt's work displays the developing midcentury dependence upon scientific notions for acquiring knowledge about the social order and for making judgments about useful social programs. While he strove to resist moral guidelines and biases in making his judgments and explanations, Sundt nevertheless displayed a lingering commitment to traditional ideas in his use of terms like *providence.* It will be clear to readers today that the meaning of morality in his work stems from a biblical conception of ethics.

The Importance of Audiences

A fourth facet of social context (implied by the other three) is the role of audiences imagined by the investigator and displayed by readers, critics, and (eventually) archivists. Useful summaries of the importance of readers and audiences appear in Darnton (1984) and Chartier (1984). In Sundt's case a variety of audience reactions are available, including the reaction of the government to his work, and the evaluation by individuals who used his work then and later.

The acceptance of Sundt's production was mixed. His career began with a positive reaction by the government to his proposal, and his studies continued with government sponsorship. It ended however, after a debate in the *Storthing* (Parliament) in 1869, when a vote of fifty-one to forty-seven opposed the continued subsidy of his studies. In this and other books Sundt responds to letters and comments about previous work. Many contain reservations about his conclusions and methods. The individuals he interviews appear hospitable, but sometimes distrust what might be extreme political positions, like those of Marcus Thrane, or are wary of a representative of the government.

Sundt was an editor of *Folkevennen* (The People's Friend) from 1857 to 1866, which ostensibly spoke for the interests of what were considered the common people. However, the readership was modest and often critical of material he included. Furthermore, in the process of preparing an entry to a contest in the mid-1860s on the role of women, he became embroiled in a public controversy over his position. He did not win the expected prize, and his work was criticized as being anachronistic and pretentious (Allwood 1957).

Modern commentators have noted the relative inattention to Sundt until recently, even in Norway. It is true that a building was named for him in the 1960s at the University of Oslo. However, Norwegian sociology shows that his contributions in this book and in his other writing were not often followed directly. Rather, similar ideas were sought through English and American sociology. As recently as 1977, a review of the rise of the field in Norway mentions Sundt only in passing. Appreciative response to his work begins to appear in English with Hillman's brief biographical sketch (1951) and Allwood's biography (1957).

As Sundt is placed within his context using these four dimensions, they can be considered a useful schema for examining similarities and differences from his contemporaries. For example, in addition to similar orientations to objects and self-conceptions, at least three concerns or macro-references within Sundt have potential linkages with others. In much of Europe there looms the problem of political economy, though it may be variously worded as "justice" or "rights." Secondly, there hovers a concern with national identity and prominence. Thirdly, the tools for social analysis were emerging, as was the interest in applying them in social engineering. Drawing on three additional cultural traditions provides brief but suggestive examples of these concerns in Herbert Spencer, Friedrich Engels, and Frédéric Le Play. These three endure as major, acknowledged contributors to modern social thought. Sundt, working largely independently and in relative isolation, struggled with similar problems and applied similar approaches. His striking comparability with the others is emphasised when specific ideas from them are juxtaposed with some of Sundt's own.

Commentary on the sociological implications of Spencer tend to suggest his ideological alignment with business and capitalism and essentially a nonsectarian, indeed agnostic, world view (Martindale 1960). But religious influences on him were profound, particularly from his mother, a follower of Wesley, and from his paternal uncle, who was a clergyman in the established church, with whom he lived for considerable stretches of time. Especially suggestive for purposes here are the many remarks in Spencer's autobiography that speak approvingly of his uncle's work to improve the conditions of the laborer against the interests of big business (Spencer 1904, 32, 33). Such sentiment is striking from this spokesperson for social Darwinism.

Sundt throughout his work spoke of the value of the true Norwegian spirit displayed in the objects of his study. The nineteenth-century priorities in the form of constitution, banks, schools, and the university all were linked to the concern with nationhood. The same currents were evident in Germany, but the task of finding a telling exemplar there is difficult, because of the shadings and complexities in sentiment. It is frequently pointed out that Bismarck became the model for much of Max Weber's approach to formal organization, and Weber's own nationalism is commonly noted. Actually, much scholarship, such as the monumental historical studies of Triestchke, was highly nationalistic. In retrospect, one looks at the writing of Marx and Engels as a foundation for international political expression and for an analytical approach dominated by cross-national emphases. At the time their ideas were clearly interlocked with the German penchant for unification, national identity, and potency. These are especially evident in the correspondence between them and in the journalistic efforts of Engels (Marx and Engels 1986, vol. 38:93, 1963, vol. 27:71, 72).

Sundt throughout his work resisted the temptation to resort to nonscientific criteria for drawing conclusions. He would appeal to providence and betray biblical standards when speaking of "morality." However, he clearly casts his lot with a modern social science that resists religious conclusions and personal biases. These Enlightment norms are commonly said to have originated in France. Of contemporaries of Sundt, though, whom best to note? The legal and administrative reforms of Napoleon Bonaparte began the century in a distinctively modern administrative spirit. Urbanization experts might point to the contributions of Georges-Eugène Haussmann (1809–1891). The attraction of de Tocqueville persists to this day (Paxton 1989). Comte is, to be sure, identified with the origin of positivism; Renan might as well be cited as an extreme exemplar, particularly in *Vie de Jesus,* 1863.

As an embodiment of contemporary scientific intentions comparable to Sundt, Frédéric Le Play is perhaps the most apt. Like Sundt, he began to use the current tools of political arithmetic. However, like

Quetelet, he rejected the use of the modal or mean representation in favor of a reliance on a variety of information generated by field studies (Le Play 1879). He stressed, as did Sundt, the utilization of careful, ethnographically generated sets of information for the reconstitution of society. His book, *La Réforme sociale en France,* provides us with telling examples of this emphasis: "I admit, without preamble, that the reform necessary to our country should be brought about, without constraint, with the help of all the classes of the society restored to some common opinions by the study of social facts. Such is the point of view which has been offered to my mind since the beginning of my work and since then has been constantly confirmed to me by observation" (Le Play 1864, 30).

There are other examples that might be noted for their correspondences with Sundt in terms of their orientation to objects of study, self-references, invocations of norms, and in the audience reaction. Contrasts in political, economic, and intellectual features could be elaborated in all countries. But during the period of transition over this twenty-five year expanse these three share with Sundt general markers of the change. It was not a changed period; it was a changing period. The old persisted, but its hold was eroding. Each of these three, along with Sundt, has left a residue of comments on their own work (particularly Spencer in his autobiography, Engels and Marx in their correspondence, and Le Play in *La Réforme sociale en France*). These sources allow the possibility of an assessment of their social context by pursuing a rich web of reference to their subjects and their self-location as well as the macro-referenced norms. All elicited vigorous response in their time and since, allowing the recovery of the final element of the social context of production—the reaction of audiences.

BIBLIOGRAPHY

Allwood, Martin S. 1957. *Eilert Sundt: A Pioneer in Sociology and Social Anthropology.* Oslo: Olaf Norlis Forlag.

Chartier, Roger. 1984. "Culture as appropriation: Popular cultural uses in early modern France." In *Understanding Popular Culture,* edited by Steven L. Kaplan, 229–54. Berlin: Mouton.

Christopherson, H. O. 1959. *Eilert Sundt: Humanist og samfunnsforsker.* Det Norske Studentersamfunds Kulturutvalg.

Collins, Randall. 1981. "The micro-foundations of macro-sociology." *American Journal of Sociology* 95:984–1014.

Current Sociology (special issue on Scandinavian sociology) 25 (November 1977). Beverly Hills: Sage.

Darnton, Robert. 1984. *The Great Cat Massacre and Other Episodes in French Cultural History.* New York: Basic Books.

Finlay-Pelinski, Marike. 1982. "Semiotics or history: From content analysis to contextualized discursive praxis." *Semiotica* 40:229–66.

Hillman, Arthur. 1951. "Eilert Sundt, social surveyor extraordinary." *Journal of Sociology* 43:49–56.

Lazersfeld, Paul F. 1961. "Notes on the history of quantification in sociology—trends, sources, and problems." *Isis* 52:277–333.

Le Play, Frédéric. 1879. *Les Ouvriers européens.* Tours: Alfred Mame et fils, Livrairer-Editeurs (Deuxième Edition en Six Tomes).

______. 1864. *La Réforme sociale en France.* Genève-Paris: Slatkine (Reimpression de l'édition de Paris), 1982.

Martindale, Don. 1960. *The Nature and Types of Sociological Theory.* Boston: Houghton Mifflin Company.

Marx, Karl, and Friedrich Engels. 1977–1986. *Collected Works.* Vols. 7, 8, 19, 22, 38. New York: International Publishers.

______. 1963. *Werke.* Vol. 27. Berlin: Dietz Verlag.

Paxton, Robert O. 1989. "The divided liberal." *New York Review of Books,* March 2, 16–18.

Piaget, Jean. 1950. *Introduction à l'épistémologie génétique.* Tome 3. Paris: Universitaires de Paris.

Porter, Theodore M. 1986. *The Rise of Statistical Thinking, 1820–1900.* Princeton: Princeton University Press.

Spencer, Herbert. 1904. *An Autobiography.* New York: D. Appleton and Company.

Sundt, Eilert. 1980 [1855]. *On Marriage in Norway.* Translated and introduced by Michael Drake. Cambridge: Cambridge University Press.

Wieting, Stephen G., and Thórólfur Thórlindsson. 1987. "The emergence and management of divorce in the early Icelandic commonwealth." Paper presented at the meetings of the Midwest Sociological Society, Chicago.

INDEX